Reimagining Anti-Oppression Social Work Practice

Reimagining
Anti-Oppression
Social Work Practice

Edited by
Samantha Wehbi and Henry Parada

CANADIAN
SCHOLARS

Toronto | Vancouver

Reimagining Anti-Oppression Social Work Practice
Edited by Samantha Wehbi and Henry Parada

First published in 2017 by
Canadian Scholars
425 Adelaide Street West, Suite 200
Toronto, Ontario
M5V 3C1

www.canadianscholars.ca

Library and Archives Canada Cataloguing in Publication

Reimagining anti-oppression social work practice / edited by Samantha Wehbi and Henry Parada.

Includes bibliographical references and index.
Issued in print and electronic formats.
ISBN 978-1-55130-979-8 (softcover).--ISBN 978-1-55130-980-4 (PDF).--ISBN 978-1-55130-981-1 (EPUB)

1. Social work with minorities--Canada. I. Wehbi, Samantha, 1969-, editor II. Parada, Henry, 1959- editor

HV3176.R45 2017   362.8400971   C2017-902775-1   C2017-902776-X

Text design by Brad Horning
Cover design by Em Dash Design
Cover photo © Samantha Wehbi, from the *Pieces of Place* series

17   18   19   20   21   5   4   3   2   1

Printed and bound in Canada by Webcom.

Canada

MIX
Paper from
responsible sources
FSC **FSC® C004071**
www.fsc.org

Contents

Section I: Supportive Critiques of Anti-Oppression

Section II: Nuancing Anti-Oppression

Section III: Engagement with Marginalized Populations

Section IV: Anti-Oppression as a Frame for Transformation

Preface:
Reimagining Anti-Oppression Social Work Practices

Tensions and Conversations

Samantha Wehbi, Professor, School of Social Work, Ryerson University

Henry Parada, Associate Professor, School of Social Work, Ryerson University

Anti-oppression practices and pedagogy have gained increasing favour in social work, as evidenced by their inclusion in the discourses of some social service agencies and in accreditation standards in Canada, the United States, and Australia. As long-time advocates of this approach we find ourselves at a crucial turn. On the one hand, it is heartening that anti-oppression is gaining acceptance as an approach to practice and research; on the other hand, there is a concern that this approach is being weakened and co-opted within the growing climate of neoliberalism shaping social services and educational institutions. Beginning from this understanding, there is a need to reengage with and interrogate anti-oppression in ways that reimagine its role within the current climate and our unwavering commitment to social justice. Brown (2012) argues for the need to be critically reflexive, "which moves beyond personal reflection or self-awareness but to purposeful awareness of our discursive practices, which may both challenge and reinforce mainstream practices of power" (p. 37) that may be reproduced within our own anti-oppression practices. As such, turning the lens inward, this book seeks to engage readers in critical reflexivity on the key concepts and theoretical tensions underlying anti-oppression social work practices.

The chapters in this book begin from an acceptance of anti-oppression as a guide for practice, albeit not without contestation and challenge. For the authors of this book, anti-oppression is not to be adopted unquestioningly as a new dogma, but as a means to accept the potential for co-optation that threatens every endeavour seeking to challenge existing social relations and conditions. To recognize the rise of a specific approach to practice is to come to terms with how it has been shaped and sculpted to fit the concrete realities and contexts of practice. These contexts, placed as they are within current retrenchments of the welfare state and the growing influence of right-leaning definitions of inclusion and citizenship, are not vacuums within which an approach, be it anti-oppressive or otherwise, can be inserted without consequence. As Cocker and Hafford-Letchfield (2014) contend, "This is certainly not about erasing the past but taking stock of new questions that have been posed" (p. 3). Hence, as detailed in this volume, not only do we need to question the approach itself for it to remain true to its commitment to social justice and transformation, but we also need to critically examine how it plays out within various realities of practice settings, populations, and communities.

Taking this critical perspective on anti-oppression forward, this book focuses on practice through a collection of chapters addressing practice principles, social issues, and work with specific populations. Each chapter responds to the central guiding question driving this book: How can we challenge or push forward our understanding of anti-oppression to enhance practice? The answers to this question provide the organizing framework of the book and its structure, which is divided into four thematic sections: providing supportive critiques of anti-oppression; introducing nuances to anti-oppression; strengthening engagement with marginalized populations; and utilizing anti-oppression as a framework for institutional transformation.

PROVIDING SUPPORTIVE CRITIQUES OF ANTI-OPPRESSION

The first section offers an entry point to discussions about anti-oppression practice in social work, and it intends to demonstrate the complexity of this approach and the practices associated with it. A common thread in these discussions is the need to engage critically with anti-oppression by pointing to its limitations and offering supportive critiques. In Chapter 1, Baskin and Davey draw parallels between Indigenous and critical approaches to social work practice, including anti-oppression, and argue for the important place of understanding and challenging colonialism. The chapter highlights the need to include critical concepts such as cultures, spiritualities, strengths, and decolonization to be more responsive to Indigenous approaches. Also highlighted is the role that anti-oppressive social work could, and should, play in supporting decolonization and healing. The authors suggest that, for anti-oppression social work, the way forward is the adoption of decolonizing approaches not only in practice but also in how we prepare future practitioners in child welfare and other fields.

Similarly, starting from an understanding of social work as a social justice–oriented profession, in Chapter 2, Wilson offers a critique of the limitations of these approaches should they fall prey to neoliberal imperatives. The author renders our understanding of social problems and responses more complex by calling our attention to how we construct social problems, especially within the context of neoliberalism. Tang and Peters (2006) note the growing encroachment of neoliberal discourses on social work as a profession, on social work practice, and on social work practitioners. Larner (2000) further argues that neoliberalism is best understood not simply as a policy framework but also as an ideology and a discourse that influence practices that could be deciphered through a lens of governmentality. Wilson touches on these interconnected facets of neoliberalism and governmentality through her detailed discussion of neoliberalism as an ideology, political project, and process. Her analysis of the institutional classification of "youth problems" in Ontario is undertaken through a Foucauldian lens of governmentality to highlight how the construction of these issues has shifted in present times. Through this discussion, Wilson helps us understand how an anti-oppression approach, or a social justice–oriented approach, can be a way to address social conflicts through our professional practice, but in ways that potentially reflect dominant discourses. Of importance in this process is the link between social work and the state and how this professional role can be implicated in reproducing oppression.

Building on these critiques, Smith, in Chapter 3, also engages Foucauldian analysis and concepts of governmentality and neoliberalism to examine the implications of activist and anti-oppressive social work for workers in child welfare and primary care. The author further complicates the picture by demonstrating how neoliberalism is being contested in the workplace by social workers, even when their subjectivities appear to be reshaped by its workings. Her chapter, based on a study conducted in Ontario, provides us with a glimpse of the contestations and negotiations that workers are engaged in to challenge what may seem like a foregone conclusion: the inevitable hegemony of neoliberalism. As Larner (2000) notes, "Only by theorizing neo-liberalism as a multi-vocal and contradictory phenomenon can we make visible the contestations and struggles that we are currently engaged in … [thereby opening the door to the] potential to imagine political alternatives" (p. 21). For Luchies (2014), these alternatives are necessary to resist the "violence of neoliberalism" (p. 100). To illustrate these points, the chapter brings in the voices of activist social workers in conceptualizing and interacting with the contextual shifts under neoliberalism. In doing so, the chapter also provides a critique of determinism and demonstrates micro-acts of resistance.

INTRODUCING NUANCES TO ANTI-OPPRESSION

The second section of the book aims to introduce nuances to our understanding of anti-oppression practice. The chapters in this section introduce key concepts and practices that hold an important potential for anti-oppression practice. A common thread throughout these chapters is the need to challenge received notions of rights, empowerment, and equality as these are being co-opted to serve a neoliberal agenda. Preston and Aslett, in Chapter 4, focus on the concept of citizen engagement through an example of working with youth, and they argue that policies and practices could be enhanced to serve the needs of youth better if they provide input. The authors echo earlier analysis by examining how neoliberal discourses and strategies have impacted engagement at the level of community practice and have shifted our understandings of participation. The authors attribute this lack of youth engagement to the impacts of funding priorities, neoliberalism, and a shift toward evidence-based practice. Also impactful is a reconceptualization of youth as currently constructed within notions of citizenship to status as service recipients, upon whom decisions are enacted. Preston and Aslett highlight the need for anti-oppression practitioners to nuance and problematize their understanding of empowerment, which has been reshaped in the context of neoliberalism. Indeed, George and George (2013) provide the example of the co-optation of discourses of citizenship rights and equality and how these have been reshaped under neoliberal restructurings of old-age policies; their analysis demonstrates how the assumed neutrality and "race blind" old-age policies have, in fact, further entrenched racism. Similarly, Preston and Aslett caution against such co-optations and argue that adopting an anti-oppression approach in community-based agencies without attention to issues of youth engagement could lead to tokenizing and ineffective engagement.

In Chapter 5, Sookraj, Phillips, and Pon rely on child welfare practice to draw our attention to issues facing social workers as they seek to engage in new or contested forms of practice to challenge racism. The authors discuss the limits of current approaches to child welfare and propose Family Group Conferencing as an anti-racist and anti-colonial alternative for working with children and families. The chapter discusses the barriers to implementation of this approach and calls for better preparation of social workers, starting with social work education. The chapter also integrates an Indigenous (Maori) perspective and, as such, fits well with earlier discussions of indigeneity and the need to push anti-oppression practice to better engage with anti-colonialism and decolonization.

Adding further nuance to our understanding of anti-oppression practice, Chapter 6 by Onishenko takes on the issue of rights discourse and demonstrates implications for social work practice through a case example of same-sex marriage in Ontario. The author provides a critical examination of how discourses of rights and citizenship are negotiated in complex ways to challenge heterosexism. Onishenko's research highlights how historically marginalized communities can reclaim tools, such as law and human rights instruments, as a form of resistance and a way of revaluing their own experiences, and how these could hold promise for anti-oppression practice. However, the author also discusses the limitations of rights-based approaches and the risk of reinforcing heteronormativity.

STRENGTHENING ENGAGEMENT WITH MARGINALIZED POPULATIONS

The third section of the book explores ways in which anti-oppression practice can enhance and advance its engagement with marginalized populations. The authors of these chapters highlight the insufficient engagement of anti-oppression practice with populations such as people with disabilities, people living with mental health issues, and people who are grieving. Indeed, Larson (2008) argues that while anti-oppression has gained favour in North American and British contexts, its principles have not become entrenched in addressing issues touching the lives of people with disabilities or those living with mental health issues. Consistent with this argument, tying the three chapters in this section together is the critique of professional discourses that tend to pathologize and individualize experiences of health, neglecting the influence of the operation of whiteness, capitalist agendas, and medical discourses on constructions of what it means to fit a norm. In Chapter 7, Sandys seeks to counter medical-model discourses and practices by offering an anti-oppressive approach to working on disability issues and with people with disabilities. Looking specifically at the example of employment, her chapter offers guidelines on how to engage in this practice from a lens that revalues the contributions and place of people with disabilities within society.

Abdillahi, Meerai, and Poole in Chapter 8 argue for the need to revalue marginalized subjectivities as one of the challenges and ways forward for anti-oppression practice. This chapter pushes anti-oppression to recognize and integrate a challenge of anti-Black sanism, an under-discussed area of scholarship and practice. Building on scholarly work in anti-oppression, anti-racism, and anti-sanism, the authors challenge all three to integrate an intersectional analysis that can revalue the experiences of Black people dealing with the conflation of racism and sanism. Abdillahi and colleagues also challenge the medical discourses that frame and impose normalcy. Their discussion highlights how an anti-racism approach combined with anti-sanism could hold promise for resisting practices that further marginalize and devalue the identities and lives of people living with mental health diagnoses.

Similarly, Ord challenges the pathologizing and marginalization of those experiencing grief. Adopting a queer theory lens, Chapter 9 addresses a topic that has not been fully addressed through anti-oppression scholarship. Like the chapters on disability and anti-Black sanism, it enriches our understanding of a topic that has yet to be fully explored from an anti-oppression lens. Inspired by Foucauldian analysis, Ord challenges the medical gaze that frames and dictates the boundaries of what and how grief should be lived. By revaluing the place of grief and emotions in our lives, and the diverse strategies we may engage to sustain ourselves, Ord presents us with a way forward through—instead of over—loss.

UTILIZING ANTI-OPPRESSION PRACTICE AS A FRAME FOR TRANSFORMATION

The final section of the book reflects on key questions related to practising from an anti-oppression perspective within the context of organizational and institutional settings and arrangements. One theme that brings these chapters together is a shifting of the lens from the lives of individuals and communities to organizations and institutions as places where oppression must be resisted. Strier and Binyamin (2014) call on social service organizations to move away from hierarchical structures that reinforce oppressive social relations and relationships with service users, to adopt instead anti-oppression principles.

The authors posit that, "Evidently, any systematic implementation of anti-oppressive practices in social services would require extensive changes in the organisational structure and culture of social services" (Strier & Binyamin, 2014, p. 2096). Advancing this argument further, Barnoff, Abdillahi, and Jordan in Chapter 10 examine the structures and processes of what it actually takes to create anti-oppressive organizations. They contend that it is important to engage in this critical reflection even within anti-oppressive organizations. Their work, which is based on years of experience in organizational practice, presents us with some of the challenges and potential responses when seeking to develop anti-oppressive practice within organizations.

Ng moves the discussion to a broader level through her examination of alliances between social work and the labour movement. Chapter 11 offers a discussion that is focused on why, and how, it is important to make links between social justice–oriented social work and trade unions/labour movement organizing. The author points to the way forward through (re)building new alliances and processes. For Ng, this path is also a return to our roots as a profession, albeit in the historical sense. Specifically, through a discussion of several examples of organizing efforts, Ng calls on us to rebuild our connections with social movements and labour organizing by reminding us of our historical links to labour struggles and attention to class issues. The author suggests the need to forge trade union and social work alliances for anti-oppressive practice to thrive.

The final chapter in the book is by Clarke, Preston, and Ajandi, who examine the need to bring the lessons of practice into the classroom through anti-racist and decolonizing lenses. Taking us back to the classroom, Chapter 12 offers us a way to revalue student experiences in order to contribute to anti-racist and decolonizing practice. Through an exploration of portfolio development and reviews as an alternative to placement experiences for Aboriginal and non-Aboriginal students, the authors note how these processes reflect and reinforce anti-oppressive practice at the level of educational institutions. In this sense, how we act with our students in the classroom is a reflection of how we wish to be in the world outside of academia. As Jones (2009) maintains, integrating transformative learning into the classroom is a way of demonstrating a commitment to social change. In aligning our vision of social justice within and outside social work education, we succeed in bridging the gap between theory and practice, not only for our students but also for ourselves as anti-oppressive educators.

In the following pages we engage with these ideas, hoping to contribute, in a small measure, to the discussion on anti-oppression approaches to practice. Bringing the practice, research, and teaching experiences of the authors to bear on how this approach plays out in the field of social work offers a glimpse into its workings in a diversity of settings. More importantly, the authors offer the contours of a debate and challenge to help keep an anti-oppression approach alive and honest to its initial aims of resisting injustice. We invite you to join us as we reflect on these tensions and propose alternatives for the way forward.

Section I

Supportive Critiques of Anti-Oppression

1 | Parallel Pathways to Decolonization: Critical and Indigenous Social Work

Cyndy Baskin, Associate Professor, School of Social Work, Ryerson University

Caitlin Davey, Psychologist, Baxter Antoniazzi and Associates

Greetings! My English name is Cyndy Baskin, and my spirit name translates into English as something like "The Woman Who Passes on the Teachings." My ancestors are of the Mi'kmaq and Celtic Nations, and I come from the northernmost point of New Brunswick. My clan is the fish, who are known as the mediators, philosophers, the ones who help others during times of struggle. I am a teacher and a helper. For this chapter, I will put these two together to explore how critical theories of social work both contribute to and are challenged by Indigenous approaches to helping.

My name is Caitlin Davey, and my spirit name translates into English to "She Who Digs in the Dirt," which means that I tend to work hard to look beyond the surface to gain understanding. My family is from the Mohawk Nation from Six Nations of the Grand River in Southern Ontario. My clan is turtle, who are known for being slow and steady, determined, humbly stubborn, and for holding a lot on their shoulders. For this chapter, I used the characteristics described above to understand and write about Indigenous perspectives on healing in social work.

CRITICAL SOCIAL WORK THEORIES

There are several critical social work theories, such as anti-racism, feminism, structural, and anti-oppression, but for the purpose of this chapter, the focus will be on the last two. Critical social work theories are attempts to understand our world as it really is. Despite the fact that there is much beauty on our planet and there are many precious people for us to admire and love, there does not seem to be a single place where the ugliness of racism, sexism, homophobia, ableism, and poverty—as well as many other "isms"—do not exist. Critical social work theory begins with this awful truth and exposes it while committing to work toward societies that will be free of, or at least lessened from, dominant-subordinate relationships.

Structural Social Work

Bob Mullaly (2010), who has been writing about structural oppression and structural social work for many years, refers to the former as:

> the means by which oppression is institutionalized in society. It consists of the ways that social institutions, laws, policies, social processes and practices, and the economic and political systems all work together primarily in favour of the dominant group at the expense of subordinate groups. At this level, oppression is often given its formal legitimization. (p. 63)

This definition certainly represents the historical and present impacts of colonization in this country as taken up by many Indigenous scholars within social work and other fields (Alfred, 2009; Allan & Smylie, 2015; Baskin, 2011; Blackstock, 2009; Bourassa, 2009; RCAP, 1996; St. Denis, 2011). Colonization has been, and continues to be, an ongoing process of deliberate displacement, cultural violence, and systemic oppression targeted at the Indigenous Peoples of the territories that make up what we now call Canada. The foundations of this country were built on the seizure of land and resources, and the imposition of foreign political, economic, educational, and religious structures on the original people of this land (Baskin, 2011).

Today, structural oppression in Canada is seen as not as overt since women can vote, same-sex couples can marry—even though they still do not have the same rights and benefits as heterosexual couples—and Indigenous children are no longer stolen from their communities and placed in residential schools. Not everyone would agree with this latter statement, however; today, the child welfare system removes more children from their families and communities than residential schools ever did (Blackstock, 2008). Nevertheless, we now have more of what is called covert oppression, which hides in the shadows and cracks of society and yet has widespread, violent impacts upon marginalized groups in all aspects of life that others take for granted, such as financial opportunities, housing, safety, and fair treatment in the criminal justice system. The over-surveillance of Indigenous Peoples is not a thing of the past nor is the trauma experienced by children and youth in systems such as child welfare and education. Not only do Indigenous scholars write about the current impacts of colonization, but so do a few non-Indigenous ones, such as Mullaly (2010) and Carniol (2010), who have openly stated that it is the Indigenous populations in Canada that have been most affected by structural barriers. Perhaps the most overarching example of this is the fact that the Indian Act, which has numerous controls over us (including issues of identity), stands as one of the few pieces of race-based legislation remaining in the Western world today (Allan & Smylie, 2015).

How, though, does structural social work fight against what is often underground in a Western democratic society believed to be mostly free of oppression? It begins with uncovering the myths in society, such as equality and that anyone can have what they need if they simply try hard enough. It reveals that the majority of the population believes that they are successful because they have taken up the opportunities that are available to everyone, and those who are not doing well did not make use of these opportunities and are, therefore, incompetent or lazy. Structural social work encourages all of us to reconsider such ingrained beliefs by taking a close look at reality and asking questions about why there are so many immigrants with PhDs who are not able to practise their area of specialty in Canada, or why over 1,200 missing and murdered Indigenous women and girls are of such little concern to the state. Rather than pathologizing people, structural social work instead focuses on consciousness-raising, advocacy, and how to dismantle the institutions that perpetuate the ongoing impacts of colonization (Absolon & Herbert, 1997; Baskin, 2011).

Anti-Oppression Social Work

Another critical social work model that acknowledges the sources of inequity in society is anti-oppression practice (AOP). Similar to structural social work, AOP also draws upon feminist, queer, and anti-racist perspectives and predominantly focuses on oppression at the structural level. Also, like structural social work, AOP acknowledges the history of global colonization whereby "much of the wealth in the First World was acquired through colonization of the Third World and theft of land from indigenous peoples" (Baines, 2011, p. 27).

AOP also fosters critical thinking, does not place the onus of positive change on those from oppressed populations, and teaches about how these populations often internalize stereotypes (Wagner & Yee, 2011). It examines privilege as well as oppression, thereby making explicit that everyone is implicated in domination (Healy, 2005) and also emphasizing how the privileged can be in solidarity and alliance with those who are oppressed (Curry-Stevens, 2011). Being an ally means to pick up the work of social justice by challenging the norms, assumptions, and behaviours of institutions and individuals. It means threatening the status quo by taking action, rather than merely talking about oppression. Allies realize that some people with privileges fear social justice as it may mean losing some of their taken-for-granted privileges in order for others to be able to participate in society on a level playing field (McLaughlin, 2005).

Putting structural social work and anti-oppression models into practice is challenging and involves both processes of resistance and the creation of new ways to practise social work (Barnoff & Coleman, 2007; George, Coleman, & Barnoff, 2007). There are no formulas or prescriptions, nothing that will work every time in any situation, and practitioners must be ever-reflexive and open to new learning (Baines, 2011). Changes to service delivery come through structural changes at the legal and political levels. For example, if we aim to stop the removal of Aboriginal children from their families and communities by child welfare workers, what is desperately needed in Canada is not simply changes to the Child and Family Services Act (Government of Ontario, 2006), but the creation of an Aboriginal Family Services Act based on the values of Aboriginal Peoples. However, while we are working toward this structural change, social work practitioners can enact smaller changes within the structures and cultures of social services organizations (Barnoff & Coleman, 2007; George et al., 2007; Strier & Binyamin, 2010). Social workers can develop partnerships with those who use their services and ensure their practice and experiences become the major sources of knowledge development. They can be mindful of the power of language when they write case notes, letters, and court reports, and speak about those who access their services. For example, is a person referred to as a "crack head" or someone who is struggling with substance misuse? Is a woman a "bad, unfit mother" if she works in the sex trade to feed her children, or is she strong and resourceful?

INDIGENOUS IMPLEMENTATION OF CRITICAL THEORIES

Cherokee/Greek author Thomas King (2003) asks readers what they do not like about Indigenous People and then goes on to respond to the question:

> Maybe the answer to the question is simply that you don't think we deserve the things we have. You don't think we've worked for them. You don't think we've earned them. You think that all we did was to sign our names to some prehistoric treaty, and, ever since, we've been living in a semi-uncomfortable welfare state of trust land and periodic benefits. Maybe you believe we're lazy/drunk/belligerent/stupid. Unable to look after our own affairs. Maybe you think all we want to do is conjure up the past and crawl into it. People used to think these things, you know, and they used to say them out loud. Now they don't. Now they just think them. (p. 147)

In some ways, the overt racism that King refers to, although painful, is easier to name and fight against because it can be literally seen and heard. The covert racism, which King also points out, is thought about, but not voiced and thus tends to be more difficult to identify because it is so ingrained in every Canadian's psyche through a Eurocentric lens via powerful institutions such as education and the media. In addition, as King alludes to, many Canadians have learned to be "politically correct" when they speak out loud.

Some Indigenous social work educators and practitioners implement aspects of critical theories in their work. Such support comes from Algonquin/Mohawk scholar and practitioner Bonnie Freeman (2011), who states, "practicing from an anti-oppressive perspective, we can slowly restructure our society to honour and acknowledge Native people rather than continuing colonial oppression" (p. 119). Freeman goes on to explain how the telling of our stories of struggle and survival, and replacing negative images of Indigenous Peoples with identities that affirm our strengths, is also anti-oppressive work.

Another component of critical social work theories that aligns with many Indigenous practitioners and educators' notions of "help for the helpers" (Baskin, 2011, p. 33) is self-reflexivity. Through such processes, social workers explore their own oppressions and privileges, consider how the power they hold in their positions impacts on those they work with, and reflect on how their values and biases influence their actions. Gord Bruyere (2010), of the Anishnaabe Nation, writes explicitly about self-reflexivity on the part of social workers when it comes to their work with Indigenous Peoples:

> Raising the consciousness of social workers in order to work in solidarity with Aboriginal peoples goes beyond an understanding of colonization. It involves making connections to how social workers perpetuate the ills of capitalism, racism, sexism (and other "isms") at personal and collective societal levels. (p. 9)

Clearly, Bruyere is speaking the language of critical theories as they connect to social work as he implicates social workers who are, in part, agents of social control benefiting from an economic system that has destroyed the egalitarian one of Indigenous Peoples. Through their power and privileges, both as individuals and as part of a profession that makes judgements about how people should parent, what behaviours and lifestyles are problematic, and what programs they need to access, social workers can oppress, rather than assist, those who must come to them for services. Many other Indigenous social work practitioners take this process further, however, by exploring these concerns not only intellectually through consciousness-raising, but through a holistic approach that includes the physical, emotional, and spiritual aspects of a person as well (Baikie, 2009; Baskin, 2011; Hart, 2002; Lavallée, 2008). This is but one gap in the literature on both structural social work and AOP regarding the roles and contributions that Indigenous knowledges and practices are making in helping and healing processes.

Another relevant critique of AOP is that because it emphasizes "multiple identities and oppressions, it becomes easy to avoid naming and talking about the impact of racism while appearing progressive" (Pon, Gosine, & Phillips, 2011, p. 399). AOP is intended to be inclusive of *all* oppressions; however, this may mean watering down the impacts of racism (and colonialism) and not addressing white privilege or supremacy. There is no doubt, despite the intersections of Indigenous Peoples' oppressions, that racism always has been, and continues to be, at the forefront of colonization, since in the West, power and privilege are held by those who have a white racial identity (Yee, 2015). The white race has gained such power through colonization, which is based on notions of superiority to justify the exploitation of those who are non-white and Indigenous (Yee, 2015). In addition, even though AOP is now being taken up by some schools of social work and social services agencies, this may mean nothing more than tokenism for the purposes of reaccreditation by the Canadian Association of Schools of Social Work or putting up a poster in the reception area or participating in a one-day training session.

The conclusion is that critical social work theories do not go far enough. Although structural social work and AOP incorporate a historical perspective and a sound analysis of oppression at the institutional and societal levels, which includes the detrimental impact of colonization on Indigenous Peoples in Indigenous–Canadian relations, they lack discussions of cultures, spiritualities, strengths, and decolonization. This is problematic from an Indigenous perspective, as most Indigenous writers stress the significance of a cultural and spiritual foundation and decolonizing processes when working with communities (Baskin, 2011). In particular, spirituality, which is defined here as "a set of personal beliefs derived from an individual's perception of self and his or her relationship to both the natural world and some metaphysical realm" (Canda, 1989, p. 37), is perhaps the most important healing component from an Indigenous perspective, yet it is omitted in mainstream theories of social work including critical theories. This avoidance of spirituality in such theories impacts how we practise social work. For example, intake and assessment processes seem to have no difficulty asking potential service users very intrusive questions such as "do you have substance abuse problems" or "were you sexually abused as a child," yet shy away from asking if service users have any spiritual practices that are helpful to them or if they believe in some form of a greater power.

WHAT ABOUT ANTI-COLONIAL/POSTCOLONIAL THEORY?

Anti-colonial and postcolonial theories tend to be positioned as relationships between the North and South areas of the world. Several social work scholars, such as Heron (2005), Razack (2000), Gray (2005), and Wehbi (2011a), agree that anti-colonial refers to historical and contemporary resistance to practices and discourses that explicitly or implicitly position the global North as superior. Simmons and Dei (2012) state that "the post-colonial has given us a way to understand, to interpret the location, the experience of bodies, which in particular have historical trajectories to certain geographies of colonization [which are the] North, South geographies" (p. 93). These theories also acknowledge the continued struggle against new forms of colonialism—neo-colonialism—such as the agendas and practices of multinational corporations that originate in the North, but oppress the people of the South (Wehbi, 2011a).

However, colonialism is obviously not confined to North/South relationships since the North has also colonized the Indigenous Peoples who live in the North. Indigenous Peoples who live in what George Manuel and Michael Posluns (1974) called "the fourth world," which is more recently described as "the unifying nature of Indigenous action in the struggles against colonialism throughout the world" (Alfred & Corntassel,

2005, p. 610), are still living in a colonial time. Those who are the original people of Turtle Island—North America—have resisted European conquest from the very beginning and carry stories of resistance that have become part of their knowledges. Postcolonialism is also about the renewal of such knowledges, which is certainly taking place across Turtle Island just as much as in any other colonized land. As long as colonialism remains, a postcolonial or anti-colonial critique will challenge this legacy while linking the struggles of Indigenous Peoples around the world.

Anti-colonial scholarship has been taken up by several Indigenous scholars in diverse disciplines with an emphasis on settler colonialism and white supremacy (A. Smith, 2012), "everyday decolonization and resurgence practices" (Corntassel, 2012, p. 97), and relationships with the land (Coulthard, 2008; Monture-Angus, 1999; Simpson, 2014). A focus on land is critical because, since colonization is about disconnecting Indigenous Peoples from their lands, decolonization and resurgence is about reconnecting to these lands and to diverse cultures and communities (Corntassel, 2008, 2012). Anishnaabe scholar Leanne Simpson (2014) refers to these processes as "radical transformation" whereby we "create a generation of people attached to the land and committed to living out our culturally inherent ways of coming to know" (p. 13). Cherokee scholar Jeff Corntassel (2008, 2012) agrees, stressing that such transformation needs to include a renewal of not only Indigenous Peoples' rights, but also of their roles and responsibilities, which must be transmitted to future generations. Beginning with the words of Taiaiake Alfred, Corntassel (2008) refers to this as "a spiritual revolution" (p. 124).

Indigenous social work academics and practitioners in Canada also push beyond critical theories like structural social work and AOP, and are moving toward decolonization (Baikie, 2009; Hart, 2009; Sinclair, 2004). Inuit social work scholar Gail Baikie (2009) succinctly explains the intertwining of anti-colonialism and decolonization:

> Anti-colonialism critiques the historical and contemporary colonial suppression of Indigenous peoples by Euro-western forces, recognizes and supports efforts to resist, decolonize and reclaim what is cultural, and brings to the fore the unique nature-and-rights based nationalism of Indigenous peoples. (p. 47)

As an approach to social work, what is unique about postcolonialism is that it has no finite formula or set theory that influences it. Rather, it is inclusive of a "body of perspectives and practices [that] has never involved a singular theoretical formation … which has been developed out of traditions of resistance to global … imperialism and colonialism" (Stoler, 2011, p. 141). Thus, it is made up of theories located in areas such as political science, philosophy, sociology, literature, and theological studies. Most importantly, postcolonial theory reflects those who envisioned it as diverse colonized voices from around the globe, and it remains open to creativity and further development (Bhabha, 1994; Said, 1978; Spivak, 1988; Young, 1990). Anti-colonialism also speaks about the revitalization of local Indigenous knowledges, which challenges colonial imposition, emphasizes resistance to colonialism or neo-colonialism, is an interdisciplinary approach, and recognizes the significance of spirituality as sources of strength within political action (Simmons & Dei, 2012).

Although the term *postcolonial* may be confusing as it could be misunderstood as implying that we no longer live in a colonized state, this is not the case as "post-colonial discourse is the discourse of the colonized, which begins with colonization and does not stop when the colonizers go home" (Ashcroft, 2001, p. 23). Of course, in the case of the Indigenous Peoples of Turtle Island, the colonizers are never going home! Postcolonial theory emphasizes that the colonial condition of Canada, like elsewhere, has not passed, and the historical context of colonialism is connected to today's neo-colonial conditions (Alfred, 2011; Hall, 1996). It is crucial to postcolonial thinkers that we deconstruct and expose the racist, imperial nature of today's colonialism in order to remove its power of persuasion and coercion. In a similar way, anti-colonial theory views those in positions of colonial power as the dominant and the oppressors who must be accountable and responsible in bringing about social change. This is succinctly explained by Simmons and Dei (2012), who write:

> By focusing on the power, knowledge and agency of the oppressed on the one hand and the challenges of accountability and responsibility on the part of the dominant bodies on the other, we come into a dialectic understanding of how change emerges (i.e., for the dominant to use their power and privilege in the service of social transformation in the contexts of the everyday resistance of the colonized). (p. 79)

Unlike other critical theories, both postcolonial and anti-colonial theories take up the topics of culture and identity (Cesaire, 1972; Gandhi, 1998; Lorde, 1984; Memmi, 1991). They both reject essentialist notions of culture and identity, but nevertheless stress their importance in the reclaiming of ways of knowing and being (Stam & Shohat, 2012). In fact, some postcolonial scholars place so much importance on culture and identity that they refer to Indigenous Peoples having "cultural citizenship" rather than "national citizenship" (Subedi & Daza, 2008, p. 2). The point here is that some Indigenous postcolonial scholars, as well as "ordinary" people, see themselves as belonging, foremost, to a specific cultural group. Thus, rather than refer to themselves as Canadian, they identify as members of their particular Indigenous Nation such as Mi'kmaq, Anishnaabe, or Haida. This way of identifying oneself leads to some Indigenous Peoples refusing to vote in municipal, provincial, and federal political elections, seeing themselves as outside of this system. Others do not stand when Canada's national anthem is played because it neglects any reference to the original people of this land. Perhaps a combination of cultural and national citizenship makes the best sense since Indigenous Peoples in Canada have a unique relationship with the state in that we talk to one another Nation to Nation—at least, that is the way it is supposed to be.

Of course, we have multiple cultures and identities across Canada, and these are complex constructions with many peoples' multiple interpretations and experiences of them. An Indigenous person may at times be an insider and at other times an outsider, depending on the community they are in and the circumstances of their involvement. Depending on the setting, we bring forward certain aspects of our identities and cultures, while placing others in the background. For example, in order to have legitimacy whereby scholars and students listen to what we have to say and read what we write, we must put forward that we have PhDs and are university professors. However, this part of one's identity is irrelevant when we participate in spiritual ceremonies in Indigenous communities.

Anti-colonial theory also speaks about one's sense of self as determined authentically by the self and as what is experienced as socially constructed or imposed upon by others (Simmons & Dei, 2012). For example, one's culture and identity are also impacted by encounters with white privilege. Globally, light-coloured skin continues to be privileged and may be desired as a cultural commodity. For example, if an Indigenous person has light-coloured skin, this may interfere with their identity since light skin is often constructed as being non-Indigenous. Thus, someone may be read as being culturally white even though they are not racially white (Subedi & Daza, 2008).

The inclusion of identity is critical in the work we do with Indigenous Peoples. Many who seek assistance, or are mandated to do so, have grown up with few signifiers that celebrate being Indigenous, but rather have lived with stereotypes, disrespect, and racism their entire lives. Often these negative responses are internalized, with Indigenous Peoples believing that they are inferior to others, which leads to low self-esteem and self-destructive behaviours. A significant part of one's journey to wellness, then, is to shed such images of the self and come to know who you truly are as strong, proud Indigenous People. Social workers can choose to be a part of this journey by offering resources, support, education, and positive role modelling.

INDIGENOUS APPROACHES TO HELPING

Are there Indigenous approaches to social work? No and yes. No, if we recognize that social work is a Western concept and not organic to Indigenous Peoples anywhere on the planet. Social work is a Western cultural creation whose transfer of knowledge has been spread in recent times to other places in the world through, for example, professional schools (Baskin, 2011; Coates, 2003; Haug, 2001). As Gray and Coates (2010) explain,

> Social work is itself a cultural construction, a product of modernity and Western thinking. It developed in Anglo-American contexts to serve the needs and address the problems of industrializing democracies. It is modern and Western in its enduring search for empirical-rational knowledge foundations, professional status and universal values. ... social work is "Indigenous" to Anglo-American cultures. (p. 20)

However, the answer is yes if we use words such as "helping" and "healing" instead of social work, as such processes have existed since the beginning of Creation. An Indigenous approach to helping grows out of our knowledges or worldviews and our unique relationship with Canada. It incorporates our identities and values. Although there is much diversity among Indigenous Nations regarding specific cultures, the worldview or foundation is consistent for all Nations. Such a worldview incorporates connections to land, people, and ancestors. It includes original languages and powerful spiritualities (Absolon, 2009; Baskin, 2011; Hart, 2002; Meyer, 2008).

An Indigenous perspective believes in, and practises, a holistic approach, which emphasizes that healing must take place in all aspects of an individual: emotional, psychological, physical, and spiritual. A holistic approach also considers the interconnectedness of people's lives, including individuals, families, communities, and ancestors (Baskin, 2011; Greenwood & de Leeuw, 2007; Hart, 2002; Reid, 2009). The prominence of healing is significant because it is through healing that people and communities are able to reclaim their identities and address the long-standing wounds of historical trauma caused by colonization.

Another important piece of an Indigenous approach is its focus on relationships. Typically, it is crucial for an Indigenous person to have a relationship with someone before they develop trust in that person and are able to confide in them. An Indigenous person will not usually ask intrusive questions of others as often happens in social work, whereby the worker asks a service user about childhood sexual abuse or substance misuse, sometimes at the first encounter. There is a strong belief in taking the time necessary to develop relationships between those involved in the helping process, which conflicts with the task-oriented, time-constrained pressures of mainstream social work (Baskin, 2011; Weaver, 2007).

As these worldviews and values are reclaimed by Indigenous service providers this, in turn, shapes their helping practices. Communities decide what helping processes they will incorporate and how these will be integrated into community action that leads to decolonization. New information is constantly needed because revitalizing worldviews and values alone will not release us from the colonial masters (Baskin, 2003, 2011). An Indigenous perspective challenges how non-Indigenous people view Indigenous–Canadian relations. The ongoing injustices and inequality faced by Indigenous Peoples in this country are overwhelming. It is not possible that the resistance of Indigenous Peoples alone can end such oppression. Non-Indigenous people have just as much of a role to play in decolonization as Indigenous Peoples do because many of them also face racism. We all live on the same land; we want to live up to our international reputation as a peacekeeping country that welcomes everyone, values diversity, and treats all with respect; and we all have responsibilities to the generations to come. In fact, because of the impact it has in the lives of Indigenous Peoples, the profession of social work ought to take a lead in this process. This may include initiatives between Indigenous communities and social work, but these would have to highlight first-voice leadership, needs driven by communities, consensus decision making, and the development of relationships between all involved (Baskin, 2011; Weaver, 2007).

Another significant aspect regarding Indigenous helping and healing is how those who help are viewed. There is much more to being a helper than attaining a social work degree. Informal, natural helpers who have cultural knowledge of the specific Nation and community are valued. Cultural and spiritual gifts of workers are recognized as life experiences. Successful, culture-based community agencies are those that hire workers from the local community who have a strong sense of belonging, as well as both collective and personal strengths and contributions (Brown & Fraehlich, 2012). Helpers are also those who have lived with historical trauma, systemic racism, and family poverty, and are engaged in their own healing (Brown & Fraehlich, 2012).

DECOLONIZATION

Both anti-colonialism and postcolonialism also take up decolonization, which other critical theories do not. Decolonization has been defined by various Indigenous scholars. For instance, Cannon and Sunseri (2011) define it as "a process of struggle whereby colonized nations and peoples reject colonial authority and (re)establish freedom, recognized self-determining governing systems, and self-determined existence on their territories" (p. 276). Alfred and Corntassel (2005) refer to it as "shifts in thinking and action that emanate from recommitments and reorientations at the level of the self that, over time and through proper organization, manifest as broad social and political movements to challenge state agendas and authorities" (p. 143). Certainly, from these definitions, Indigenous Peoples globally are engaged in various processes of decolonizing.

Other Indigenous scholars, such as Baskin (Mi'kmaq; 2011), Hart (Cree; 2009), and Tamburro (Shawnee Piqua; 2010), discuss decolonization as critical to everyone living in Canada, which includes the white descendants of the colonizers as well as racialized populations. Even though people who are not white are not in the same position as those who are, they live on Indigenous land and benefit from that. Both anti-colonial and postcolonial theories discuss decolonization for those who are colonized and those who are in dominant or white bodies. However, neither of these theories seems to take up the role of marginalized bodies who are not white, but who live on Turtle Island. These are conversations that may be even more difficult than those between the colonized and the colonizers.

Yet, such a position also invokes possibilities for marginalized people coming together as allies and resisters of colonization. Simmons and Dei (2012), both anti-colonial theorists who critique postcolonialism, state:

> The "post" conveniently implicates all, while the "anti" identifies the "bad guy" and carries with it a radical critique of the dominant, as the colonial oppressor whose antics and oppressive practices continue to script the lives of the subordinate and colonized even as we resist such dominance. (p. 68)

All non-Indigenous people need to educate themselves about past and present colonization and how they are implicated in it. They need to discard their false consciousness about this country and Indigenous Peoples. They need to address the wrongs in meaningful ways and do their own healing. All of this must be done because "the colonization and marginalization of Indigenous peoples is not just an Indigenous story, but also the story of Canada" (St. Denis, 2011, p. vii).

Interestingly enough, decolonization today will be best realized if all of us return to the original relationship formed by our ancestors in 1664 through the Guswentah or Two Row Wampum of the Haudenosaunee—"People of the Longhouse"—Confederacy (Cannon & Sunseri, 2011). This Confederacy, originally made up of five distinct Nations—today there are six—united to create peaceful ways of decision making. It is referred to as the oldest participatory democracy on earth (Haudensosaunee Confederacy, n.d.). The Two Row Wampum is an agreement or treaty made on a Nation-to-Nation basis between the Haudenosaunee and the newcomers to Turtle Island, which "symbolizes the river of life on which the Crown's sailing ship and the Haudenosaunee canoe both travel. The three white rows are recognized as symbolizing an everlasting peace, friendship, and respect between the two" (Williams & Nelson, 1995, p. 3). This Wampum also clearly speaks to the value of non-interference and the political stance of separate jurisdictions, as these two Nations

> were to co-exist as independent entities, each respecting the autonomy of the other. The two rows of purple wampum, representing the two governments, ran parallel, never crossing. The two vessels travel together, as allies, but neither nation tries to steer the other's vessel. In the relationship envisioned by the Two Row Wampum, neither government has the authority to legislate for the other. (Johnston, 1986, p. 11)

Again, however, today we need to consider a third group of people in the decolonization process—those who are racialized and did not participate in the colonization of Indigenous Peoples. Perhaps we need to update the position of the Two Row Wampum to include three canoes!

CONCLUSION

In terms of theories, it is only the anti-colonial and postcolonial that take up Indigenous knowledges and decolonization processes and are written by Indigenous Peoples. Because of this, they are the theories that are closest to Indigenous approaches to helping and healing. However, critical theories such as structural social work and anti-oppression, although arising out of Western perspectives, are in line with Indigenous approaches in terms of their recognition of historical and present-day colonization, thereby making them useful to allies of Indigenous Peoples. The way forward is to see the limitations of critical social work theories and work toward putting their principles into practice, so social workers can meaningfully participate in decolonization, which is of benefit to *all* peoples.

2 | Long-Standing Social Conflicts and Local Problems of Population Governance

Reorganizing for Future Theory Development and Community Practice

Tina Wilson, Vanier Scholar, Doctoral Student, School of Social Work, McMaster University

In school, I was taught that there is a tension in social work between care and control that can be traced back to our origins in the charity organizing societies and the settlement houses. This inherited conflict was promoted further through distinctions made between casework and community work, and between mainstream social work and critical social work. My sense is that we make these sorts of distinctions as a way to benchmark efforts to shift the discipline we have inherited, and as a means to express our willingness to acknowledge critiques of the oppressiveness of professional social work. The emergence of anti-oppressive practice frameworks is part of this ongoing acknowledgement and change work.

My aim in this chapter is to emphasize the historicity of social work knowledge–practice, including social justice–oriented alternatives like anti-oppressive practice. Maurer (2007) provides a fruitful entrance point into this history with her argument that social work provides us with a memory of social conflict. The argument goes like this: Social work provides a calming response to social transformations and perceived social problems through our work to relieve some of the damage caused by such things as nation building and colonization, capitalism and neoliberal globalization, patriarchy and sanism, and so on. The evidence—the memory—of these social conflicts can be found in our theories, our practices, and our institutions. Both anti-oppressive practice frameworks and child welfare institutions are examples of this evidence–memory. Maurer's point is not that social work embodies the *right* way to think and act in response to social conflict, just that we *do* think and act in response to social conflict. Social work's knowledge–practice is thus the manifest tip of the iceberg both to long-standing social conflicts and to processes of social change.

The idea that our work calms social tensions is a more ambiguous account of older distinctions made between care and control, between social justice–oriented and mainstream social works. Thinking along with Maurer (2007), developments in social justice–oriented perspectives like anti-oppressive practice are similarly a documentation of more popular alternative responses to social conflict, alternatives that also serve an ameliorating function. More broadly, the retraction of a welfare state approach to mediating capitalism provides evidence of social conflict being addressed differently, and of a consequent amendment to the relationship between government and citizens. These changes—in relationship and in response to social conflict—are altering the relationship between social work and government, and between social work and client sub-populations.

To what extent are social work theories able to illuminate the historicity of these shifting relationships and conflicts, and our role—anti-oppressive oriented or otherwise—in quieting the social conflicts of our present? How do we even begin to think about our imbricated relationship with government, and with social conflicts that are simultaneously indications of inequality (e.g., poverty) and local problems of population governance (e.g., homelessness)? What might we learn from the absorption of earlier grassroots advocacy efforts into the fold of mainstream social services, and of critiques of professional social work into frameworks like anti-oppressive practice? What new calming responses are in the process of being institutionalized today, and what alternative ameliorating responses might we propose? Finally, can our history teach us something useful about the instability of all attempts to foster and shape progressive social change? This chapter presents a loose theoretical framework and a sub-population-specific example from which to begin to engage with these sorts of questions.

In the first half of the chapter, I operationalize Maurer's (2007) thesis that social work activities provide evidence of social conflict by piecing together a theoretical scaffold that emphasizes the relationships between *population governance*, the construction of *social problems*, and the naming of *sub-populations* thought to require social work interventions. Three layers of theory will be outlined in brief: (1) governmentality, a perspective on governance in liberal democracies made popular by Foucault but much extended by scholars in sociology and policy studies over the past 20 years; (2) political scientist Murray Edelman's (1988) work on the construction and use of social problems; and (3) the philosopher Ian Hacking's (1999, 2007) work on the "making up" of different kinds of people. In the second half of the chapter, I illustrate both Maurer's thesis and these theoretical anchors through a mapping of the ways in which the idea of "problem youth" has changed over the past 25 years alongside the emergence and intensification of neoliberal projects in a Canadian province. In doing so, I hope to make clear the utility to social work of locating, in time, fluctuations in how we conceptualize community, distinguish sub-populations, and build assumptions about progressive social change into our knowledge–practice.

CONNECTING LOCAL PROBLEMS TO ONGOING SOCIAL CONFLICTS: A THREE-PART THEORETICAL FRAMEWORK

Governmentality

The question of whether those of us in the West can even imagine a professional social work practice that is not dependent on the possibility of state-level redistribution suggests a closer look at the relationship between social work and government is in order. Governmentality is a perspective that explores the "how" of governance. The extent to which different concepts and methods are emphasized in governmentality-focused work varies by disciplinary entrance point, project focus, and author (Lemke, 2011; McKee, 2009). In the most general sense,

> governmentality refers to government, not as centralized in a single institution, set of institutions or even a person or group, but rather as the outcome of a multitude of thoughts and practices that shape assumptions about what government is, how it should be exercised, by whom, and for what purposes. (Murray, 2007, p. 162)

More particularly, governmentality investigates the tension between individual freedoms and governmental aims, exploring how, in Foucault's words, "the conduct of conduct" is carried out in everyday life. Stated otherwise, the means through which individuals come to voluntarily act in ways that are, for the most part, congruent with overarching governance projects. This linking of the political with the personal reflects Foucault's genealogical work into both the development of liberal forms of governance and of particular types of subjectivity. "Governmentality is fundamentally a political project—a way of both problematizing life and seeking to act upon it, which identifies both a territory (i.e. social space) and means of intervention" (McKee, 2009, p. 468).

Focusing on the relationship between social work, government, and client groups, a central argument from a governmentality standpoint is that state-level governance depends on the social sciences to produce knowledges that enable individuals and populations to be known and acted upon (Lemke, 2011). Moreover, the state is not the most important actor. Rather, we should also attend to the practices of non-state institutions and actors—education, health, and social services, among others—in teaching, coaching, and socializing people to think and behave in particular ways (Murray, 2007). A third general premise is that these expert knowledges and everyday practices shape the options available for thinking about others and ourselves. Knowledge and practice encourage particular forms of subjectivity that, once embodied, propel further rounds of knowledge production and institutional practice (Chambon, 1999). An alignment between state priorities and non-state actors is accomplished in part through the imprecise circulation and operationalization of knowledge, what Foucault termed power/knowledge and what poststructuralism would define as the effects of dominant discourse. The knowledge–practice of social work, including our anti-oppressive alternatives, is part of these alignments and these shifts. Governmentality thus provides a partial explanation for how governments, increasingly neoliberalized social policies, and social justice–oriented social work can end up using the same language to imagine social change (e.g., community-based research).

The divestment and decentralizing of government-facilitated social, health, and education services commonly noted in critiques of neoliberalism is understood from a governmentality perspective as the material outcome of a shift in rationality or logic. It is a different approach to managing social conflicts and their local manifestation as problems of population governance. The move is toward more diffused, informal types of governance activities conducted by an array of non-state actors including social work and non-profit community organizations (Murray, Low, & Waite, 2006). The state, however, does maintain some control over these actors (McKee, 2009). This dispersal of responsibility to the community for population management, attended as it is by cuts to many actual material supports, is both intensifying and making more visible the governance functions of social work (Wilson, 2008).

Of particular relevance to anti-oppressive social work, neoliberal governmentality shapes the possibilities available for people to embody in ways more specific than earlier forms of liberal governance (Lemke, 2011).

> Strategies of welfare sought to govern through society. Advanced liberal strategies of rule ask whether it is possible to govern without governing *society*, that is to say, to govern through the regulated and accountable choices of autonomous agents— citizens, consumers, parents, employees, managers, investors—and to govern through intensifying and acting upon their allegiance to particular "communities." (Miller & Rose, 2008, p. 216)

As my youth-specific example will demonstrate in the latter half of this chapter, this exaggeration of affiliation for the purpose of governance is easily misinterpreted as recognition, with this ostensible recognition functioning to calm social conflict.

In these ways, governmentality as a broad perspective emphasizes the role of knowledge production, experts including social work, and institutional practices including those of community organizations, in encouraging people to act in ways commonly believed to be in their own best interests. As neoliberal governmentality, it refers to the ways in which particular interests think about the organization of society and shape activities as a means to advance diverse neoliberal projects. While presented in a linear fashion here, governmentality as a perspective also emphasizes how complexity, chance, and the actions of individuals inevitably interrupt the direct application of ways of thinking about society and population management in practice, and thus intended outcomes are rarely wholly realized (Dean, 1999; McKee, 2009).

Problem Formulations

Attending to the construction and use of social problems, Edelman (1988) emphasizes that many damaging conditions recognized as social problems endure because they are of benefit to some segment of society. Acknowledging selected problem aspects over the profit aspect of a given condition is a way to minimize social conflict: for example, widely empathizing with the personal difficulty caused by unemployment, and more quietly acknowledging the benefits of supply-side economics to employers. Edelman goes on to underscore that social policies aimed at fixing a given social problem are typically partial and contradictory, trying as they do to meet to some degree the interests of multiple social groups—those that are harmed and those that benefit. For social work, this tension is evident in the more and less equitable intents we encounter in our organizations, and perhaps most overtly in government-funded intervention programs (Wilson, 2008).

The final piece from Edelman (1988) relevant to this discussion is that the name given to a social policy—this argument can also be extended to the program goals and deliverables for funded community intervention programs—communicates a sense of certainty that things will change for the better; that progress is inevitable. This confidence elides the inconstancies, contradictions, and competing interests that underpin all levels of social intervention, from policy to direct practice. It also serves to distract us from the relatively stable nature of many social conflicts (e.g., the systemic nature of poverty) and functions to justify temporary needs-based interventions.

Social Classifications

The philosopher Ian Hacking (2007) takes this consideration of the construction and use of social problems to greater levels of specificity. Hacking is interested in the emergence and development of social classifications over time, what Foucault called "dividing practices" and what Hacking terms "making up people." If governmentality would focus on the knowledge, institutions, practices, and rationalities involved in the governance of people who are poor, and Edelman (1988) would explore how the problem of poverty is articulated in such a way that social conflict remains hidden, Hacking would be interested in the construction of people who are poor into distinct category(s) or sub-population(s):

> Classifications evaluate who is troubling or in trouble. Hence, they present value-laden kinds, things to do or not to do. Kinds of people to be or not to be. Partly because of

implied values, people sorted under those kinds change or work back upon the kind. … Classifications can change our evaluations of our personal worth, of the moral kind of person that we are. (Hacking, 1999, p. 131)

Hacking (2007) identifies five components involved in the development of distinct kinds of people that overlap with the governmentality emphasis of the role of knowledge, experts, and institutional practices in governance activities: (1) a classification, or what social work would more often term a vulnerable sub-population; (2) a group of people who are in distress; (3) formal institutions such as schools and social service organizations; (4) expert and popular knowledge; and (5) the experts, including social workers, who both develop and operationalize knowledge within institutions and with the kind of people "made up" by these five components. Social problems, social classifications, knowledge production, and institutional practices are thus imbricated with one another over time and are, from a governmentality perspective, a main way in which governance is accomplished in liberal democracies.

The three layers of theory outlined here provide a loose scaffold from which to reflect on the shifting relationships between government, social work, and client sub-populations, and on the evolving role social work plays in calming local manifestations of social conflict in the present day. Governmentality emphasizes the role of knowledge from the social sciences and of non-state actors like social work in governance activities; Edelman's (1988) work underscores the stable nature of long-standing social problems like poverty, the political uses social problems are put to, and the multiple competing interests embedded in social policy and intervention programs; and finally, Hacking's (1999, 2007) work reminds us that social classifications are neither essential truths about actual people nor static constructs. As a way to illustrate these theoretical anchors—particularly what social classifications and problem formulations can show us about changing responses to social conflict—the following section briefly reviews how young people have been understood over the past 25 years by the Ontario provincial government. This is the time period in which the phased, shifting priorities of neoliberal interests became visible through changing social policy responses to social problems.

AN EXAMPLE: 25 YEARS OF PROBLEM YOUTH IN ONTARIO[1]

The historical character of our present is increasingly recognized as a resource from which to imagine that things might be otherwise. This interest in the past is perhaps exemplified by Hoy (2009), who has gone so far as to suggest that critical genealogy is to poststructuralism what critical theory is to the Frankfurt School. The analysis included here, while most certainly not of the depth of actual genealogical research, was inspired by those social work scholars who have undertaken detailed explorations into what Foucault termed the "history of the present" (see Chambon, 1999, 2012, 2013; Skehill, 2007). Methodologically speaking, the type of broad historical anchoring described here is more closely related to Foucault's looser archaeological work, though again, this data and analysis are not nearly as detailed.

For those less familiar with either of these traditions, "archaeology tries to unearth the structures or rules that govern discourses. Genealogy uncovers the power relations that form our very subjectivity" (Hoy, 2009, p. 204). In these ways, both genealogy and archaeology have much to offer social work as we engage in the ongoing work of re-establishing our social justice projects. Inspired by both approaches, the work reported below is helpful in that it allows us to step back from the disciplinary, sectorial, and institutional discourses in which we are all entrenched, to reconnect a particular sub-population of interest—in this case young people—to broader social conflicts and their local manifestation as problems of population governance. My aim is to illustrate, through history, how the ubiquitous categories of social policy and community services euphemistically integrate with the marked social identities we are more likely to recognize within social justice communities. This amalgamation is often difficult to keep at the forefront of our attention, even within anti-oppressive social work, because our paid practice is located at the fraught convergence of status quo–maintaining population management and ongoing processes of social change.

The data presented here is a simple keyword search of the Ontario Legislature's Hansard transcripts (http://hansardindex.ontla.on.ca/hansarde.asp). Each issue of Hansard contains the legislative proceedings for one day. A keyword search of the database returns a list of transcripts, or days, in which the term was mentioned at least once. Containing more than 25 years' worth of legislative debates, this open-access data source is useful for mapping shifts in which social conditions are constructed as social problems, and which aspects of the condition are emphasized over time, by this provincial government.

The 25 years between January 1, 1985, and December 31, 2009, were searched using 27 terms related to 6 overarching problems: postsecondary education, child welfare, youth employment, youth mental health, youth homelessness, and youth crime. Returned transcripts were clustered into five-year blocks and charted. The overall proportion of each term, as well as fluctuations in their size over time, illustrates which discourses—problem formulations and related social classifications—about young people dominate in the province of Ontario.

Over the 25 years between 1985 and 2010, "youth," "teenagers," and "adolescents" were talked about on roughly 2,260 days in the Ontario Legislative Assembly. This attention has almost doubled, from discussion on 340 days in the earliest 5-year period to 640 days in the most recent. We can look at the six overarching problems of education, child welfare, employment, mental health, homelessness, and crime in terms of their size over time, where changes in the amount of attention they receive suggests influence.

Figure 2.1: Problem Weighting over 25 Years, Ontario Hansard Data

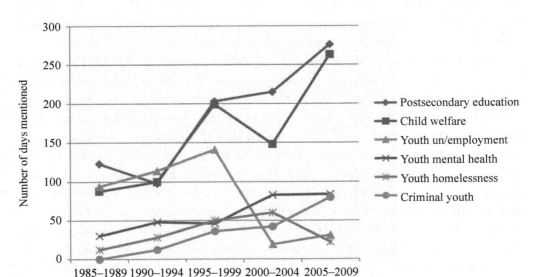

As illustrated in Figure 2.1, with a small dip in the early 1990s, attention to postsecondary education has doubled, from discussion on 123 days in the earliest period to 276 in the most recent. Youth unemployment received steady attention between 1985 and 2000—mentioned on average 115 days in each 5-year period—but disappeared rather abruptly around the turn of the century; it was mentioned only 50 times in the last decade. Corroborating the work of Ian Hacking (1999) and Karen Staller (2010), among others, we can see the growth of child abuse as a recognized social problem since the late 1980s. This problem was mentioned on 88 days in the first 5-year period and continues to trend upward, with 263 days of discussion in the most recent period. Attention to youth homelessness, which was never all that common, has been outpaced by attention to mental health, and most recently, by a steadily increasing discourse on criminal youth.

Demonstrating the "making up" of human kinds as discussed by Hacking (1999, 2007), the various named sub-populations within each of these broader problem formulations have also shifted over time. "Children's mental health" started and continues to be one of the largest concerns attached to young people, as shown in Figure 2.2. The idea of "youth mental health," however, only emerged in the last decade. The problem of homeless youth took off and then collapsed during this time, largely fuelled by the debates around the Safe Streets Act and the visibility of squeegee kids in Toronto. "Youth crime" emerged as a social problem in the 1990s and "youth violence" in the period between 2005 and 2010. Recalling Edelman's (1988) argument that certain elements are emphasized in the construction of social problems, the emergence of "at-risk youth" as a kind of young person mirrors almost exactly the social problem of youth violence. It also provides a counterweight to the apparent decline in "delinquent" young people. Euphemistically obscuring long-standing social conflicts (e.g., imperialism and capitalism), these problem formulations and problem kinds refer to the management of young people who are for the most part poor, racialized, and, in the case of criminalized youth, male.

Figure 2.2: Problem Sub-populations over 25 Years, Ontario Hansard Data

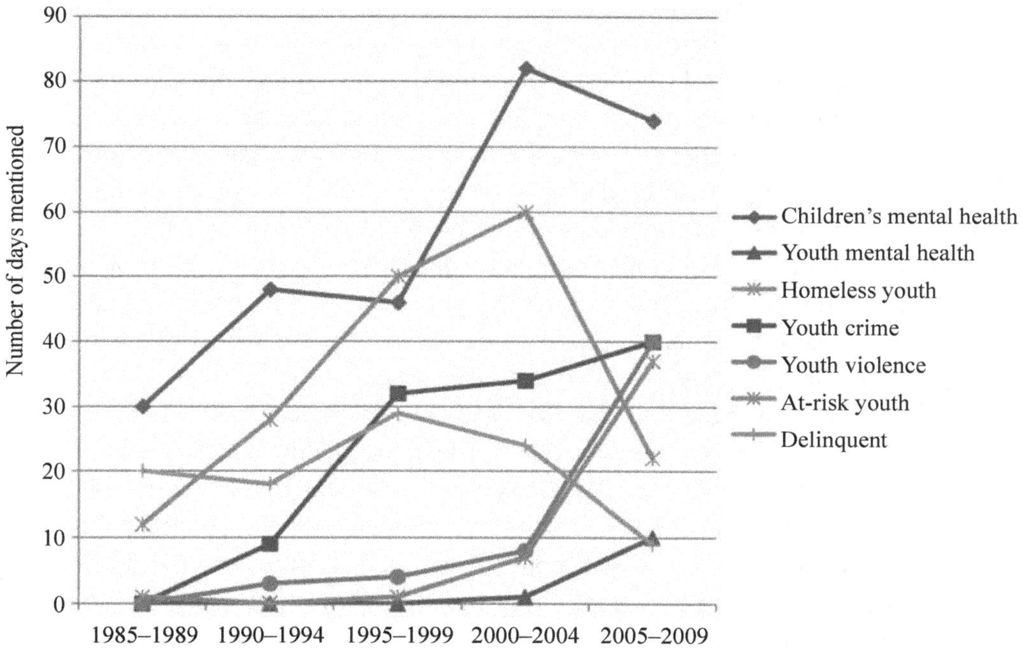

This brief mapping of social problems and problem kinds of young people over the past 25 years suggests an evolving rationality of neoliberal governmentality that emphasizes particular kinds of young people requiring particular strategies of population governance. The mounting governmental attention to young people shown here provides an important indicator of emerging approaches to quieting contemporary iterations of long-standing social conflict that will, to some degree, impact entire generations. Thus, the struggles of young people today are increasingly understood as problems of education, problems of mental health, and problems of crime. More broadly, the struggles of families are increasingly conceptualized as problems of child welfare. The shift in managing social conflict is, therefore, away from acknowledging problem social conditions and calming conflict through the financial inclusion of employment and the stability of housing, and toward emphasizing problem sub-populations and calming conflict by encouraging targeted groups to adopt pro-social affiliations and keep occupied in particular ways.

The all-encompassing nature of some of these emerging categories is one way that neoliberalization processes are able to be so nimble and responsive. Take, for example, the shift from the term *delinquent* to *at-risk youth*. While fewer young people could be classified as delinquent, all youth, at some point, can be conceptualized as being at-risk in some fashion (Bessant, 2002). A more holistic iteration of mental health as a social problem similarly enfolds an extensive range of phenomena, privileging experiences and symptoms over material conditions. The dominance of these sorts of universal social problems permits both innocuous generalizations about concern for the well-being of young people and targeted, needs-based interventions that can be shifted from special sub-population to special sub-population in an adaptive, if not reactive, fashion. The calming functions of recognition are in these ways transposed from social conditions to categories of affiliation. Of relevance to social work theorizing, while earlier material methods of managing social conflict were more amiable to certain types of social justice projects, the newer, individualized, and ephemeral recognition of neoliberal governmentality is much trickier to build upon. Moreover, if in our practices we provide recognition without recourse, it is likely that we will foster within our clients a certain level of resignation toward inequality.

Neoliberalism has been called a "rascal concept" because of the diverse and contradictory ways in which it is described and critiqued within and across disciplines (Brenner, Peck, & Theodore, 2010). The sociologist Tomas Lemke (2011) identifies three main critiques of neoliberalism: that it is a faulty ideology that can be overcome by a true knowledge of how things really work; that it represents the domination of economics over the state thus requiring the state to reassert itself; and that it is a destructive, "anti-humanist" force harming individuals and society. Lemke offers a caution of particular relevance to social work given our imbrication with both government and enduring social conflicts: By founding arguments on dichotomies, these forms of critique reinforce the conceptual strength of the very discourses they are attempting to counter.

Neoliberalism is a political project, but unlike liberalism, it is not a coherent, principled philosophy from which to govern society (O'Flynn, 2012). The general priorities of the thing we call neoliberalism are the protection of capital and the concentration of power (O'Flynn, 2012). Neoliberalism is an uneven *process* that continues to shape society in diverse ways (Brenner, Peck, & Theodore, 2010), and it is a social and political *movement* fostering neoliberal regimes of government both of states and by states (Dean, 2014), through which elite interests generate and shape responses to social conflict. Dean (2014), following Mirowski, suggests we understand neoliberalism as a diverse, flexible, and political "thought collective" rather than as an ideology or type of nation-state. Dean stresses the intelligence of this "neoliberal intellectual movement" and, similar to Edelman (1988), draws attention to the ways in which this collective operates through "a doctrine of double truths," one for the public and one for elites.

With an enviable ability to make productive use of critical events, neoliberal interests operate through current socioeconomic circumstances and the styles of government available (Dean, 1999, 2014). These interests commonly manifest at the level of the state as short-sighted, delay-tactic policies that shift pressures among social actors rather than addressing underlying causes, and as frequent, overt policy failures that drive the creation of new experiments (Brenner, Peck, & Theodore, 2010). The speed in transition from failure, reflective absorption of critique, to recreation is noteworthy, if not frankly intimidating. Remarkably discourse-savvy, neoliberalization processes and goals are in these ways difficult to isolate from broader sociocultural shifts and governmental activities (e.g., the move from "delinquent" to "at-risk"), or from discourses and interventions within social work and community-based practice (Wehbi & Turcotte, 2007; Wilson, 2011). The tensions inherent to attempting social justice–oriented social work practice are thus becoming more complicated as a result of this intelligent, articulate flexibility, and resourceful use of the tools at hand.

THE WORK AHEAD

All academic disciplines are facing the question of what's next for theory now that a certain level of post–related epistemological saturation has been achieved. The role of intellectual critique, the tools of critique, and the targets of critique are similarly unresolved matters of concern (Latour, 2004). The increasingly uncertain prospect of attaining a socialist state government—the gold standard of protection from capitalist excess—let alone retaining our welfare state, and the ascent of both evidence-based advocacy over democratic protest (Laforest, 2004; Laforest & Orsini, 2005) and philanthropic volunteerism over structural change (Buffett, 2013), are significantly undermining the utility of traditional alternative responses to inequality. It is against these shared uncertainties, and in the face of cuts to actual material resources, that social justice–oriented social work is attempting to articulate practical theoretical direction for everyday community work with people who are marginalized through the long-standing conflicts of our society.

My aim in this chapter has been to emphasize the importance of history to contemporary social justice–oriented social work knowledge–practice, including our anti-oppressive alternatives. Operationalizing Maurer's (2007) argument that our work provides us with evidence of conflict, the layering of ideas presented here provides a range of entrance points into exploring the governmental functions of expert knowledge and non-state actors such as social work and community organizations; the political uses and competing interests embedded in the construction of many enduring social problems, and relatedly, in our interventions; and finally, the ways in which troubling people are classified and targeted over time. Historically locating the emergence of sub-populations and the broader problem formulation that serves to justify them can help us keep pace with the evolving ways in which inequality is rationalized and managed. In the genealogical tradition, this is a very preliminary way to detect "the birth of universals and their transformation into principles of domination" (Hoy, 2009, p. 235). Thinking along with Dean (2014), these rationalizations and forms of management can be understood as the public face of the neoliberal intellectual movement as it makes productive use of local forms of inequality.

The identity of social justice–oriented social work in the West is arguably founded upon the possibility of advocating for the inclusion of marginalized groups so that they too receive the benefits of full citizenship rights within liberal democratic society. At this time, however, it is difficult to ascertain when our community-based interventions foster actual inclusion within liberal democracy and not simply participation in capitalist relations (see Preston & Aslett, this volume, for a discussion of the complicated absence of democratic youth engagement from community organizations in Ontario). To whom, to what extent, and with what permanence democracy provides recognition, opportunity, or material resources has arguably been answered, but there is much more work to be done to understand what the philosophy behind both the original concept and its critiques might suggest is worth salvaging from this powerful idea.

Liberal democratic traditions, neoliberal projects, and justice-oriented social work share many organizing concepts (Maurer, 2007). Our task, therefore, is to differentiate all-important nuances within these alignments. Brown (2012), emphasizing differences in epistemology, provides a useful illustration of some of the ways in which this overlap manifests within anti-oppressive practice discourses. As important as they are, postmodern and poststructural theorizing do not provide us with sufficient grounding in the classic political philosophy required if we are to engage with state-level government, liberalism, democracy, and capitalism in their contemporary Western forms. Latter-day epistemologies, and perhaps especially postcolonial and de-colonial critiques, are essential to reorganizing justice-oriented social work, but we must also establish a firmer grounding in the political philosophical traditions that underpin our work.

Our challenge in the present day is to identify the broad socioeconomic shifts in favour of elites that are occurring behind diverse local manifestations of population governance, including our anti-oppressive alternatives. In the case of young people in Ontario, we must be especially careful as we engage with what is produced by the mounting attention to education, mental health, crime, and child welfare. Moreover, we must find ways to recognize and carry with us gains made over the past 100 years in favour of some marginalized sub-populations, and weigh these gains against damage done in our evolving assessment of social progress. The boundaries imposed by social categories produce all sorts of things including, sometimes, much-needed recognition and access to resources. Historically locating social shifts, social service interventions, and social justice–oriented alternatives allows us to understand ourselves as actors in the messiness of time. There is nothing inevitable about our present.

With the possibility of innocent (Rossiter, 2001), heroic (Todd, 2005), or paid critical (Wilson, 2008) social work practice increasingly suspect, similarities, shared history, and shared aims—both within increasingly neoliberalized state governments and amongst our allies—may very well be a place from which we can develop new strategies for ameliorating social inequality in our everyday community work and, as a discipline, attempt to imagine beyond the limits of liberalism and democracy as governmentalities. If difference-attentive activism has schooled us in the violence, mass inequalities, and mass failures hidden behind grand metanarratives, including that of liberal democracy and the welfare state, 30 years of evolving neoliberalization processes have also taught us the dangers of failing to hold on to even flawed dreams or to collectively propose alternatives. Reorganizing social work, therefore, also requires that we propose alternative forms of governance that we can imagine we would be willing to accept for our clients and ourselves.

NOTE

1. This data set is an extension of work previously published in the *Canadian Social Work Review, 28*(1), under the title "Embodied liability: The usefulness of at-risk youth." The data used here include more items than were originally reported, and that earlier work focused more specifically on current conditions for young people.

3 | Ontario's Child Welfare Transformation and Primary Health Care Renewal

The Allure of Change

Kristin Smith, Associate Professor, School of Social Work, Ryerson University

Rapid and dramatic transformations have been taking place within health and social service organizations over several decades throughout Western countries. These transformations are part of larger processes that critics describe as neoliberal restructuring (Baines, 2004a, 2004b, 2007; Dominelli, 1999; Fabricant & Burghardt, 1992). Across Canada, during the 1990s to early 2000s, all governments, to varying degrees, moved to enact cuts to health and social service programs. These cuts caused rising pressures on social service workers to provide more supports with fewer resources to marginalized community members who were facing far more complex problems (Baines, 2004b, 2007). In response to these growing pressures, service delivery systems were reorganized, often along the lines of corporate-like managerial practices (Clarke & Newman, 1997). In line with these restructured workplaces, service providers faced new expectations to demonstrate commitments to "efficiencies" and "accountability" within their work practices (Baines, 2004b, p. 6).

By 2008, a worsening global economic recessionary crisis prompted what many believed to be a leftward shift in the willingness of Western governments to intervene in the economy. Indeed, to many, it seemed as though governments of all political stripes were now racing to distance themselves from free-market ideology and, instead, pledging to realign themselves with a decidedly more Keynesian economic plan (Weisbrot, 2008). Amidst a world economic recession, unlike any since the 1930s Depression era, most economists conceded that "stimulus measures"—deficit financing, infrastructure spending, and social and economic protection measures— would be necessary to address a failing economy (Clark, 2008).

Certainly, for many progressive social and health policy-makers and social service providers, increased government intervention in the economy is seen as a necessary shift away from the hardships of free markets toward more collective models of social provisioning (Jessop, 2003; Midgley, 1999, 2014). However, some have suggested that rather than a rediscovery of Keynesian economic principles, the apparent leftward swing in the political pendulum could be more accurately analyzed as the adaptive potential that characterizes new forms of neoliberalism (Peck & Tickell, 2002). This argument sees neoliberalism not as a retreat from a regulatory economy (i.e., a dismantling of the social welfare state), but rather as a series of market-oriented governance techniques designed to intervene in the social and economic lives of all (Peck, 2010). For instance, Peck and Tickell (2002) identify deliberate stretching of the neoliberal policy repertoire to include new models of institution building such as the selective appropriation of "community" and "partnership" modes for public service delivery (p. 390). Hall (2005) refers to this appropriation in the UK as the "double shuffle" (p. 332), whereby New Labour defends its massive departures from social democratic values by rhetorically "spinning" its continuity with them. Taken together, these authors argue that the new regulatory processes effectively extend the neoliberal project through the management of its contradictions.

In this chapter, I explore the implications of these expanded forms of neoliberalism for activist or anti-oppressive social work practice. In order to understand the new regulatory potential of neoliberalism, I explore and analyze the practice stories of social workers labouring in contexts characterized as "transformed" and "renewed" in Southern Ontario, Canada. While the discussion in this chapter is limited to Ontario, the conversation has a broader reach to other locales and practice settings experiencing similar shifts. The context for my study involves significant policy changes, announced by the Ontario Liberal government in 2005, which would transform two important care sectors that employ social workers. The new programs resulting from these changes would be known as *Child Welfare Transformation* and *Primary Health Care Renewal*. I draw on research in which I conducted qualitative interviews with 17 self-identified activist social workers with extensive work experience—ten years or more—in either Ontario's child welfare system or its primary health care sector in order to explore what the changes have meant for their social justice–based practices. I use the term "activist social worker" to refer to those within the profession who draw on feminist, anti-racist, anti-oppressive, and other critical theories, in order to link "the personal and the political" (Hick & Pozzuto, 2005, p. x). Activist social workers seek not only better ways to understand the world but also how to change it based on the principles of social and economic justice.

The purpose of my research is to explore what seems to be a profound and meaningful shift in the social policy and practice landscape in Ontario, where prior austerity measures are seemingly being transformed into a more robust social safety net. I asked my research participants to reflect on questions of power in the workplace, their sense of identities and purpose, and their thoughts on possibilities for critical practices during a time when the terrain for debate and struggle had shifted—what some have called a "pendulum swing" (Dumbrill, 2006, p. 6). What does it mean to be an activist social worker when hope for change is seemingly on the rise? What kinds of subjectivities, knowledges, and work practices do activist social workers bring to a context characterized not by regressive reforms but by the allure of transformative renewal?

INTRODUCING TRANSFORMATION AND RENEWAL

Described as a "total transformation" of the health care system, the new primary health care program known as *Renewal* promised 50 multidisciplinary teams located in 112 communities across the province. These Family Health Teams, consisting of networks of social workers, doctors, nurses, and other health care professionals, would eventually serve as many as 2.5 million Ontarians (Ontario Ministry of Health and Long-Term Care, 2016). Government documents describing the new program, available online at the Ontario Ministry of Health and Long-Term Care website, emphasized the need for "flexibility," "choice," and "equity" within health care services. The documents emphasized that the 50 multidisciplinary teams would work "collaboratively" with local "community partnerships" in order to provide expanded access to patient-centred care located close to where people live, and that their focus would be on effective "health promotion" and "illness prevention" (Ontario Ministry of Health and Long-Term Care, 2005, 2016).

Interestingly, at this same point in time, Ontario's child welfare system was also undergoing "a significant shift in culture" (Child Welfare Secretariat, 2005, p. 23) under the program known as *Child Welfare Transformation*. As outlined in a government document available on the Ontario Ministry of Children and Youth Services website, this program promised more "flexible" approaches that emphasize differential responses to child welfare concerns. The various responses include kinship arrangements, mediation, and family conferencing, which were all designed to "build on family and community strengths" (Child Welfare Secretariat, 2005, p. 8). Mirroring changes in primary health care, child welfare was adopting a more "collaborative" approach with families and community partners while placing greater emphasis on early detection and prevention of risks to kids across the province. Taken together, *Transformation* and *Renewal* appeared to be long-overdue breaks from the austerity measures enacted by two previous Conservative governments. Not surprisingly, for many social workers in my study, the troubling conditions of prior reforms, including long wait-lists, huge caseloads, and other "cookie cutter" approaches to care, were expected to be remedied through improved access to an expanded array of flexible service intervention.

METHODOLOGY

In order to gain an understanding of how *Transformation* and *Renewal* shaped social workers' practices, my study included interviews with self-identified activist social workers, all of whom were recruited from my professional networks, using purposive sampling (Palys, 2008). The 17 participants represented a diverse group, including both managers and direct service providers. In terms of social location, the participants self-identified as 15 women and 2 men between the ages of 26 and 65. Three social workers identified as Aboriginal, 2 identified as Black, and 12 identified as white.

My aim was to invite social workers to reflect on the varying subjectivities, knowledges, and work practices that they brought to a context now characterized by progressive reform. In order to encourage social workers to talk about how a changing work context impacted their practice, I conducted individual, in-depth interviews using open-ended questions designed in a way to elicit stories (Hollway & Jefferson, 2000). I analyzed the interviews using a method of discourse analysis developed by Davies (2000) and later used by Bansel, Davies, Gannon, and Linnell (2008), in which the concept of "positioning" (Davies, 2000, p. 70) is utilized to carefully examine how people's identities are constituted through everyday practices. According to Davies (2000), positioning is the discursive process whereby selves are located and become subjectively coherent. This process can happen in several ways, including "interactive positioning" where one person positions another, and "reflexive positioning" when one positions the self (p. 91). Discourse analysis draws attention to the many ways that discourse "works on and through people" (Bansel et al., 2008, p. 675) to produce not only certain kinds of subjects but also the actions they engage in, and the feelings they experience. These research methods were important to the aims of my research because they helped me to learn how social workers' individual social locations—in relation to marginalization, oppression, and/or privilege—influenced their work practices in contexts characterized by expanded forms of neoliberalism.

THEORETICAL FRAMEWORK

In this chapter, I suggest that social workers' responses to the contradictions experienced under *Transformation* and *Renewal* can be analyzed, in part, as emerging forms of self-governing identified by Michel Foucault as neoliberal governmentality (Foucault, 2008). For Foucault (1991), governmentality referred to the emergence of political rationalities where governing becomes the calculated management of the lives of each and all in order to reach certain objectives as efficiently as possible. This perspective is significant because it directs our attention to the ways in which strategies for the regulation of conduct operate through processes that Foucault (1994) called "techniques of the self" (p. 87)—all the ways that individuals experience, understand, judge, and organize their own behaviour or performances of the self to be in relation to a particular technology of power. Foucault (1994) explained techniques of the self are procedures, either "suggested or prescribed to individuals in order to determine their identity, maintain it, or transform it in terms of a certain number of ends, through relations of self-mastery or self-knowledge" (p. 87).

In other words, the governing of the self is a matter of placing the imperative to "know oneself" (Foucault, 1994, p. 87) in its neoliberal context. In the context of my research, this imperative might be restated in the form of the following question: Who are activist social workers becoming now under the terms of neoliberal governance?

Foucault (2008) views neoliberalism as the emergence of more versatile forms of governing whereby the state retains its traditional functions, but continues to develop an array of indirect techniques for managing the lives of individuals without simultaneously being responsible for them. Instead, the responsibilities for social risks are shifted onto the domain of the individual. As Foucault (2008) explains, neoliberal governance "does not involve providing individuals with a social cover for risks, but according everyone a sort of economic space within which they can take on and confront risks" (p. 144). To accomplish this aim, the ideal subject under neoliberalism must be self-governing and entirely occupied with producing the self as enterprising, productive, and responsible. From this perspective, the new subject of neoliberalism is an inherently malleable creation and manages to perpetually adapt to new economic and social imperatives, including modifications in the context of social work practice. However, in this chapter, my findings suggest that this analysis of governing is overly determinist. Consequently, it fails to account for alternative positionings of the self. Specifically, this failure obscures how some social workers position themselves, to varying degrees, in opposition to emerging neoliberal discourses in the workplace. Often this resistance is related to specific biographical histories, and sometimes related to racial, gender, and class oppression. The findings I discuss in the rest of this chapter provide an alternative interpretation of neoliberal governance, one in which the "making up" of the activist social work self often results in far less predictable outcomes.

SUBJECTS OF TRANSFORMATIVE CHANGE: BECOMING CAPABLE OF TEAMWORK AND COLLABORATION

Social workers employed in either child welfare or primary health care recall how their work sites were immediately flooded with themes of change as soon as *Transformation* and *Renewal* were announced across the province of Ontario. They eagerly anticipated the new ways of working that were outlined in the programs, including less hierarchical and more egalitarian team arrangements, and the development of collaborative networks involving service users and other service providers in the community. In the beginning, social workers were clear: Partnerships, teams, and collaborative work arrangements offered greater opportunities for their input into policy and procedural decisions, as well as creating more room for innovative case planning and management. Many expressed hope that through better integration of community supports and enhanced resources, social workers could offer more comprehensive solutions to the problems faced by service users and their families.

Despite feeling overwhelmed at times, many social workers found the themes of change appealing. Some felt the new programs conveyed a distinctly emancipatory agenda that reminded them of why they went into social work in the first place. As one frontline child welfare worker shared, "it was the whole feeling of when I first got into social work in school, 'we're going to change the world, and we're going to make it better!' And I thought WOO-HOO! This feels great!" Several participants anticipated that the new programs signalled renewed commitments to "front-end" or preventative interventions in the lives of service users, including interventions aimed at expanding opportunities for the prevention of crises, many of which had been virtually shut down during the regressive years under Premier Mike Harris, a Conservative who implemented massive cuts to services in Ontario. Recalling the constraints imposed on her practice during the time of the Harris government, Joy,[1] a white child welfare frontline worker, explains,

> I think that was a period for me when activism was impossible because it was so difficult to do our job. It was so difficult to go see the client who had no money. It was so difficult to help when there's no services … it was just one thing after another. You were inundated with trying to keep your head above water.

Many social workers described how they believed that the new work arrangements represented a break from past practices when top-down surveillance and tick-box approaches were emphasized over more comprehensive care practices. Expressing relief and exuberance about the new forms of care work, Anita, a white frontline child welfare worker, exclaimed, *"Differential Response* has really allowed me to come out of the closet! It's really about letting me practice the way I've always wanted to, the way I envisioned it would be, and it's a *partnership*!" Lydia, another white social worker with many years of experience working frontline in health care services, believed passionately that primary care was an ideal site for mental health care services because, unlike many other services in the post–Mike Harris era, primary care was supposedly universally available. Lydia describes the "phenomenal potential" of interdisciplinary teams for solving many persistent social problems and for simultaneously minimizing the strain on an already overburdened provincial health care budget:

> We have social workers, we have dieticians, we have pharmacists, we have a lactation consultant, we have nurse practitioners, and there are a lot of potential resources that you can draw upon. And we are more and more working together. Like the dietician is supposed to do a weight loss programme, and she said "weight loss alone doesn't work" … this is not a good thing. So now we're doing a self-esteem/body image group together. That makes so much more common sense.

For many social workers in my study, there was a palpable yearning observed in their narratives that indicated a desire to return to forms of practice that they believed could make a real difference in people's lives. In many instances, it was apparent that social workers labouring under *Transformation* and *Renewal* were enthusiastically making themselves up to be subjects of transformative change. Using Foucault (2008), it is possible to argue that, despite their transformative discursive packaging, social workers are mobilizing a particular technique of the self in the service of neoliberal governmentality. Adika, a Black child welfare social worker, expressed this positioning in the following way: "We were going to try and be more family-based, family-oriented, least intrusive measures are best, kind of thing ... working with families instead of against families." Similarly, another frontline mental health service provider recalled thinking that her move to the new program in primary care would mean a return to creativity and patient-centred care. She believed that people would receive better care with fewer stigmas in a far less institutionalized setting. The themes of change so prevalent in *Transformation* and *Renewal* programs represented a long overdue and welcomed shift in service arrangements. And, at least initially, many of my research participants embraced these themes with great enthusiasm.

Catherine Casey's (1999) work can be used to explain how it is that social workers come to position themselves in alliance with expanded forms of neoliberal governance in the workplace. She writes about how new organizational cultures depend on the deliberate installment of incontestable and universally attractive discourses that are designed to signal the sharing of skills and labour directed toward the attainment of shared goals. In particular, Casey takes up the increasing use of teams in the workplace and considers the psychic effects of these institutional practices on individual employees. She argues that the discursively constructed notion of "team" manages to elicit and simulate warm feelings of belonging while simultaneously serving as a regulatory and disciplinary device in the workplace. Casey (1999) describes this process as a "discursive colonization of the employee self" (p. 159), and in doing so, she underscores how systemic and totalizing the process can be for workers. Missing from Casey's analysis is how teams and partnerships can obscure differences between individuals based on socially produced hierarchies of power, and how resistance can sometimes be forged from embodying such difference. The success of teams requires that we forget how the workplace, much like the world around us, is materially organized along socially produced lines, including race, gender, class, ability, and so forth. In the following sections, I build on Foucault's (2008) and Casey's (1999) analysis to explore how activist social workers positioned themselves within the discourses of transformative change while simultaneously drawing on alternative discourses related to important emotional attachments and investments in their lives.

EMERGING DOUBTS AND OUTRIGHT BETRAYALS

Once the *Transformation* and *Renewal* programs were well underway within their workplaces, many social workers began to observe a troubling disconnect between promises of change and the realities achieved. For instance, in the child welfare sector, social workers were shocked to learn that the Ministry of Children and Youth Services suddenly froze the new funding for *Transformation*. Some observed how this abrupt change in plans occurred after intense negative media scrutiny following the release of a report by Ontario's Auditor General revealing questionable expenditures by several children's aid societies (Office of the Auditor General of Ontario, 2006). One supervisor expressed the belief that the real reason for the disruption in the plan's funding was that Ministry personnel had gravely miscalculated how expensive it would be to implement the kinds of transformative changes that would keep children out of care. According to her, the rollout of *Transformation* began, "and then they found out 'oh my god, this *Transformation* funding was going to be billions and billions of dollars to make these things happen.' And suddenly, it wasn't there." In her version of what happened, the negative publicity over allegations of inappropriate spending by a few children's aid societies provided the Ministry with the necessary cover to rein in spending for the *Child Welfare Transformation* program across the entire province. This supervisor's observations show how *Transformation*, much like *Renewal*, is connected to the economic rationality at the heart of neoliberal governmentality. In other words, good and responsible social and health services are now fiscally responsible ones, and it falls onto individual practitioners to implement this rationality.

Concerns were also expressed by social workers about the inexplicable contradictions in which the new funding model in child welfare "rewarded" apprehensions and "penalized" innovative care plans that could potentially keep kids out of care. Participants explained that such regressive models of care surfaced in two ways. Firstly, agencies continue to receive the most funding when a case involved high-risk and intrusive apprehension measures. In contrast, and perhaps most puzzling, efforts to ward off apprehensions through "front-end" counselling or other forms of ongoing therapeutic work with families were deemed to be "mandate drift" and, therefore, discouraged. Secondly, children placed with foster families are covered by publicly funded medical benefits and caregivers are provided with financial support to help offset day-to-day living expenses.

In sharp contrast, and contrary to the spirit of *Transformation*, extended family members who agreed to care for children within the new kinship care agreements would receive nothing by way of financial assistance. Many research participants who worked in child welfare pointed out that this produced a double standard and had the effect of shifting responsibilities for publicly funded care arrangements over to the private realm. In the words of one child welfare supervisor, "It reminds me of the Mike Harris thing back in the 90s, where he cut, right? Told people to go to their families … told them to go to their extended family, as well. It's the same thing with *Transformation*. Go back to the extended family. Go to the communities. But there's no funding for them." Social workers were able to identify that under *Transformation*, those who would now shoulder the burden of the costs of care would be family members and extended kin, typically women, who themselves were often already struggling financially. Positioning the self within a social change project so characterized by contradictions left many social workers feeling doubtful about their own transformative potential. As one child welfare supervisor shared, "there is this feeling that I should know what I am doing … but I have a sneaking suspicion that I am a crappy supervisor. What am I doing to people?"

Child welfare workers were also troubled by the ongoing, dominating presence of Ministry-led audits and service reviews. Social workers complained that evaluation methods were too narrow and that the government-inspired rating systems captured little by way of service quality issues. Citing the inevitable competition between agencies to secure "best performance outcomes," Ali, a white supervisor in child welfare, observed that pressures to comply with thin standards established through audits and reviews led to a "race to the bottom" that discouraged innovation and creativity on the part of service providers. As she explained, "the problem is you're always going to get that agency or group of people that always meet all the compliances. And then that's what the Ministry focuses on—'Well, if they can do it, why can't you?'" In this instance, Ali demonstrates how neoliberal governmentality is a subjective process. Certainly, social workers are feeling the pressures to be responsible through compliance with fiscal bottom lines. Yet, consistent with my critique of Foucault's (2008) and Casey's (1999) overly determinist conclusions about identity formation, Ali reveals a kind of micro-resistance practice through her ability to critique *Transformation*.

Within the context of primary health care, similar questions were raised about the transparency and accountability of the new funding arrangements. Several social workers voiced concerns that the *Renewal* funding was being diverted to costly renovations to physicians' private clinics. Although physicians' offices served as the workplaces for the new Family Health Teams, social workers observed that renovations to these spaces seemed overly excessive, especially given the lack of resources being directed toward expanding direct services for patients. Although research participants from primary health care expressed appreciation for upgrades to workplaces where publicly funded care took place, they shared doubts about whether these particular advancements actually improved patient access and quality of services. Some wondered if the private business interests of physicians were eclipsing the growing crisis of access in primary care in Ontario.

In response to pressures created by the lack of resources, it was not uncommon for social workers in primary health care services to rack up extensive overtime hours in vain attempts to protect the meagre access to services that existed, especially for patients seeking mental health care. Referring to the unrelenting pace of her working conditions, Didi, a white frontline worker, decried the negative impact on her direct service with patients. As she explained, "I've had days where I've booked 9 people. I can't see 9 people! By the ninth person, I feel very bad for them, that they're getting me at that point ... I mean, I book every hour that I'm there." Didi's account resonates powerfully with Davies' (2005) discussion of what it means to be a neoliberal subject. Drawing on Sennet (1998), Davies describes how survival in the neoliberal workplace requires that one sets the self adrift from the values of social justice. Instead, the neoliberal self is kept busy "fearing" (p. 9), and the appropriate(d) self at work is produced because it is too risky to do otherwise. Didi clearly struggled with anxiety about how new work practices conflict with her values. She also feared that the developing practice expectations would interrupt her capacity to engage in "good" anti-oppressive social work. As Didi explained,

> The social justice piece takes time and it's the first thing to go when you're booked back to back. And you know, you can bring the analysis into your workplace but in terms of actually going out there and trying to bring about change ... well, it's harder to do that when there isn't a spare minute in the day.

The majority of social workers from my study expressed growing concerns about the lack of accountability and transparency found in the plans that were intended to transform their sectors of care work. Kathy, an Aboriginal child welfare supervisor, conveyed the bitter sense of betrayal felt by many colleagues as they began to perceive that government had reneged on important aspects of the promised changes:

> At least with Mike Harris, you knew what you were getting, right? Whereas, I feel with this, you've gotten sucked into this wonderful theory generated by social workers for social workers; for families that will serve families. But the funding and the community capacity-building isn't there. Like you know, again, "put your money where your mouth is." There's nothing behind it. There's no foundation to the bridge. The bridge is great, it looks fabulous ... but if you step on it, it's just falling apart.

Despite harbouring inner doubts, many social workers emphasized how important it was to position themselves as enthusiastic supporters of the new programs in their workplaces. Key to this positioning was the ability to perform "teamwork" and "collaboration" even though the necessary resources and time were not allotted to do so effectively. Davies, Browne, Gannon, Honan, and Somerville (2005) argue that the demands of neoliberal workplaces, including ongoing audits, time pressures, funding constraints, and the discourses of flexibility, place pressures on working bodies that are difficult to oppose. Many of the accounts provided by social workers in my research revealed that striving to make oneself up as "successful" in the workplace did not necessarily result in transformative change such as improved flexibility in services but, rather, in the constitution of greater "flexibility of the person" (Scourfield, 2007, p. 107). In many cases, this meant the making up of selves capable of tolerating a high degree of contradiction.

CONDUCT UNBECOMING OF "TEAMWORK" AND "COLLABORATION"

In the emerging culture of work organizations, where there is a reliance on teams and collaboration, it is often assumed that employees will bring their knowledge, skills, and experiential expertise to all aspects of planning and delivering a program (Casey, 1999). It seems fair to assume that this culture nurtures empowerment and, subsequently, high degrees of tolerance for differences in opinion. However, contrary to these assumptions, some social workers in my research found that there was a steep price to pay for deviating from what it meant to be a "good team player" who was, by necessity, compliant, loyal, and unquestioning. Consequently, those social workers whose work performances could be perceived as "unbecoming" of teamwork confronted barriers that placed their economic survival at risk and also increased their exposure to stressful work conditions.

Social workers explained that some of the most painful and difficult circumstances they encountered took place when the new modes of service assumed regulatory functions in ways that collided with their sense of ethical being and purpose at work. One social worker in primary health care referred to these circumstances as "the point at which I go into moral crisis." This collision of values is exemplified by Rita's observation about major power and philosophical differences across so-called community partnerships involving women's shelters, child welfare, and the police. She worried that forced partnerships under these conditions silenced more critical analysis of violence against women and other views that challenged dominance and systemic forms of oppression. Increasingly Rita, a Black woman who refers to herself as a survivor of male partner abuse, expressed concerns about her own capacity to speak out under the new conditions imposed through "teamwork" with other professionals. As she explained, "I learned the hard way what to say and what not to say." Although Rita tried to proceed in her work more carefully, she worried about how long she would be able to remain at her agency if "playing the game" required her ongoing silence and complicity. Rita felt betrayed by her managers and shared that, on one occasion, when she openly criticized a police officer for not following a policy related to domestic violence, she came close to losing her job because "one of the worse things you can be at this time is a 'bad team player.'" Similarly, another social worker shared that, despite the rhetoric of teamwork, a willingness to speak up with even mild criticism at her agency could jeopardize her ability to advance in her career—the equivalent of becoming "benched on the sidelines." Casey (1995) explains that in the new participatory culture and diminished hierarchy of the transformed workplace, speaking up and making contributions is apparently valued and encouraged. Yet, in her study of a large multinational corporation, Casey highlights how workers must learn the difference between acceptable and unacceptable verbal commentary under these new conditions. An implicit censorship operates and workers are expected to learn subtle rules governing discourse and internally regulate themselves: "Appropriately acculturated, self-censored employees will know automatically the difference between welcome speaking up and troublemaking speaking out" (Casey, 1995, p. 141). Citing her own experiences of being tagged as a "trouble-maker," Marie, a frontline child welfare worker and a member of the Afro-Caribbean community, was shocked at how her efforts to raise issues of systemic racism in police services were met with disapproval from senior managers who warned her against public criticism of a partner organization:

> I feel that we are in position and in a place to start to challenge … if we're really, truly looking at being an anti-racist organization, to move beyond tokenism … we then have to start to also challenge the other systems that oppress our clients, you know? And I feel that we don't. We get slapped on the hand when we want to challenge the police for being oppressive and abusive in some instances to women. We get in trouble for that.

Like many other social workers in the study, Rita, Marie, and Pauline worry about punitive reprisals if they openly criticize the new work arrangements. They find various ways to "swallow" or outwardly mask their conflicts and tensions so that they can continue to be recognizable as "appropriately" transformative social work subjects. For example, Pauline, a white primary health care social worker, has recently started to miss team meetings while cloaking her absence through sending regrets that she is just too busy. Pauline explains that she decided to avoid these meetings after concluding that they were essentially opportunities for management to ensure that employees are "toeing the line." She observes troubling similarities between expectations in her workplace and her earlier life experiences when she lived in another country under a repressive military regime. From that earlier time in her life, Pauline has learned to be deeply suspicious of any processes that are not inclusive, transparent, and open to challenge. As Pauline describes her work meetings, her disdain and anger are palpable:

> There's something about how those meetings are conducted … I find things go from top to bottom. They don't use the resources of people. There is no room for looking at the talents that all of us have … I call it a funnel meeting … you open up your mouth and they are going to throw all this information in and you swallow it.

In some cases, these social workers take risks and challenge the new arrangements. However, these risks always pose potential costs and, consequently, the practice of anti-oppressive social work can begin to feel like a series of double binds. Every act of resistance must be veiled with apparent compliance. Social workers' stories reveal their positioning within expanded forms of neoliberalism to be unruly and existing in a constant state of tension between techniques of the self that assure performances of compliance and a "plurality of resistances" that are at varying times "possible, necessary [and] improbable" (Foucault, 1977, p. 96).

Rita, Marie, and Pauline carry biographical histories that intersect with the new requirements of work in ways that make them feel trapped between the need for survival at work and loyalty to communities with which they feel a deep affinity. As Marie explains, "A lot of times, clients will look to me and say, 'this is what's happening. Is there anything that you can do?' And then I feel like, no, there isn't. And who do I go to? Who do I go to? It's really frustrating!" Walkerdine (2006) writes thoughtfully about how those who occupy subject positions deemed "other" can work in fear of becoming "caught at the border" (p. 13) within new workplace restructuring arrangements. Walkerdine conceptualizes the border as a site of pain, loss, and exclusion. She explains that those who are rendered unable to perform the embodied flexibility required for success under neoliberalism often struggle at this border due to conflicting emotional investments that are tied to racialized, gendered, and class-marked histories. When applying Walkerdine's ideas to my research participants, it is possible to see how social workers who bring biographical histories and social locations from the margins find themselves persistently caught at a point of conflict. The point of conflict is between a workplace characterized by "*Transformation*" and the knowledge that employment conditions work against meaningful, transformative change. Walkerdine (2006) describes this as tension between "what is supposed to be produced and what is not supposed to be there" in the new workplace (p. 13). For some social workers, especially those whose lives embody "difference" in a setting dominated by whiteness, this experience of being stopped at the border of their workplace leaves them feeling permanently on the outside.

Success, for workers such as Rita, Marie, and Pauline, demands a willingness to leave important parts of themselves at the door, and as Walkerdine (2006) suggests, an acceptance of conditions that make them resigned to feeling like "imposters, always on the edge of being found and cast out" (p. 18). Self-governing for these social workers is often about managing the tensions between maintaining stable employment and living with the risk of betraying important commitments to families and broader communities.

CONCLUSION

When I interviewed my research participants, several years had passed since the introduction of *Transformation* and *Renewal* to their agencies and clinics. Social workers were able to share their hopes about the potential for such programs, but perhaps more importantly, they also expressed growing concerns about emerging tensions, conflicts, and contradictions experienced under these initiatives. There were three major areas of concern expressed by my research participants. First, much of the new funding had not materialized as promised, nor was the available money being directed in an accountable and transparent fashion. For many in the study, the lack of transparency led to doubts about whether funding would be used to fulfill promises of expansions to direct services. Second, stringent government-driven audit and accountability-review systems continued to be applied in ways that increased top-down surveillance, control, and decision making over frontline practices. It was believed that these command-and-control processes prioritized financial efficiencies, narrowed creativity, and diminished innovation at the local level of care, and that they fostered dispiriting forms of competition between agencies and individual service providers. Finally, participants described the variety of ways that the new practice interventions continued the "Harris legacy" by downloading the provision of public services onto the private realm. In other words, in this new era of "transformed" health and child welfare, responsibilities for care increasingly fell to the individual, family, and community.

Based on their own direct observations, many social workers who took part in my research expressed serious doubts about the ability of the new programs to achieve the promise of change. However, public debate and criticism of *Transformation* and *Renewal* remained curiously muted, even though the harsh legacies of the Harris government continued to persist in the province. In fact, far from critiquing the new programs, many social workers in Ontario moved quickly to establish a strong professional presence within these renewed sectors of practice. Citing their abilities to navigate complex service systems, their expertise for working with vulnerable populations, and their special knowledge for understanding complex human problems, the provincial social work association claimed that its members were best positioned to provide strong leadership for change in the new programs (Ontario Association of Social Workers, 2005a, 2005b). From the vantage point of my research participants, it is possible to see how different social workers' positioning can variously collude and collide with the techniques of neoliberalism. As a result, it would appear that what it means to be an activist, anti-oppressive social worker within expanded forms of neoliberalism is difficult to pin down. Social workers' positioning tends to reflect strong desires for ethical selfhood. Yet they also reflect the contradictions of the work world where there is little clarity and a decidedly blurry line between what is right and what is wrong. This new reality points to the fact that despite their "transformed" and "renewed" forms, current child welfare and health care places of work can be messy and unsettling spaces where knowing and not knowing, belief and rejection, allegiance and betrayal can all coexist in varying complementary and contradictory degrees.

Foucault's (2008) ideas about the self-constituting effects of neoliberal governing provide insights into the stories of compliance and resistance shared by activist social workers labouring under *Transformation* and *Renewal*. In many instances, social workers reveal ways they learn to perform a self that is capable of proactive entrepreneurialism, including "teamwork," "partnerships," and "collaboration." While these subject positions can be analyzed simply as social workers performing those traits valorized under neoliberalism (du Gay, 1996), this analysis fails to grasp other forms of self-governing at play.

Throughout this chapter, I have discussed the various ways that activist social workers in my research grappled with the tension between their desires for progressive changes under *Transformation* and *Renewal*, and their growing awareness that those changes are being betrayed in practice. The ongoing presence of service and funding constraints continued to make the possibility of developing meaningfully transformative practices unachievable. It is apparent that some social workers manage these contractions by stubbornly holding onto hope. Often, the allure of change was seductive and compelling, even to the point that people were willing to deny and minimize evidence that change was illusory. Still, others drew on powerful biographical life experiences and found ways to recognize that many of the changes represented not "renewal" and "transformation," but rather an extension of prior patterns of exclusion and marginalization. However, almost all of the social workers found ways to perform a messy, complicated mix of self-governing and identity work that enabled them to walk a fine line between outward compliance and their inner defiance.

The work–life narratives shared by social workers demonstrate the many ways that people negotiate, collude, and sometimes collide with new work discourses circulating within *Transformation* and *Renewal*. At times, they manage to variously position themselves within competing discourses generated from their diverse biographical histories and intersecting social locations. Despite variations in self-governing, the narratives explored here reveal how social work selves become constituted as "subjects of transformative change"—individuals who hold onto hope after a harsh decade of decline in social provisioning under successive Conservative regimes. Social workers' work–life stories also reveal pressures to perform as "transforming subjects" who are willing to adapt, to be flexible, and to absorb tensions and contradictions in the new programs. Žižek (2008) insists that the most dangerous narratives emerging after a crisis event—such as the Harris years faced by Ontario social workers—are those that enable us to continue to dream. This chapter reveals how dreams for change following the difficult time of the Harris regime can contain the seeds of danger. Social workers' hopes and dreams can obscure how neoliberalism continues to evolve, mutate, and adapt, in order to more effectively, and efficiently, extend market principles into "practices of care."

Du Gay's (1996) work on new organizational identities alerts us to some of the implications when notions of change begin to circulate within the discourses that shape our working selves. While assumed to represent a positive change in organizational development terms, du Gay points out that this assumption is misleading and fails to address how the change really involves a reimagining of the social as a form of the economic. When social workers facing similar conditions constitute themselves as collaborators, partners, and team members, they risk engaging in what has been referred to as the "performative principle" (Lyotard, 1984, as cited in du Gay, 1996, p. 156). Those who engage in the performative principle are capable of adapting to modifications and demands made in the environment of work. When performing in this way, social workers become particular kinds of persons who are more likely to pursue goals valued by commercial interests and less likely to pursue the goals of equity and social justice. However, the stories shared by social workers in my research convey varying levels of discomfort with the idea that they are participating in processes that extend rather than remedy prior regressive restructuring projects. At times, social workers seem content to live with hopes for change, despite knowing that these hopes will seemingly not be actualized in practice. Yet, importantly, activist social workers also strive to reconcile the breach between what is desired and what is actually known about the new practice arrangements. Despite constraints and obstacles, they remain committed to the social justice goals of their work.

NOTE

1. In order to protect the confidentiality of participants, I use pseudonyms in place of their real names.

Section II

Nuancing Anti-Oppression

4 | Youth Engagement in Governmental and Community Organizations

Contradictions and Recommendations

Susan Preston, Associate Professor, School of Social Work, Ryerson University

Jordan Aslett, Instructor, School of Health, Education and Human Services, Yukon College

Political bodies are concerned with citizen participation as an element of democracy to promote citizen voices (MASS LBP, 2008; Stoker, 2006), most notably in policy development. Such engagement is sought to inform policy/programs, test new ideas, and foster interest in political issues (Barnes, Newman, Knops, & Sullivan, 2003). Similar to anti-oppressive practice (AOP), citizen engagement has the potential to place value on localized knowledge and centre the voices of people with lived experience (Dalrymple & Burke, 2006) related to the effects of organizational policies and programs. Practices of citizen engagement range from polling to deliberation (Callahan, 2007; Gastil & Levine, 2005), with purposes varying from gathering tokenistic feedback to participating in full decision making (Arnstein, 1969; Tritter & McCallum, 2006). In this chapter, we explore how citizen engagement is enacted in the context of youth services by examining recent literature and current practices in government and community agencies, as well as our own experiences. We then offer recommendations for future practice and policy at both levels of service provision.

Commitment to citizen engagement in government policy (Volkery, 2004) may be framed as a democratic principle, and having the practice enshrined in government policy suggests a stronger likelihood of making it happen. The Government of Canada promotes citizen participation in specific policies and directives (Treasury Board of Canada Secretariat, 2007); meanwhile, provincially, in Ontario public consultation is seemingly haphazard, sometimes named in legislation (e.g., Environmental Assessment Act), while other times only implied within prescribed reviews of legislation (e.g., Child and Family Services Act). Municipally, implementing public consultation processes is at the discretion of individual municipalities; in Toronto, it is promoted as a form of civic engagement (City of Toronto, n.d.a). We also see the value of stakeholder participation in community-based organizations. Parallel to these larger political deliberations, human services agencies often seek stakeholder input.

Mandates and practices of engaging citizens and stakeholders vary according to organizational context and personnel, as do the purposes or intended outcomes of engagement; as such, there are both positive and negative practices of citizen engagement, along a continuum from meaningful, effective practices to tokenistic, ineffective practices. Negative ineffective practices of citizen engagement can include a reliance on a single staff member to support and maintain an engagement program, tokenism, and the possibility of homogenizing stakeholder experiences into a singular identity (Woodford & Preston, 2013).

Staff subjectivities can either advance or hinder the process of engagement. In most organized formal participation projects, staff from the relevant government department or an organization's specific program are assigned to oversee the citizen or stakeholder participation project. These staff have considerable influence over the process (Rutter, Manley, Weaver, Crawford, & Fulop, 2004), and as such, their attitude about and commitment to meaningful engagement will impact the effectiveness of the engagement experience. Additionally, their capacity to foster a meaningful engagement process will influence the experience, and the philosophical foundation of the training they may or may not have received to this end also will have an impact.

Tokenism as a problem of meaningful or impactful participation has been noted in both government and organization engagement (Abele, Graham, Ker, Maioni, & Phillips, 1998; Sheedy, 2008). In this way, input may be sought to satisfy an external expectation about citizen/stakeholder insight into decision making, but there is not a genuine commitment to such influence by the public/organizational policy-makers (King, Feltey, & Susel, 1998; Woodford, 2010). In such circumstances, participants may either engage in the process and then be disappointed when their input is not acted upon, or recognize the process as tokenistic and thus not fully engage in it—both of which defeat the intent of participation. Additionally, we note that citizens with marginalized identities, such as racialized people, youth, or people living in poverty, often do not experience meaningful participation experiences and/or are involved in tokenistic ways (Couch & Francis, 2006), both of which can minimize the importance of their issues and the impact of their consultation and engagement (Wharf Higgins, 1999).

In any kind of scheme that reaches out to a particular demographic, there is the risk of homogenization, wherein diversity within the group can be glossed over and a singular identity assumed. When targeting participants, engagement schemes may have a tendency to ignore the varying degrees of lived experiences within the target group. Considering that participation in general requires a level of feeling empowered on the part of the participant, engagement schemes may be prone to attracting certain participants from certain demographics and life experiences (Nairn, Sligo, & Freeman,

2006), which may be the more privileged sector of a group, rather than attracting a truly representative deliberative body (Lowndes, Pratchett, & Stoker, 2001).

Notwithstanding these and other critiques (Bessant, 2003; Woodford & Preston, 2011), including those noted by Wilson in this book, it is important to recognize that participatory deliberation can be effective and serve many useful purposes (Sheedy, 2008), such as enhancing a sense of ownership and accountability (Carpini, Cook, & Jacobs, 2004), developing teamwork and communication skills (Halvorsen, 2003), and increasing political participation (Fung & Wright, 2003). On an organizational level, it creates a systematic process for gathering feedback to improve services and governance (Rogers, Finley, & Galloway, 2001), which can create a sense of partnership between clients and the organization and improve organizational policy (Dusenbury, Liner, & Vinson, 2000). However, assuming any participatory process is "good engagement" ignores the difficulties in the practices and intentions of some participation schemes (MacKinnon, Pitre, & Watling, 2007), as noted above.

Citizen engagement practices are not restricted to the adult population, having been implemented with youth organizations and governmental institutions. UNICEF (2001) notes, "one cannot just build in a little participation element to what is already being done. Rather, a participatory approach is a different way of seeing young people, and of acting in the world" (p. 11). We recognize that our chapter tends to discuss "youth" as a singular identity, giving the impression that youth are a homogeneous group. In actual practice, youth-serving agencies serve many youth across many backgrounds and lived experiences. It is not our intention to deny individual youth identities and experiences, but to recognize that all youth regardless of lived experience need to be engaged by decision-makers. We thus think of youth as a broader group, with a mix of common and different identities and experiences.

In this chapter, we build on the assumption that if youth service users have input into the policies and programs that affect them, those policies and programs will better fulfill their mandates (Beresford & Croft, 1993). In reviewing the literature about youth engagement and reflecting on our own practice, we note its growing importance in the human services. We discuss its prominence in human rights discourse, as well as its importance in AOP. Drawing on an environmental scan of community-based agencies and governmental and quasi-governmental bodies operating in a large city in Ontario, we note that in spite of the importance placed on youth engagement in the relevant literature, government policy, and the international community, there is a dearth of such programs in community agencies. Surprisingly, it is more commonly practised in governmental/quasi-governmental bodies. We see this lack of youth engagement as a missed opportunity for community-based agencies, and discuss how agencies might replicate practices similar to those in governmental bodies. We conclude with recommendations for youth engagement practices that focus on affecting change within organizations, noting the need for better funding toward these ends.

THE CURRENT CONTEXT OF YOUTH ENGAGEMENT

Moving away from "youth socialization" schemes of government, critiqued by Wilson in Chapter 2 of this volume, the United Nations in 2003 called on member states and youth-serving agencies to implement authentic youth engagement practices and policies, noting the "great importance of empowering young people by building their capacity to achieve greater independence, overcoming constraints to their participation and providing them with opportunities to make decisions that affect their lives and well-being" (UN General Assembly, 2004, p. 2). Furthermore, UNICEF (2001) frames youth participation as a human right within democratic principles, acknowledging its value for skill development, while noting that "participation builds effectiveness and sustainability" (p. 9) and has value to society overall.

Youth engagement fits well with AOP as a way of bringing marginalized voices to the centre and demonstrating a commitment to structural changes within organizations and communities (Barnoff, 2011). Youth engagement can be a form of resistance to ageism whereby youth voices are valued and the agency of youth as citizen subjects is recognized (Armstrong, 2011). With the recent turn toward an anti-oppressive approach within community-based agencies, we would expect several examples of youth engagement in those agencies.

As the cornerstone of social work education in Canada (CASWE, 2012), AOP is becoming more prevalent in practice, including the community-based contexts in which we—the authors—previously worked. In our roles as youth workers, we witnessed broad policy directives from administration to deliberate with youth in various ways, with programmatic details to be worked out among staff. As such, practices varied according to how engagement was envisioned and operationalized, sometimes consisting of nothing more than client satisfaction surveys or focus groups as a way of responding to new expectations from funders that agencies conduct program evaluation. Other times, youth engagement had a wider scope, incorporating official channels for enacting policy change and social advocacy. As the funding and service climate shifted toward evidence-based practice (EBP), youth engagement directives became more focused on formal research methods such as program evaluation, thus losing some of the potential for creating partnerships for organizational change and empowering youth.

Current scholarship views youth engagement as having a positive impact on youth, government, and community-based organizations. The literature emphasizes therapeutic benefits (Donaldson, 2005), the promotion of positive ethnic identities (Luluquisen, Trinidad, & Ghosh, 2006), and meeting adolescent developmental goals (Sherrod, 2007). Historically the primary goal of such programming has been youth development (Paterson & Panessa, 2008), such as increasing leadership and communication skills (Checkoway & Gutiérrez, 2006), similar to Wilson's point about pro-social youth programming—in this volume. However, the focus on benefits to organizations through youth engagement is a burgeoning area of interest and is garnering more attention (Carlson, 2006). While past literature has often paid lip service to these benefits (Checkoway & Gutiérrez, 2006), they are now becoming an area of increased concern.

Recent literature emphasizes to organizations and policy-makers the benefits of having youth participate in citizenship engagement practices (Camino & Zeldin, 2002; Zeldin, McDaniel, Topitzes, & Calvert, 2000). Sometimes this emphasis on organizational benefits is the primary focus (Camino & Zeldin, 2002; Zeldin et al., 2000), but even when not primary, it still is seen as beneficial (Carlson, 2006; Jennings, Parra-Medina, Hilfinger-Messias, & McLoughlin, 2006). Hence, we see consensus across the literature on the value of youth engagement toward organizational and policy change. As UNICEF (2001) suggests, the importance of youth engagement toward creating organizational change has to be a primary rather than secondary focus, though it often is overlooked in practice. This led to our investigation of current practices of youth engagement in governmental and non-governmental organizations in Ontario, with a focus on seeking out programs that emphasize youth input for organizational change.

LOCAL PRACTICES OF YOUTH ENGAGEMENT

Given the push for further youth deliberation in our own practice and the increasing emphasis from international bodies, alongside the movement toward AOP in Canadian social work practice, we were surprised to find that youth engagement programming seems absent from many community organizations that serve youth. An environmental scan that reviewed the websites and annual reports of ten large youth community organizations in the City of Toronto yielded no mention of programs geared toward youth deliberation on organizational policies or advisory councils. In our environmental scan we looked at the annual reports and websites of the following youth-serving organizations: Central Toronto Youth Services, East Metro Youth Services, Oolagen Youth Mental Health, Geneva Centre for Autism, The George Hull Centre for Children and Families, Griffin Centre, The Hincks-Dellcrest Centre, Turning Point Youth Services, Youthdale Foundation, and YouthLink. While these results were unexpected, some literature suggests that undertaking youth consultation and engagement faces a number of barriers, including inconsistent funding commitments and shifting agency priorities (Carlson, 2006) as well as a lack of sustained engagement even when programs are implemented (Camino & Zeldin, 2002).

We anticipated similar findings in our scan of governmental and quasi-governmental bodies, which included the Government of Canada, the Province of Ontario, the City of Toronto, the Toronto District School Board, the United Way of Toronto, Toronto

Community Housing, and Toronto Police Services. However, we were surprised to find the opposite. For example, the recent directives from the Government of Ontario—"Stepping Up: A Strategic Framework to Help Ontario's Youth Succeed" and the "Youth Action Plan"—outline their stance on youth engagement, emphasizing the importance of youth involvement in democratic processes and decision making, including within community-based organizations. As a quasi-governmental sector example, Toronto Community Housing (TCH) has implemented a youth elections process, creating official channels through which youth can influence decisions. Across these two sectors, many organizations are implementing schemes to engage youth in meaningful ways.

Government enactment of engagement can be tokenistic or ineffective (Bess, Prilleltensky, Perkins, & Collins, 2009), which has been a strong criticism of many forms of citizen participation, both federally and provincially (Phillips & Orsini, 2002; Wilson, this volume). Surprisingly, our scan of local government and quasi-government youth engagement showed commitments to both enacting and sustaining meaningful participation in decision making by youth. Many programs are long-standing (e.g., Toronto Police Service youth consultation process), and new initiatives are packaged with substantial funding commitments (e.g., TCH youth elections process). This is promising because youth engagement initiatives are often short-lived (Head, 2011) and underfunded, thus having minimal tangible impacts and short lifespans (Stoneman, 2002). A commitment by these organizations to creating sustainable programs advances the institutionalization of youth engagement (Zeldin, 2004) and thus enhances their potential for affecting change.

UNDERSTANDING THE LACK OF YOUTH ENGAGEMENT IN COMMUNITY-BASED ORGANIZATIONS

Reflecting on our own practice, current scholarship, and our environmental scan, we propose political, citizenship, and funding explanations for the current lack of youth engagement schemes in community-based organizations.

Political Issues

Two trends in political arenas contribute to the lack of youth engagement in community-based organizations: neoliberalism and EBP. Similar to Wilson's chapter in this book, we note the current political and policy climate of neoliberalism in Canada has impacted community-based agencies through practices of new managerialism and economic rationality (Clark, 2002). Neoliberal political orientations often come with the expectation that publicly funded organizations will demonstrate the effectiveness of their programs as efficient processes that lead to their intended outcomes (Briskman & Muetzelfeldt, 2003; McDonald, 2006). Youth engagement programs may not meet these expectations, firstly because the outcomes most valued by funders often focus on individual change, rather than the organizational change emphasized in youth engagement (O'Donoghue, Kirshner, & McLaughlin, 2002; Zeldin et al., 2000). Secondly, processes that affect organizational change are complex, and thus contrary to neoliberal linear processes that progress along a definitive, short-term, and easily followed schedule.

EBP reviews often are mandatory, with precedence over any focus on participatory deliberation with clients. Conducive to a neoliberal agenda, EBP valorizes easily measureable definitions of effectiveness and accountability, often determined outside the organization. When client stakeholders are considered, it is done as outcome-focused program research rather than as a participatory deliberative process to affect organizational change. The expectation of using research to inform practice as a means of efficiency, and the challenge of not being able to "demonstrate" the value of stakeholder engagement in decision making, may explain the lack of youth engagement programs in community-based agencies. In a neoliberal policy climate, these programs can be seen as invalid and thus are not funded (Evans, Richmond, & Shields, 2005).

Citizenship Issues

Citizenship is at the core of engagement schemes, analogous to participation as an element of democracy. While mostly considered in the political realm, citizenship participation also takes place outside formal political arenas, such as non-political or quasi-private milieux. Deliberation and participation create spaces where participants can act, not simply as service recipients but as citizens with rights and responsibilities toward making decisions about their own wellbeing (Golombek, 2006). We can see persons enacting their citizenship in spaces such as neighbourhood councils, sports and recreation programs, and parent councils. In these contexts, while recognizing that not all people are equally valued or feel equally validated, there is an assumption that everyone has a right to contribute. We wonder if this understanding of citizenship is consistent in all community-based organizations or if there is variation depending on what services are being provided, and in which community context.

We considered the possibility of differing stakeholder subjectivities as citizens in community-based organizations. Outside the agency, the person might be considered a "citizen"—even as a young person—and a member of their community. However, inside the agency that same person perhaps no longer receives the same rights, benefits, and responsibilities of community citizenship, instead becoming a "service user" subjectivity, an identity that can be judged as deficient and thus needing service (Bessant, 2003). Through their "problem" or "needs" identity and the services provided, they are subject to practices of observation and surveillance, including research and evaluation. They in effect become the recipients of decisions and programs rather than providing input to decisions and programs.

The perception of a person as having citizenship rights seems further diminished in relation to any negative stigma of service needs and provisions; for example, community organizations that provide services regarding mental health, corrections, and addictions may be less amenable to including the voices of the people they serve in their operating policies and decision-making processes. In the context of youth services, this is compounded by young people being dismissed due to their age, wherein adults assume deficiencies in youth comprehension, maturity, and ability to take on responsibility, while inflating assessments of their own abilities to make decisions (Singh, 2013). Reasons for exclusion were not evident in our scan of youth-serving agencies, though we clearly noted a lack of youth voices in decision-making processes. Perhaps this also reflects the trend of citizen disengagement with democracy articulated by Wilson in this volume.

Funding Issues

A possibly more debilitating factor in the lack of action by community-based organizations toward including youth in policy deliberation is inconsistencies in government funding benchmarks for social services. In Ontario, funding allowances are tied to the ability of agencies to demonstrate the effectiveness of their programs and services. For example, the accreditation process for children's mental health agencies prioritizes their ability to provide outcome-focused evidence, and thus the ability of an agency to deliberate and engage with youth in their care is not a priority. We anticipate this trend extending beyond children's mental health, with the recent expansion of accreditation to other health and social services (Canadian Centre for Accreditation, 2017).

Meanwhile, the Government of Ontario's Youth Action Plan stresses the importance of engagement with youth, noting that "no one is more knowledgeable about what programs work than youth and community members themselves [and] ongoing youth and community engagement must be an important goal of any action plan" (Government of Ontario, 2012). This government has invested time and financial commitments to creating their own youth engagement schemes, such as the Premier's Youth Council. This suggests engagement as a government priority; however, provincial funding to community-based agencies for deliberative processes and youth engagement is scarce. Similarly, the City of Toronto released two reports on engaging youth. *Involve Youth* stresses the benefits of participation in decision-making processes. *Involve Youth 2* focuses on how organizations can implement youth engagement, while also describing the challenges for organizations in implementing these processes. Absent from these documents is a discussion about funding or any commitments by the city to finance initiatives for youth engagement within community-based organizations. This lack of commitment stands in contrast to the city funding its own Toronto Youth Cabinet, which is "the city of Toronto's official youth advisory body" (City of Toronto, n.d.b). The city seems committed to maintaining its own initiatives, but reluctant to support other organizations to do the same. We question this disconnect between what governments articulate about the value of youth engagement for community-based organizations and their lack of funding to support it.

The politics of neoliberalism, differing understandings of citizenship, and conflicting commitments for funding to community-based agencies may explain this lack of youth engagement programming. We consider this a missed opportunity for community organizations to support youth in ways that are empowering for them, while also beneficial to organizations. Below we offer our assessment of youth engagement's value, in the social work context of community-based organizations.

WHY DOES ENGAGEMENT IN COMMUNITY-BASED AGENCIES MATTER?

Similar to our earlier discussion of the value of engagement, we argue for the value of youth engagement in community-based organizations and its potential to effect change. Engagement is another way that agencies can more fully actualize AOP social work in their organization. By countering the marginalization of young people, particularly those who are trying to access stigmatized services, engagement can promote their status as active citizens in decision-making processes. Creating these processes can foster a sense of partnership with workers toward building a common vision (Karabanow, 2004) and promote some elements of self-determination by informing decisions about both the youth's own individual services (Fook & Gardner, 2007; Prilleltensky, 2003) and the larger service-delivery context (Prilleltensky, 2003; Zeldin et al., 2000). In addition to youth engagement's potential in enacting AOP, it also can foster tangible changes to policies, particularly in government. For example, the Toronto Youth Cabinet has had numerous successes in changing municipal policy, including lobbying city council to fund youth-led initiatives and to hire more city-based youth workers. These achievements are testimony to the potential for youth engagement programs to contribute to any organizational contexts, including community-based organizations.

We recall our own practice experiences of successful youth engagement in organizations. For example, in a residential care facility, youth were directly involved in every decision, from small operational details such as food and leisure to policies around staffing and report writing. Procedures for deliberation were institutionalized to the point of being a common, everyday practice as opposed to being tokenistic. When asked for feedback about their experiences, youth reported a sense of belonging and empowerment. In another example, youth involved in a youth advisory board at a counselling service spoke of having increased confidence in their potential for success in school and employment, as well as their own efficacy as citizens to affect change. Organizationally, there were direct changes in program delivery, including how client information was gathered and hours of service delivery. However, the youth advisory board was not formally recognized as a decision-making body, and the vague mandate meant the group's role varied according to the intentions of individual youth members and the staff responsible. Sometimes the group was simply tokenistic, to satisfy funders or as a public relations tool.

The literature demonstrates how effective youth engagement programs can be in creating better organizations (Ginwright & James, 2002; Zeldin, 2004), including creating agencies that are more representative and inclusive, and helping agencies clarify their mission and their programming intentions (Zeldin et al., 2000). Given the outcomes and potential benefits, below, we offer recommendations on how community-based organizations can implement youth engagement programs while emphasizing the importance of government support for them.

RECOMMENDATIONS

Forms of citizen engagement can be applied to youth participation schemes; however, youth engagement mostly benefits from practices that are flexible, informal, and situation specific to the context of the organization (Head, 2011). With this in mind, we offer recommendations to support meaningful youth engagement in community-based organizations, ranging from suggestions about social work education through to government commitments to funding.

Given youth engagement's fit with the current emphasis on AOP in social work education and agencies, we suggest that schools of social work incorporate youth engagement into their curriculum. Policy courses could explore provincial and municipal documents on youth engagement. In practice courses, the theory and skills of youth engagement could inform readings and assignments. In research classes, students could be introduced to research approaches that measure the effectiveness of engagement programs alongside other methods of program evaluation. In agencies, staff could implement principles of democratic decision making in small group contexts such as residences and day-treatment programs or by enhancing self-determination in individual counselling. This level of youth engagement does not necessarily require agency support or funding as workers can choose to enact it as part of their daily practice.

Social group work also holds promise for contributing to youth engagement in agencies. Groups can be a space for developing and practising skills of engagement for both group members and group leaders. Drawing on democratic principles of mutuality and shared leadership, groups also can be a model for how social workers can employ those principles in other forms of practice. Group members often negotiate with group leaders to advocate for change in how the group operates; this negotiation process may be a guide in how workers could approach agency administration about organizational change toward youth engagement. Finally, group work also has a strong theoretical and empirical base to support the value of democratic principles as effective means of change (Lindeman, 1980; Cohen & Mullender, 1999), and such knowledge can be transferred to recognizing the value of youth engagement for organizational effectiveness.

Until government and other funders recognize and financially support youth engagement as a form of participatory democracy in agencies, perhaps the clinical benefits of youth engagement can be incorporated and evaluated as one way to meet programmatic benchmarks. This approach has been used in social group work; for example, groups that have social advocacy and action as their primary mandate also evaluate the therapeutic benefits of these social action groups (Donaldson, 2005).

For youth engagement to be a priority across an agency it must be supported by administrative personnel. It is equally imperative that board members be sought that recognize or have experience with the importance of youth engagement, perhaps by drawing members from public administration and social work where citizen engagement and youth engagement is more common. Primarily, we stress the presence of youth themselves on boards of directors and decision-making bodies, similar to what is done in quasi-governmental organizations such as the Toronto District School Board and the Toronto Police Service.

Having a board of directors and administration that understands and supports practices of youth engagement may create criteria for hiring staff that includes knowledge of, and experience with, youth engagement models. By doing so, agencies may more quickly implement youth engagement practices, without having to begin with related training. This also supports the value of incorporating such knowledge in education for social work and related disciplines. At the same time, top-level support is needed to institutionalize youth engagement within the organization. In particular, encoding youth engagement schemes as part of an agency's constitutional bylaws and as responsibilities within job descriptions will promote its sustained presence in the organization's practice (Bevan, 2011). As an ingrained element of the organization's culture, it is hoped that practices of youth engagement also will emerge organically in the everyday intentions and practices of all staff.

Perhaps the most significant recommendation we offer is for governments at all levels to better fund youth engagement programming. We noted the support for citizen participation at the international, federal, provincial, and municipal levels. However, while governments may support the idea, their commitments do not extend beyond funding their own implementations of youth engagement to inform policy decisions in government. If governments expect community-based organizations to practice youth engagement, they must fund it. There is a need for strong voices supporting youth engagement from community and other leaders, including board members of community-based organizations that serve youth and professional associations of public administration and social work, to lobby government for funding. At the same time, youth, parents, and youth workers can pressure agencies to lobby government, while also lobbying government themselves, as constituents, asking for funding for such programs.

CONCLUSION

We find it ironic that the same governmental agencies that have implemented youth engagement practices are not emphasizing this type of engagement within the community-based agencies that they fund. Perhaps community-based organizations are not considered political spaces, whereas a governmental youth council is seen as the proper place for politics. This speaks to common conceptions of politics in representative democracies, wherein politics exist at the level of party and parliament, but not in the micro-transactions of negotiating community resources. AOP recognizes all forms of social work as political spaces, and as such, youth engagement fits well with the current climate. In the end, this chapter calls upon community organizations to consider how they can enact meaningful engagement with their service users as stakeholder citizens and asks government to support those practices in agencies similar to what they themselves do, having seen the benefit of such practices in their own organizational context.

5 Breaking Barriers

Obstacles to the Use of Family Group Conferencing

Nyron Sookraj, Former Manager, Catholic Children's Aid Society of Toronto; and Coordinator, Family Group Conferencing, The George Hull Centre for Children and Families

Doret Phillips, Social Worker

Gordon Pon, Associate Professor, School of Social Work, Ryerson University

Nyron Sookraj, the first author, sadly passed away on October 1, 2016. He was a cherished friend and colleague, a loving father and husband, who dedicated his life to helping children, youth, and families for over 33 years in the child welfare sector. After retiring from an illustrious career in senior management in child welfare, he returned to frontline work as family group conference coordinator at The George Hull Centre for Children and Families. He valued and deeply respected the strengths, resilience, and expertise of families, particularly those who were dealing with intersecting oppressions. His values and respect for children, youth, and families were reflected in his passion and deep commitment to family group conferencing. He touched the lives of many who knew him. He was a humble, generous, kind, and social justice–oriented person. It was a joy, honour, and privilege for us to co-author this chapter with Nyron.

In this chapter, we discuss barriers that prevent social workers from making referrals to family group conferencing (FGC) or family group decision making (FGDM) and offer recommendations for addressing these obstacles. FGC and FGDM are similar processes and the names are used interchangeably within Ontario. For the purpose of this paper we will be using the term *family group conferencing*. It was introduced into Ontario child welfare legislation in 2006 (Dumbrill, 2006) as an alternative dispute resolution process. FGC originated in New Zealand as one method to address racism and colonialism in their child welfare system as it pertains to the Maori people (Love, 2002; Tauri, 1999; Walker,

1996). FGC was introduced to some provinces in Canada with a goal to include families in plans of care for their children, support for families dealing with domestic violence, and more recently as an alternative dispute resolution process.

Despite the legislative support of FGC and the positive feedback from participating families and child welfare staff, a limited number of referrals to FGC are being made by child welfare agencies in Ontario. Barriers to referrals include ideology; history of child welfare; training; high workload; families declining referrals to FGC; and worker fears of liability, losing control, being critiqued, and the negative perception of involving fathers. Working from an anti-oppression, anti-racism, anti-Black racism, and anti-colonialism framework, we draw on the work of Irving and Moffatt (2002), who embrace a postmodern stance of not knowing, to suggest that this perspective could help to address some of the barriers to FGC. We conclude by recommending the following: (a) the language of the legislation be changed to be more compelling, and accountability mechanisms around the use of family group conferencing be implemented; (b) increasing advancement of postmodern theories and approaches such as anti-oppression, anti-racism, anti-Black racism, and anti-colonialism to social work and education; (c) using FGC to address overrepresentation of Aboriginal and Black children in the care of child welfare agencies; (d) training and more extensive promotion so that all child protection families know that FGC is an option for them; (e) research on barriers to FGC; and (f) ensuring the availability of adequate funding.

Anti-oppression perspectives emerged in the late 1990s and seek to eradicate all forms of oppression as generated by such social differences as class, race, gender, sexual orientation, (dis)ability, and so forth (Carniol, 2010; Clarke, Pon, Benjamin, & Bailey, 2015; Pon, Gosine, & Phillips, 2011). Four tenets of anti-oppression perspectives are power-sharing, reflexivity, combining the micro and macro pictures, and an emphasis on multiple and interlocking identities and oppressions such as racism, classism, sexism, heterosexism, ableism, and ageism (Carniol, 2010; Pon, Gosine, & Phillips, 2011).

Anti-racism in social work emerged in the early 1990s and is a political practice and theoretical framework that seeks to address individual, structural, and systemic forms of racism and other interlocking oppressions (Clarke et al., 2015; Pon et al., 2011). Anti-racism uses race as the primary lens through which to view and address interlocking oppressions. This entry point is a political stance that seeks to counter the widespread denial of racism in Canada (Dei, 1996).

Anti-Black racism refers to a pernicious form of racism directed at Black people on the one hand, and resistance by Blacks to this oppression on the other (Benjamin, 2003; Clarke et al., 2015; Pon, Gosine, & Phillips, 2011). Benjamin (2003) notes that anti-Black racism stems from grassroots activists and is best understood as encompassing both oppression and resistance.

Anti-colonialism in social work is gaining momentum, particularly in the new millennium. Anti-colonialism is the political struggle and active resistance of colonized peoples against the ideology and practice of colonialism (Ashcroft, Griffiths, & Tiffin, 1995; Baskin, 2011; Dei, 2000; Hart, 2009; Sinclair, Hart, & Bruyere, 2009; Smith, L. T., 1999). It emphasizes decolonization and affirming Indigenous knowledge and culture, and Indigenous sovereignty (Sinclair et al., 2009).

In our experience, it would appear that the model for Child Protection Services in Europe and North America has remained fairly stagnant for many decades. However, one creative and innovative initiative is family group conferencing. Whitaker states, "Family Group Conferencing is the most intriguing child welfare innovation to arise in the last quarter of a century" (as cited in Burford & Hudson, 2000, p. xii). Much of the innovativeness of FGC lies in it being family focused. Cameron and Vanderwoerd (1997) note that more intensive family-focused services are likely to offer more depth to practice and increase the potential for workers to both protect children and support families. The hallmark of a family-centred approach is practice that encourages partnership, focuses on strengths, and incorporates empowerment values and principles (Sandau-Beckler, Salcido, Beckley, Mannes, & Beck, 2002). Finding the balance between family expectation and the care and safety requirements of statutory agencies rests at the heart of FGC practice (Connolly, 2006).

Empirical research demonstrates that family group conferencing has very positive outcomes. In Toronto, a study examining the first seven years of the FGC program revealed that 90 percent of children who were the focus of conferencing remained with or returned to their family groups (Cunning & Bartlett, 2006). Another study from Texas using family group decision making found that families who participated in the process experienced a decrease in foster care and an increase in placements with relatives (Texas Department of Family and Protective Services, 2006).

Family group conferencing originated in New Zealand in 1989 in a new child welfare legislation known as The Children, Young Persons, and Their Families Act (Connolly, 1994). This Act provides the means through which the extended family can be brought together in partnership with professionals and contribute to the process of finding safe solutions for children (Connolly, 2006). The catalyst for this shift stemmed from concerns about the overrepresentation of Maori children in the care of the state, and the exclusion of families from active participation in child welfare decisions. It was also evident that the child welfare system operates from a white, European perspective of family life and decision making. This Eurocentric approach ignored the Maori culture, epistemology, and ontology that emphasizes community and collective decision making. This shift in philosophy was articulated in a government briefing paper:

> The procedures are based on the belief that, given the resources, the information, and the power, a family group will make safe and appropriate decisions for children. The role of professionals such as social workers and doctors should not be to make decisions, but to facilitate decision making, by providing information, resources and

expertise which will assist the family group. Professionals will have a crucial role as the resource people. (Department of Social Welfare, 1989)

The New Zealand legislation represented an emphatic response to racial disproportionality, and made clear that families were to be included in the decision-making process by virtue of the FGC model that was developed. It was made mandatory that all children who are considered to be in need of care or protection are referred to the FGC process.

The definition of family group conferencing differs between jurisdictions. The Toronto Family Group Conferencing Center defines FGC as "a culturally sensitive decision making process that brings the family together—nuclear and extended family as well as friends and service providers to develop a plan that meets the needs for the safety and wellbeing of the child within the family" (Toronto Family Group Conferencing Project, 2006, p. 15). A Eurocentric perspective of family generally refers to the nuclear family system. However, non-Western cultures often view family more broadly. This broader family system may include immediate family members, extended kith and kin, friends, service providers, and the community at large. Burford, Connolly, Morris, and Pennell (n.d.) write, "societies that focus on the nuclear family—mother, father, and children—may find the notion of involving extended kinship networks in decision making much more challenging than societies in which collective responsibility for children is a cultural norm" (para. 13).

Several guiding principles and theoretical assumptions underpin the FGC model. These include the following: (a) every child has the right to be raised in an environment of safety and wellbeing; (b) the safety and wellbeing of the child can be assured through family participation in planning and decision making; (c) families, being the experts on themselves, are central to all planning and decision making; (d) families have underutilized strengths and resources to solve problems for their children; (e) culturally sensitive and appropriate responses should be applied; and (f) partnership with the family in decision making and planning for child safety and wellbeing should be shared among service providers and the family (Toronto Family Group Conferencing Project, 2006).

The family group conferencing process involves three primary stages when participants convene. Stage 1 involves the introduction of all the participants and the sharing of information from Child Protection Services and other involved service providers. Information would include a brief history of child welfare involvement with the family, identification of family strengths, and the child protection concerns. This is then followed by Child Protection Services articulating their bottom lines or non-negotiables. The introduction period is also a time for all participants to articulate their hopes for the conference and a moment for family and/cultural rituals such as prayers.

Stage 2 is referred to as the private family time when the family engages in developing a safety, wellbeing, and permanency plan of care for the child. Stage 3 involves the family and Child Protection Services reconvening, and the family presenting their plan and responding to questions from Child Protection Services. If the family's plan is satisfactory to Child Protection Services, they will approve it. Approval of the plan, on occasion, will be tentative until certain assessments are completed (i.e., kinship). If the plan is not approved, then there could be a follow-up meeting, or the matter could be dealt with through the court process if necessary.

Recall that FGC originated in New Zealand to mitigate racial disproportionality in the number of Maori children in state care. While FGC may not have been introduced in other countries for the explicit purpose of addressing racial disproportionality, including Canada, it is starting to be seen in American states, such as Texas, as a way for dealing with the overrepresentation of African-American children in state care. Similarly, Canada struggles with racial disproportionality in the child welfare system (Pon, Gosine, & Phillips, 2011). Racism and colonialism have been identified as factors in this overrepresentation (see Baskin & Davey, this volume; Strega, 2007; Swift & Callahan, 2009). Strega and Esquao (2009) estimate that 25,000 of the 65,000 children in out-of-home care in Canada, or 38 percent, are Aboriginal. However, Aboriginal children account for only 5 percent of all children in Canada (Trocmé, Knoke, & Blackstock, 2004).

In the Canadian province of Manitoba, nearly 80 percent of the children living in out-of-home care are Aboriginal (see Trocmé et al., 2004). Aboriginal youth aged 0–19 represent less than 3 percent of the total child population in Ontario, Canada's largest province, but 14.4% of Aboriginal children are in care (Ontario Association of Children's Aid Societies, 2008). Discussing the overrepresentation of Black children and youth in the child welfare system in Canada (Clarke, 2012), the Child Welfare Anti-Oppression Roundtable (2009) notes that in an urban Ontario city, Black youth represent 65 percent of the children in group care, despite the fact that the Black population in this urban centre totals only 8 percent. A recent *Toronto Star* article noted that 41 percent of the children in the care of the Children's Aid Society (CAS) are Black, while the Black population represents only 8 percent of the city (Contenta, Monsebraaten, & Rankin, 2014).

Involvement with child welfare has been found to implicate intersecting social differences such as class, ability, single parenthood, and race. One response to these dynamics is anti-oppression practice (Strega & Esquao, 2009). Anti-oppression emphasizes self-reflectivity (Wong, 2004) and the critique of privilege, bias, power, and oppression in relation to aspects of social differences such as race, class, gender, sexual orientation, (dis)ability, and so forth (Wong, 2004). The goal of anti-oppression is to promote social justice and combat all oppressions, including racism, classism, sexism, heterosexism, ableism, and so forth (Wong, 2004). Child welfare systems continue to serve clients who are marginalized and oppressed. Those people who are at high risk for receiving these services are experiencing poverty and are often racialized (Clarke, 2012). Research suggests that being a single parent or living in poverty is a risk factor for involvement with the child welfare system (Strega, 2007).

Many studies highlight the efficacy of family group conferencing in keeping children in the care of relatives and lowering the disproportionately high numbers of Aboriginal and racialized children who are placed into the care of child welfare agencies (Pennell, 2009). Support for family group conferencing as a model in child protection is extremely high among social workers and the families who have experienced it (Merkel-Holguin, 2004; Merkel-Holguin, Nixon, & Burford, 2003; Schmid & Pollack, 2004; Velen & Devine, 2005; Waites, MacGowan, Pennell, Carlton-LaNey, & Weil, 2004). While the concept of FGC seems relatively simple to understand and the research supports its efficacy, we wonder why there are such low referral rates to this decision-making process. This leads us to ask the question: What is getting in the way of referrals to FGC? Theorists such as Brown (2007), who examines how innovative ideas are diffused through organizations, have pointed out that "the decision to adopt or reject a new idea can be influenced by a range of factors such as the origin of the innovation, the characteristics of the adopters, the environmental context and the organizational context and structure" (p. 322). Below, we describe a postmodern pedagogy that we believe may explain some of the barriers to referrals to FGC, while offering a way to mitigate some of them.

POSTMODERN PEDAGOGY AND ITS APPLICABILITY TO CHILD WELFARE PRACTICE

In this section, we propose that some of the barriers to family group conferencing referrals can be addressed by a focus on anti-oppression, anti-racism, anti-Black racism, and anti-colonialism, in combination with Irving and Moffatt's (2002) postmodern approach to teaching and learning. In their work on pedagogy, which can be understood as the study of teaching and learning, Irving and Moffatt (2002) offer the notion of the "carnival classroom" that challenges traditional ways of teaching and practising, which are premised on Enlightenment principles that value reason, science, objectivity, and linear progress. Enlightenment refers to a Western intellectual movement beginning in the 17th century, which witnessed the rise of science, eventually supplanting religion as the authority on knowledge (Goldberg, 1993). Instead, the postmodern classroom recognizes that Enlightenment ideals fail to acknowledge the emotional, spiritual, contradictory, and precarious nature of human subjectivity and relationships. Irving and Moffatt, therefore, propose the notion of the teacher as occupying a position of not knowing, while embracing the carnival classroom where the emotions, body, spirit, and mind can all be present and engaged. This not knowing stance runs counter to the prevailing notion that educated professionals must know and have mastery of professional competencies. In this way, the carnival setting is akin to a place for liberation and transformation. We contend that social workers and family group conference coordinators can similarly occupy a postmodern position of "not knowing" and work with the messiness of human subjectivity, including all the contradictions, unknowns, pains, fears, anxieties, and dramas of our existences.

Irving and Moffatt (2002) explain that carnival is not simply a party, but much more revolutionary. Stam (1989) argues that it embodies an "oppositional culture of the oppressed, a counter model of cultural production and desire ... where all that is marginalized and excluded takes over the center" (pp. 86, 95). For example, in a recent *Toronto Star* article, a woman named Patrina told her story of overcoming adversities, including substance use and violence, to be reunited with her children through the FGC process. This reunification was against tremendous odds because her children were Crown wards, and it is not often that youth legally designated as such are returned to their mother's care (Contenta, Monsebraaten, & Rankin, 2014). The FGC process demonstrates how Patrina and her extended family, who occupied highly marginalized subject positions, were able to contest, disrupt, and challenge the hegemonic discourse of "bad mothers" (Swift, 1995). By regaining custody of her children, Patrina was able to triumphantly demonstrate her family's strengths, resilience, and capacity to parent and care for their children. However, for this to have happened required that the dominant discourse of bad mothering be displaced, and the ways of knowing and being of Patrina's family had to occupy the centre. The carnival classroom, like FGC, disrupts the taken-for-granted way of viewing, seeing, interpreting, and doing by virtue of its contestation of Enlightenment ideals of reason, objectivity, and linear progress.

Irving and Moffatt (2002) utilize the metaphor of carnival to "reflect our postmodern contradictions, ambiguities, multiplicities and complexities" (para. 3) and thereby allow professors and students to inhabit the "chaos, fragments and messiness of a postmodern world" (para. 3). They argue that this carnival classroom is "an emerging space of intensity for articulating endless uncertainty about both the professor's and students' positions, identities and stance" (para. 3). If we apply this analogy to the social work encounter, we see that much of the same principles can aid child welfare workers to confront our own limits, fears, worries, and anxieties, particularly as they impede referrals to family group conferencing. These fears implicate the worker's own subject location, privileges, and biases, particularly how these factors may influence how they are working with the family. The workers may, for the first time, realize that they are implicated in replicating oppression against the family. This resonates with what Irving and Moffatt (2002) would call the textures and complexities of client lives: the fissures and rawness of the inescapable realities of racism, classism, sexism, ableism, and community and societal violence that clients have to live with. These truths can be unsettling for social workers because they are what Britzman (2000) calls "difficult knowledge." Often times, social workers may not be prepared and are not able to deal with the visceral aspects of what a carnival setting signified by family group conferencing could unleash.

BARRIERS TO FAMILY GROUP CONFERENCING

Despite the high levels of satisfaction on the part of families who participated in family group conferencing, numerous global studies have noted low levels of referrals to FGC in countries such as Sweden, the United Kingdom (Huntsman, 2006; Sundell, Vinnerljung, & Ryburn, 2001), the United States of America (Gunderson, 2004; Jones & Finnegan, 2003), and Canada (Helland, 2005). Nixon, Burford, Quinn, and Edelbaum (2005) surveyed 225 FGC professionals across 17 countries and found that the usage of family group conferencing was very low.

In Ontario, the legislation states clearly that "if a child is or may be in need of protection, a Children's Aid Society must consider whether a prescribed method of ADR (Alternative Dispute Resolution) could assist in resolving any issue related to the child or a plan for the child's care" (Child and Family Services Statute Law Amendment Act, 2006). ADR includes FGC, mediation, and certain Aboriginal approaches. However, despite this legislation and reported high levels of satisfaction by families, relatively few referrals are made (Contenta, Monsebraaten, & Rankin, 2014). As Rautkis, McCarthy, Krackhardt, and Cahalane (2010) indicate, while much evidence exists highlighting how FGC benefits families, it is still a marginalized practice in child welfare. Several systemic and structural factors have been identified as reasons that underlie the low referral rates to family group conferencing, which include ideology, practices, processes, and attitudes (Boxall, Morgan, & Terer, 2012).

At the ideological level, scholars and advocates such as Doolan (2004) contend that neoliberalism and colonialism, which continue to prevail in Canada and other Western nations, serve as a barrier to family group conferencing. He argues that the neoliberal emphasis on individualism, self-reliance, and independence from state support makes it difficult for social service workers to introduce concepts such as family empowerment into their practice. For Doolan, the touted neoliberal rhetoric of family responsibility shifts public welfare into a private family matter. This translates into a reduction of state funding for social services such as child welfare. Concomitant with the neoliberal reduction in state funding is a rise in managerialism in social welfare agencies (Baines, 2011; Carniol, 2010; George, Coleman, & Barnoff, 2007; Lundy, 2004; Mullaly, 2001). Managerialism in social work refers to an ethos that believes that for-profit business models should be applied to better manage public social services (Baines, 2011). This ethos results in workers and managers often feeling that initiatives such as FGC are too time consuming and not cost effective. There is very little evidence to support these concerns.

The concept of the postmodern carnival classroom is helpful for countering the neoliberalism, managerialism, and individualism that characterizes contemporary social work ethos and practices. The postmodern approach makes us question the validity and efficacy of applying business models championed by neoliberalism to the work of supporting families in communities that are historically, socially, economically, and politically disadvantaged. This postmodern perspective would also assist workers and managers in being more open-minded, taking a risk, and examining what the process would look like in terms of time commitments, costs, and outcomes. It may be that the process reveals pleasant surprises.

Parada (2004) also argues that, increasingly, child welfare agencies in the current neoliberal era have shifted their operations to a managerial focus on efficiency, accountability, and a technocratic approach to social work. This neoliberalism often moves the work of social workers away from relationship building to an emphasis on administrative work (Gunderson, 2004). As Gunderson (2004) points out, "case and data management keep Social Workers at their desk leaving very little time for the fundamentals of relationship building" (p. 2). The impact of this sociopolitical context of neoliberalism is that workers are left without ideological support to engage in the work of family group conferencing, which is premised on relationship building and bringing family members and professionals together for the purpose of shared decision making. This renders many aspects of the FGC antithetical to the hegemonic neoliberal discourse of efficiency, technocracy, and individualization of social problems. These counter-hegemonic aspects of FGC are consistent with the postmodern notion of the carnival classroom.

Further, as Beck and Pennell (2013) argue, the rugged and vaunted individualism in nations such as the United States contradicts the principles of interconnection and cooperation that underpin initiatives such as family group conferencing. This self-reliance is linked to a reluctant support for the welfare state since progressive social programs run counter to the rhetoric of "pulling oneself up by the bootstraps." Romanticized discourses of rugged individualism that abound in countries such as the United States, according to Beck and Pennell (2013), are "rooted in maleness and whiteness" (p. 139). Indeed, Sundell and Vinnerljung (2004) argue that a significant barrier faced by FGC is the prevailing paternalistic culture in Westernized nations such as Sweden and the United States (Merkel-Holguin, 2004). This paternalism shapes the welfare state by valuing social control emphases in interventions with certain families, such as the poor, Aboriginal and racialized, disabled, sexual minorities, and so forth. This paternalism places little emphasis on valuing the expertise and opinions of families when formulating professional interventions and corrective service plans (Merkel-Holguin, 2004). Such ethos contradicts the principles of FGC and potentially contributes to low referral rates.

Similarly, Thobani (2007) notes that the paternalism characterizing the child welfare system finds an underpinning in the rise of the welfare state in nations such as Canada. She argues that, historically, the welfare state exalted whites as national subjects or venerated citizens, while concomitantly demonizing Aboriginal and racialized communities as constituting threats to the nation (Thobani, 2007). In other words, she argues that whites were viewed as superior to racialized people. Thobani (2007) contends that racism, sexism, classism, and colonialism were constitutive of the emergence of the post-war welfare state in Canada.

In nations such as Canada, the welfare state, including the child welfare system, is argued to have replaced the Indian residential schools (Chrisjohn & Young, 1997; Desmeules, 2007; Kundouqk & Qwul'sih'yah'maht, 2009; Pon, Gosine, & Phillips, 2011; Sinclair, 2009; Thobani, 2007). The establishment of the Indian residential school system in Canada was an attempt to "strip Indigenous peoples of their culture and identity" (Kundouqk & Qwul'sih'yah'maht, 2009, p. 32). Beginning in the 1950s and accelerating in the 1960s, child welfare services removed large numbers of Aboriginal children from their parents' care and placed them in predominantly white homes (Sinclair, 2009). This practice, often referred to as the "Sixties Scoop," coincided with the closing of many Indian residential schools.

The Sixties Scoop involved the broader social construction of Aboriginal and racialized families as dangerous, backwards, and pre-modern (Thobani, 2007). Numerous researchers have asserted that clients of child welfare are often viewed very negatively, at times even demonized by some workers (Swift, 1995) as being untrustworthy. There is also the belief that the "apple does not fall too far from the tree," an argument which is used to pathologize whole families, including extended family members. The often diminishing and pathologizing view that some workers may have internalized about families on their caseload can be best understood in the socio-historical context of the evolution of the child welfare system in nations such as Canada. These worker attitudes should not be viewed solely as individualistic aberrations, but also as systemic latent reflections of child welfare's genesis. The carnival classroom concept speaks to the need to look at every family without the biases that are so prevalent in the child welfare system.

The discursive devaluation of child welfare clients creates an ideological-level obstruction to referring families to family group conferencing. Brown (2007) researched three sites in the United Kingdom that offered FGC and found that some workers viewed the model as potentially dangerous, as it handed power to members of ostensibly dysfunctional families. Marsh and Crow (2000), for example, found that social workers who were introduced to the model and who were supportive of the underlying principles of FGC nonetheless maintained the opinion that it "won't work" for "their" families. These negative perceptions of child welfare clients often preclude imagining them as capable of sharing decision-making powers with professionals and being involved as potential protective factors for children. It is unfortunate that these types of perceptions exist, because they fail to provide children and their families the opportunity to access FGC, and the social worker may never get the chance to experience the efficacy of this process.

Current Ontario Legislation

Another reason for low referral rates to FGC in provinces such as Ontario is linked to the legislation where the language, although mandatory, is also permissive, as it leaves the primary responsibility for making a referral to FGC in the hands of the social worker. In New Zealand, the model is legislated with mandatory language, whereas other jurisdictions use more permissive language, therefore making it optional for other child welfare agencies to implement or not. This Ontario legislation allows the social worker to determine whether they have considered the use of FGC, and there is no system or mechanism in place to monitor whether this consideration is actually happening. It is understandable that when there are so many mandatory demands on child welfare workers and they are then given the option to make a referral or not, workers may choose to decline making the referral to FGC. Therefore, the language of the Ontario legislation acts as a barrier to the use of FGC.

Liability

Interconnected with neoliberalism are concerns and fears among social workers around individual, professional, and agency liability (Brady, 2006; Merkel-Holguin, Nixon, & Burford, 2003; Schmid & Goranson, 2003; Sundell et al., 2001). One area of concern in regard to the paucity of referrals could be the fear that if harm were to come to a child who was placed within the extended family, then blame would fall upon the social worker. In one study, 19 social workers were interviewed. Fourteen expressed reservations about family group conferencing, either because of distrust concerning the involvement of the extended family in the decision-making process, and/or because of the fear of losing control (Sundell et al., 2001). This concern about liability on the part of social workers and child protection agencies may hinder referrals to FGC.

Fear of Losing Control and Being Critiqued

Related to the concerns of liability on the part of workers and agencies is the concomitant fear of losing control and power (Sundell et al., 2001). Connolly (2006) believes that family group conferencing exposes the child protection worker to the vulnerable position of having their professional practice scrutinized and critiqued by family members and other professionals. This scrutiny puts intense pressure on the social worker during the FGC process (Connolly, 2006). The FGC process, therefore, must entail a willingness of the worker to cede professional control and power in this regard. Connolly asserts that this makes the Social Worker very vulnerable in FGC when presenting their information. This leads to Social Workers often feeling very powerless and intimidated by the dynamics of FGC. Some workers may understandably fear this loss of control and therefore eschew family group conferencing.

An anti-oppression, anti-racism, anti-Black racism, and anti-colonialism framework combined with the postmodern notion of the carnival classroom can be effective for dealing with these worker fears. The postmodern perspective encourages and supports social workers to occupy a position of being open to possibilities and not expecting that things will unfold in a way they anticipate. This stance acknowledges and appreciates how workers may feel because of the contradictions, ambivalence, unknowns, pains, anxieties, and intense dynamics that are sometimes associated with FGC. This can be operationalized in practice, for example, by the worker acknowledging her or his own feelings of discomfort, anxieties, and fears of the unknown vis-à-vis FGC. Child welfare managers and supervisors can verbally state their support for a forum where workers can freely express such fears and be supported through this process. A parallel process would involve FGC coordinators working with both families and workers in advance of the conference to prepare and support them, particularly with regard to feelings of fear and anxiety.

Training

Another systemic barrier to usage of FGC is the lack of training for social workers (Boxall, Morgan, & Terer, 2012). Sundell (2000) found that the high staff turnover rate in child welfare agencies meant that new workers did not have training in or knowledge of FGC, resulting in lower referral rates to the service. Pennell (2005) reports a need for training to help workers not only become aware of FGC but also to better understand its underlying principles. Adams and Chandler (2004) assert that many conference facilitators are also in need of training about FGC. It is important that such training include anti-oppression, anti-racism, anti-Black racism, and anti-colonialism perspectives, and be implemented in all stages of the FGC process.

Adams and Chandler (2004) further point out that FGC training often must undo traditional forms of training that workers may have received. They argue that some social workers tend to believe that child welfare families do not have the capacity to be decision-making partners. Concomitantly they found that social workers may have been trained to facilitate assessments that focus on the deficits of the family and not their strengths. This training leads workers to view families as incapable of being partners in decision making (Adams & Chandler, 2004). Therefore, traditional mainstream forms of social work training may obstruct referrals to FGC.

Workload

Another significant barrier to referrals to FGC is the high workload carried by child welfare workers, which leaves them feeling that they do not have the time to commit to initiatives such as FGC (Merkel-Holguin et al., 2003; Schmid & Goranson, 2003). Related to the workload issue is that many workers are reluctant to make referrals to FGC because of the weekend or after-hours work that would be required (Adams & Chandler, 2004; Boxall, Morgan, & Terer, 2012; Brady, 2006; Nixon, Burford, Quinn, & Edelbaum, 2005). Clewett, Slowley, and Glover (2010) note that the reluctance to commit to the weekend and after-hours work often associated with FGC can also be exhibited by other professionals involved in the process. This dynamic can make child welfare workers very hesitant to make referrals to FGC, knowing that it would place unwelcomed expectations on them and other professionals to work on the weekend or after hours.

Absence of Fathers in Child Welfare

The cultural ethos of child welfare that often ignores or manufactures what Brown, Callahan, Strega, Dominelli, and Walmsley (2009) call "ghost fathers" hurts the advancement of family group conferencing, because this initiative requires that workers embrace the fact that fathers and their family members can be resources, not liabilities (Jones & Finnegan, 2003). Without an affirming view of fathers and their family members, workers will be hesitant to make referrals to FGC. Kinney and Merkel-Holguin (2013) argue that in child welfare, several systemic barriers lead to workers not identifying and locating fathers. These barriers include: (a) high worker caseloads, (b) lack of standards and guidelines for searching for fathers, and (c) biases among some workers who view fathers as liabilities or as threatening or abusive people who cannot make meaningful contributions to child development (Kinney & Merkel-Holguin, 2013).

Discomforting Dynamics of Family Group Conferencing

Also exacerbating the vulnerability of workers in the family group conferencing process is what Connolly (2006) describes as social workers not being comfortable to speak clearly and honestly about child protection concerns. In Connolly's study, coordinators spoke about workers being exposed during the FGC for not being upfront with families, especially during the investigative phase. This exposure puts workers in the very uncomfortable position of having to clearly explain the tasks they have completed and justify their actions (Connolly, 2006). Workers can circumvent these challenging and exposing dynamics by simply not making referrals to FGC.

Families Declining Family Group Conferencing

Another barrier which causes low referral rates is linked to family decisions to decline invitations to family group conferencing (Boxall, Morgan, & Terer, 2012; Helland, 2005;

Jones & Finnegan, 2003; Sundell, 2000; Sundell et al., 2001). In Sweden, many social workers report that numerous families actually rejected offers of FGC. This raises many questions as to why families do not see the usefulness of this model. Cultural reasons, as they pertain to the meanings and definition of family, may be a factor. For example, there are cultures where kinship and kith relationships are affirmed as part of the family. In other cultures, the nuclear family predominates. This is an area that requires more research.

Family refusals of family group conferencing are linked to a myriad of possible reasons, including having no extended family available or not wanting extended family to obtain intimate details of what can be a stigmatizing and shame-filled involvement with the child welfare system. It may also be the case that parents do not trust their extended family members. Social workers may also present FGC in a negative light, which sways families to decline the referral (Sundell, 2000). Chandler and Giovannucci (2004) have further identified language as being a potential barrier to FGC usage and referral. As such, there is a need for more research around referral rates to FGC for families whose mother tongue is not English.

CONCLUSION AND RECOMMENDATIONS

In conclusion, in order to address the barriers to referrals to family group conferencing, we recommend the following: (a) the language of the legislation be changed to be more compelling and accountability mechanisms around the use of family group conferencing be implemented; (b) increased advancement of anti-oppression, anti-racism, anti-Black racism, and anti-colonialism approaches to social work and education, which would include pedagogy on whiteness and colonialism; (c) using FGC as a proven strategy for addressing the inequality in the overrepresentation of children and families from the Aboriginal and Black communities; (d) training and promotion; (e) research on barriers to FGC; and (f) ensuring adequate funding to support the growth and development of FGC across Ontario, so that the service is available in a timely manner to any family involved with child welfare.

We believe that, given the reported efficacy of family group conferencing, particularly in relation to ameliorating the overrepresentation of Aboriginal and racialized children in state care, FGC should be legislated to be more compelling. Currently, without changes to this legislation, a myriad of structural systemic barriers may lead to a paucity of referrals to this innovative and promising practice. Contenta, Monsebraaten, and Rankin (2014) state:

> Changing legislation to remove the word "consider" so that children's aid societies are compelled to offer family group conferencing or child protection mediation in all cases would shift the power dynamic in child welfare and lead to more family-focused care, advocates say. (para. 8)

Secondly, we propose that some of the barriers to FGC can be addressed by adopting an anti-oppression, anti-racism, anti-Black racism, and anti-colonialism framework that embraces a postmodern turn encouraging and supporting social workers to occupy a position of not knowing. This stance would facilitate working with the confusion of human subjectivity, including all the contradictions, unknowns, pains, fears, anxieties, and dramas of our existences.

Thirdly, the origin of FGC is related to an overrepresentation of the Maori children in the care of Child Protection Services in New Zealand. Also, the state of Texas has implemented the use of FGC to address a similar concern with Black children in the care of Child Protection Services. We believe that with Ontario experiencing similar challenges with its Aboriginal and Black communities, the need to apply FGC as a strategy for addressing this concern is prudent and necessary.

Our fourth recommendation is that there should be increased training of social workers around family group conferencing, including the conferencing model of practice. There are challenges to working with a process that involves the gathering of large numbers of family members and the potential for the expression of intense emotions. It is important that agencies support and encourage workers who endeavour to participate in FGC. This support must recognize the precariousness, uncertainty, challenges, and intensity inherent in the process of FGC. Support can also be manifested as acceptance that the FGC process may not reflect taken-for-granted, normative, Enlightenment modes of linear progress, and that outcomes may not be as quickly achieved as one may desire. This support must acknowledge the tremendous potential gains that can be derived from this process of FGC.

Although this service is meant to be available for all families who are involved with child welfare agencies, there are very few who know that it exists. Every effort should be made to widely promote this extremely useful service so that the families have the option available to them. This could be done through media, direct contact with families, and educating all collateral agencies so they can support the families in choosing this option.

Fifthly, support for FGC can also be achieved by supporting the social workers and supervisors so that they are able to attend these conferences. This support requires senior leadership to embrace the concept of FGC and establish it as a priority for the organization. Conferences should be held at a convenient time for the family. This includes evenings or weekends. More effort needs to be made to explore other possibilities such as weekdays when possible.

We recommend that there is an urgent need for more research in order to fully understand the dynamics in play that prevent child protection agencies from capitalizing on this model of service delivery. The research will need to focus on the CAS, families, the Ministry of Children and Youth Services, the Ontario Association of Children's Aid Societies, unions, and community organizations, among other stakeholders. Having a clearer picture of the barriers will allow for effective responses to address these obstacles. It is imperative that funding is available to support the development of FGC, so that it becomes a service that is available to all families who are involved with child welfare agencies. This will clearly support the spirit of the legislation that speaks to collaboration with the families in finding solutions for the safety and wellbeing of children in our society.

6 | Equal Rights Discourse
Transformative Possibilities?

Dawn Onishenko, Associate Professor, School of Social Work, Ryerson University

The past couple decades have witnessed a burgeoning—almost exclusive—emphasis on discourses of human rights and equality to redress social inequality and platforms of reparation, in the form of human rights codes, acts, tribunals, charters, and judicial decisions, which have served to dictate the way in which society responds to its marginal citizens. The role of equal rights is a topic that is timely, and the political arena in which it has been constructed is one that will inevitably impact the ways in which we practise our profession as social workers. More and more oppressed groups are embarking on legal challenges and embracing the language of rights and equality as a means of challenging injustice; increasingly, social change and community organizing is taking place in the courtroom as opposed to on the street (Brown, 2002), thereby privileging law as an agent of enfranchisement (Lahey, 1999; Porter, 2006; Sycamore, 2006; Warner, 2002a). In Canada, rights rhetoric has emerged as a critical means of remedying inequity experienced by subordinated peoples and groups, particularly since the protection of minority rights under the Canadian Charter of Rights and Freedoms (Brown, 2002; LaRocque, 2006) with the 1985 inclusion of Equality Rights (section 15) in the Charter, and for the LGBTQ population since being declared an analogous group in 1995.

Consequently, human rights and equality have come to be understood as a kind of communal shorthand for inclusion, fairness, amelioration, and the eradication of prejudice and discrimination (Kennedy, 2002). Moreover, the profession of social work has historically included a branch steeped in a tradition of promoting social justice and human rights (Baines, 2007; Killian, 2010; Lundy, 2011) and, more recently, regulating bodies have formally adopted the language of human rights as a strategy of social change (Lundy, 2011; Reichert, 2011; Woodford, Newman, Brotman, & Ryan, 2010). Accordingly, within social work, an equality lens has been taken up as a site of resistance (Ife, 2012). However, the value of an equal rights discourse/outcome is not without question; while some activists, academics, and subjugated citizens regard rights-based activism as an integral and fundamental—albeit partial and inadequate—instrument of social change (Lahey, 1999; Turpel-Lafond, 1997; Valdes, 2003a, 2003b; Williams, 1991; Yamamoto, 1997), others counter that the attainment of formal equality rights offer little more than empty promises and hollow hope for redressing social inequality (Boyd, 2004; Cossman, 2002; Eskridge, 2000; Gavigan, 2006; Kennedy, 2002; Leckey, 2014; Roithmayr, 2001). In light of competing opinions, the privileging of legal equality and human rights as the means to a transformative outcome is a strategy worthy of consideration, particularly in the realm of anti-oppressive social work practice.

The LGBTQ community[1] quickly realized the utility of joining the equality rights tide for the purpose of gaining access to mainstream society and increased social inclusion, turning to the legal sector and the pursuit of equal rights with great fervor (LaRocque, 2006; Lehr, 1999; Sanders, 1996; Smith, M., 1999)—a shift that has repositioned LGBTQ activism from a fragmented and disparate collective movement realized in a grassroots community-based space of oppositional politics, contesting the hegemony of heteronormativity, to a homogenized group of individuals relying on "elites" and professional associations utilizing legislators, the judiciary, and the media to gain greater access to the rights of citizenship (Boyd, 2004; Cossman, 2002; Gavigan, 2006; Smith, 2005). Nevertheless, access to equal rights does not necessarily secure full inclusion, nor does it guarantee a transformative outcome (Leckey, 2014; Lehr, 1999). In fact, the facade of equality may give the false impression that disparity has been resolved and make it much more difficult to dismantle systematized structures of subordination (Valdes, 2003b). Yet the language of human rights and notions of equality may also reframe marginal issues into familiar language (Brewer, 2003; Hull, 2001), enlist state power to give legitimacy to minority claims (Ignatieff, 2000), and allow excluded people to participate in political discourse (Dorf & Tarrow, 2014; McIvor, 2004).

Discussion about the merit and effect of LGBTQ equal rights activism has occupied a prominent place on the public agenda in recent years (Brewer, 2003), as well as within LGBTQ discourse (Robinson, 2004; Warner, 2002b). While equality rights have been critiqued as limiting and restrictive (Boyd, 2004; Cossman, 2002), they have also been declared necessary and liberating (Smith, 2005). Law is both a coercive and discursive field within which change and struggle occurs and, as such, it can be both a site of empowerment and control (Cossman & Fudge, 2002); equality rights claims may produce benefits for constituents even as they simultaneously subdue and suppress their identity. Thus, "rights struggles can be contradictory and complex" (Stychin, 1995a, p. 49), and the pros and cons of engaging in such an approach must be weighed carefully.

The Equal Marriage Charter challenge and accompanying/subsequent discourse provides a framework from which to understand the influence of the codified language of rights on LGBTQ Canadians and explore the take-away learning for anti-oppressive social work practice. Indeed, in Canada, social work organizations lobbied in favour of same-sex marriage (Woodford, Newman, Brotman, & Ryan, 2010); to this end we must at least consider the impact this has had on the profession of social work. The law was changed in Ontario in 2003 and in the rest of Canada in 2005, making Canada the fourth country in the world to legalize same-sex marriage. In order to consider the effect of judicial activism and equality rights claims, this chapter utilizes findings from a qualitative research study of legally married same-sex couples to gain insight into the personal and political meaning of claims to equal marriage. The participant pool included 30 females and 12 males ranging between the ages of 22 and 78 years old and identified as white/Caucasian, African-Canadian, Aboriginal, Métis, and Middle Eastern; spanning the spectrum, they self-defined as lesbian, gay, bisexual, trans, transgendered, gender-queer, dyke, homosexual, Two-Spirited, butch, femme, fluid, and queer. Couples were together prior to marriage between 1 year and 37 years and, at the time of the interview, had been married between 1 month and 6 years. Interview participants, at least tangentially, reflected upon marriage as an act of transgression and indicated that marriage often became an occasion of dissent and defiance in the face of the dominant discourse. Accordingly, submerged subtexts and veiled stories were drawn to the surface and explored from the perspective of rights activism as a component of citizen engagement, social movement activism, and social change.

This chapter posits how we can better understand the nature and possibility of the legal activism and accompanying rights discourse as a mechanism for, or moment of, jurisgenerative praxis. In order to understand the way in which the reliance on the language of equal rights impacts a marginalized population, this chapter incorporates an analysis of the role and function of legislated equality in advancing, and/or limiting, transformative opportunities for LGBTQ people. Drawing on the narratives shared by the research participants, this chapter offers an overview of the ways in which the language of rights, manifest in the equal marriage debate, provided a space of claiming rights and incited/empowered some queer individuals to recognize and resist the collective and systemic nature of oppression. It introduces a discussion of the impact of increased equal rights for LGBTQ people accessing social services in Canada and considers the message, and stumbling blocks, for anti-oppressive social work practitioners. Finally, it speculates about how anti-oppressive practitioners can utilize an equal rights discourse as a strategy of change and a space of resistance.

LEGISLATED EQUALITY

Research participants noted that, while they were reluctant to allow the state to confer legitimacy on their relationship, there is power in the law: "Although my younger, more outrageous self, might say f#*k the state—who cares whether the government likes it or not, there is validity in the state" (Bev). "For me I would not have considered marriage in a same-sex setting if it had not been a political act just because I did not want to be a part of the status quo or to be a part of the norm" (Jessica). The passing of inclusive laws and legislation is part of a larger structural change, which in turn forces compliance and tolerance, if not inclusion and acceptance, as "law makes people obey and then change occurs" (Dale).

Participants observed that social change begins at the level of the state and in the law: "I think that sometimes you have to change laws in order to change social attitudes" (Zahra), and it is the reallocation of "social meaning codified in law that shapes popular understanding of these issues" (Terri). Law compels organizations and structures, even if reluctant and averse, to become more inclusive and, in so doing, formalizes a space of participation and conscientization. Hence, while legislation demands only formal remedy and substantive change cannot be legislated, legislation may *in practice* provoke substantive systemic transformation.

Organizational and social inclusion, protected by law, has the potential to lead to personal acceptance, and law provides a place from which to lay claim to entitlement.

> Although same-sex couples were already covered under common law and it did not change so much in terms of policy, marriage changed things in terms of meaning—it gave same-sex couple[s] equivalency. I think it is like the fight to have gender identity added into the Charter and the Ontario Human Rights legislation—trans rights are already protected—under sex and sometimes disability. ... So the argument, by some, is that we do not need to include gender identity specifically in the Charter as it will not change anything policy wise, and that is true, it will not change anything policy wise, but with that issue, without it being explicit, employers, trans people themselves, the public, do not know it is protected. There is not a public awareness—that needs to be there. (Terri)

As indicated by critical legal theorists, the explicit identification of minoritized populations in a legal context is important in its function as a tool to increase personal and societal consciousness regarding social and structural obligation (Matsuda, 1995; Yamamoto, 1997). Law is an integral part of the sociopolitical process that generates structures of meaning and identity (Chappell, 2002). Although change may or may not be tangible and immediate, and regardless of whether or not legislative correction leads to acceptance and transformation, changes to law and legislation create a legal space of inclusion from which education and awareness can be realized.

Interestingly, all participants were aware of the Charter and identified it as a critical element in the expansion of LGBTQ equality rights in Canada. The Charter not only provides a tool by which to lobby and petition for equality but also acts as an ideological and cultural framework that serves to shape and give direction to social attitudes and sensibilities. "The philosophy behind [the Charter] is that the opinions of the majority cannot make decisions that override the rights of the minority. So I think that philosophy is ingrained in Canada and Canadians and that relates to the Charter specifically" (Ian). Moreover, the Charter has a profound effect on the social landscape as it enables marginalized and minoritized populations to claim their position of equality in the face of disenfranchisement and alienation. The Charter provides a valuable signpost of enfranchisement for disenfranchised populations; as excluded individuals and groups come to see themselves as protected and included in law, there comes a sense of belonging and power from which they can assert their identity and "otherness" (Majury, 2002). The significance of the Charter and equal rights litigation may not reside so much in its measurable outcomes but rather in its ability to mobilize and empower marginalized groups and offer them symbolic strength.

Thus, while the equal marriage case was about a limited action seeking a specific type of remedy, the very act of having to engage in the struggle for acceptance and the consequent backlash created a climate ripe for the recognition of broader notions of injustice and inequality (Klarman, 2013). A *subaltern-counter-public voice* was engendered as members of a subordinated group came together to oppose hegemony and found a space of mutual support, identity formation, and self-understanding (Hobson, 2003), mobilizing LGBTQ people to lobby for inclusion and recognition (Dorf & Tarrow, 2014). Legislated inclusion creates enclaved spaces of civic engagement and facilitates the discourse of membership whereby the excluded can determine their degree of participation and insert themselves into society, even when society is defining them as Outsider (Onishenko & Caragata, 2010). Legislated equality has an instrumental role to play in empowering marginalized populations and stimulating dialogical exchange and, in so doing, challenging and shifting intransigent beliefs and opinions.

PUBLIC DISCOURSE

Many participants related that equality discourse surrounding marriage provided the opportunity and space from which they could, and did, claim their sexual identity in a setting that before had no, or few, openings to share that part of their life: "We were never able to discuss our relationship with a lot of people in our lives and the straight community. Now we can" (Alex). Relationship recognition gave participants the confidence and self-assurance to claim their relationship in the public arena: "I was going to say as well that what it does is give me a quiet confidence about my status. Before we had the legal papers that we kept in our wallets and we could bring them out on the occasion when we did end up in the hospital or someplace and had to prove that, but it's true, I always felt that I had to prove that" (Arianna). Recognition conferred by access to equal rights contributes to a sense of self and, while rights may have been previously available, marriage—legislated equality—offers the place of strength and power from which to claim these rights.

The equal marriage debate saw the elements of private life launched into the public sphere for dissection and appraisal, thereby blurring the distinction between private and public. Participant narratives reveal the way in which they perceived the public profile and dialogue as a necessary, if not welcome, gateway to inclusion and recognition. Although "maybe that debate causes discomfort [...] that discomfort may not necessarily be a bad thing. Discomfort may be a part of the process of accepting people for who they are and maybe that eliminates marginalization to some degree" (Anjali). While the conversations are at times painful and complicated, and may even provoke hostility and critical opposition,

> it is important that there is dialogue. These issues need to be brought up. It takes a while for people to be on the radar of people not affected. There is opposition, then there is a tipping point with public awareness—it tips when people are aware—opinions shift and policies can change—then the policy feeds back into that and then helps shape opinions. (Terri)

Public deliberation is the embryo of greater public understanding and social transformation: "The good thing is it seems that the tone of the debate is changing—people are shifting bit by bit. We've come a long way" (Alice). Seeking denied equality in the context of legislated change serves both a dialogical and discursive function, as it generates public debate while also precipitating and solidifying the construction of an individual and collective social identity (Klarman, 2013).

Ongoing conversation that occurs in the media forges allies and compels ambivalent or oblivious natural champions to enter the discussion.

> Oh yeah, I absolutely think so [change from dialogue], because the longer it went on, the more conversations that were happening, the more actual groups, whether they were unions or even religious groups, came on board and really started to do the work—became part of the group and through that they became part of the current change. (Gail)

In the dialectical exchange, recognition—or rejection—by others contributes to a deeper recognition of self and, in turn, a stronger understanding of one's own place in the larger context of oppression is found (Dorf & Tarrow, 2014).

> I know for me it started out being a gay and lesbian issue and it transformed for me over those three years to an issue of equality and inclusion for everybody. To me it has nothing to do with gender or sexual orientation. It's anybody who experiences discrimination. (Barb)

This discussion is significant in its contribution to social change as "[d]iscourse is important. You can see that currently with trans issues. You can see changes occurring there too. Opposition and public discussion and visibility begins to shift perceptions"

(Terri). In the example of equal marriage, "somebody heard, and somebody listened and something shifts. I think that was a very big part of the success of the same-sex marriage case—it was all of the talking that was done" (Barb). Thus, the Charter challenge facilitated a formal venue from which to engage in informal politics. In keeping with Habermas's (1996) notion of discourse theory, social transformation takes place in the interaction between the informal public opinion and the institutionalized process of communication; the Charter challenge served a communicative function in elevating counter-hegemonic voices to increased parity with powerful hegemonic voices.

Furthermore, formal relationship recognition contributes to the increased social recognition, which in turn provides a place from which to exercise the reallocation of economic goods (Hull, 2003; Phillips, 2003) previously denied to LGBTQ people. Silence and invisibility have been used to oppress individuals and deny them access to rightful benefits; thus, even when redistribution has occurred via law, people may not feel empowered to lay claim to these rights for fear of reprisal and retaliation (Lahey, 1999, p. xxi). Certainly, as participants noted, there are many accounts of individuals afraid to demand spousal health benefits, spousal deductions, or bereavement leave at their places of employment due to anticipated negative repercussions such as job loss or lack of promotion associated with having to "come out" in order to access these rights. For example, Jason described being a teacher and having same-sex health benefits. Nevertheless, before equal-marriage, he did not feel inclined to put his spouse on his benefits as it required disclosure to the principal to do so. However, admittance to institutional and hegemonic establishment may provide the space from which to claim those rights; while individuals may be fearful in their workplace or community to apply for rights due to anticipated hostile responses or negative ramifications, increased profile and removal from being placed in a "special" and separate category may serve to make redistributive rights automatic and routine. Hence, there may be an economic good attached to the public recognition of private relationships in a commonplace and familiar institution.

> It was interesting because we had, as far as I was concerned, we had all the rights with one exception—which was to be married. I guess for myself it was interesting to see that if I wanted Barb on my benefits I had to prove that we were in a relationship, a cohabiting relationship, I'm sorry common-law relationship. You gotta be living together for three years and you have to prove that you've been living together. ... Whereas all I had to do now was check off married to and then I could send my marriage certificate—and that was whether we've had known each other for three days or six years, it doesn't matter. I think for me that was the one thing—when, if I had to, walk into a hospital or anywhere and it would be "what's your relationship?"—partner. That was always one of those things that I had a hard time with—because I would say it is my partner and they would ask, "is that your business partner, your lover—what you mean by that?" (Gail)

Invisibility in *both* the private and public sphere has contributed to the exclusion from civil society and denied LGBTQ people the opportunity to be included in the public discourse (Sanders, 1994). Accordingly, recognition and legal protection in the private sphere is central to queer politics in its capacity to ensure that LGBTQ people have the opportunity to participate in civic society and contribute to the social definition of family and make choices regarding their public and private identity (Sanders, 1994). Rights denied, whether or not the community experiencing the denial of those rights wants to take advantage of them, preserves dominant social codes and permits oppression (Nash, 2005). Equal marriage is not so much about marriage in isolation as it is about the larger notion of equality and access to alternatives for all people. It should be available to all—to accept or reject—as their sensibilities dictate (Calhoun, 2000). Individual freedom, in this case, is merely the end product of the struggle for collective sovereignty; as individuals fight for, and claim the option of, equal marriage in the face of rejection and controversy, they do so as a progression of past struggles and as a gateway to subsequent social transformation (Crenshaw, 1994). In using their privileged positionality, those advocating for equal rights may create an opening in civil society for the inclusion of voices of other sexual minorities and maybe, by extension, other marginalized populations to contest established and deleterious social structures. As individuals come to view themselves as part of a larger collective resistance movement, fostering an allegiance and sense of belonging, they are able to generate and sustain more expansive acts of social change and social activism. It may be that the cultural reframing of same-sex marriage as an equality rights issue is a strategic discourse that thrusts queer identity into the focus of mainstream culture—potentially shifting and altering social perception. In terms of social work practice, it can be argued that enlisting a discourse of rights can provide spaces of legitimacy for marginalized service users; engender dialogue that shifts oppressive attitudes, values, and policies; and be used to advocate for equitable access to and redistribution of limited resources.

THE TAKE-AWAY FOR ANTI-OPPRESSIVE PRACTITIONERS

Participants were not ignorant of the fact that they were entering into an institution considered to be the traditional domain of heterosexuals; they were clear that their non-heterosexual status was a difference that would continue to exist long after marriage—marriage alone was not about to erase their queer identity nor would it ensure hetero-privilege. While participants felt that marriage *should* be an equality right, there was no illusion that marriage would suddenly create equality, eliminating all historical and current realities that come with membership in a sexual minority group: "It is not all won." Joyce reflected,

Queers still get killed for being queer. Queer kids still kill themselves. I am terrified for the two beautiful trans kids of my friends. So we have not won it all. Just because we have same-sex marriage does not mean that there is nothing left to fight.

Furthermore, participants agreed that marriage would not be an overnight cure for societal oppression, and that their relationships would continue to be defined by their collective and individual narratives of marginalization, as well as by persistent external characterization and depiction:

I hoped marriage would be transformative. I thought maybe I would feel safer at work and my family would accept me more. That has not been the case. In some ways it was easier when I was not really out—I was not in the closet, but in the shadows of the closet—I did not have to face the overt discrimination or rejection in the same way. I could choose what and how much people knew. (Kadeem)

Thus the proliferation of a rights discourse, increased representation in the media, and the concurrent shifting perception of inclusion for LGBTQ people demands that we consider the neoliberal context, which constructs social service agencies as "safe" for sexual minorities. As CJ states:

I originally became involved with the marriage case because I thought that the case and the legal recognition of same-sex marriage could be a site of transgressive action, one that would socially reform notions of family. However, in practice, I feel that equal marriage has amounted to the widening of neoliberalism to include and acknowledge same-sex marriage. It has allowed for further privatization of family, has reified the nuclear family formation and heteronormativity. What has been and continues to be important to me though is the notion of choice. I now have the right to choose whether I want to be legally married to my partner or not. It is this choice I feel is central and important.

Despite progressive legal rights in Canada, homophobia still exists (see Abramovich, 2013; Allen, 2014; Ciszek, 2014; Lahey, 2010; Taylor & Peter, 2011), particularly for racialized, non-status, youth, older, and differently abled sexual minority individuals, as well as for individuals and groups that remain outside of the normative representation (Abramovich, 2013; Bauer & Scheim, 2015; Broverman, 2009; Lahey, 2010; Onishenko, n.d.; Parks, 2010; Rehaag, 2008; Teitel, 2014b). Indeed, defining sexuality with fixed and static parameters maintains the invisibility of transgendered persons; ignores notions of sexuality as flexible, fluid, and contextual; and reifies Western hegemonic notions of gender and sexuality (Rehaag, 2008). Thus, one must consider the impact of an equal rights discourse on anti-oppressive practice and begin to tease out ways in which legislated inclusion and the notion of rights can be utilized as a transformative strategy of change, while continuing to be vigilant about the oppression and marginalization that may be further concealed in an era of equal rights.

TRANSFORMATIVE POSSIBILITIES

Much contestation of oppression and hegemony occur in rights claims and counter-claims, and law, as a site and symbol of power, is all-pervasive and infiltrates the consciousness of ordinary people, shaping their thinking, identity, self-perception, and cultural perspective (Chappell, 2002; Majury, 2002; McIvor, 2004; Porter, 2006). The discourse of equality and human rights has permeated all elements of social services, and the right of access to services for marginalized populations is included as a matter of routine; hence, the anti-oppressive social work practitioner must seek ways to utilize this re-languaging of social problems as a new form of resistance.

The role of equality rights as sanctioned by legislation, law, civil codes, charters, international conventions, and other avenues of codified inclusion works to institutionalize the influence of public discourse over law-makers and create a space whereby dissident citizens are given a platform from which they can demonstrate an alternative lived reality (Yamamoto, 1997). This self-expression serves to contradict or agitate the dominant structures; the public claiming this identity creates social consciousness and demands a response—positive or negative. Public discourse, fuelled by opposing and disparate opinions and perspectives, can serve to alter definitions of the good life, as well as mobilize the public to participate in the re-definition and reconstruction of society's norms and values (Dorf & Tarrow, 2014; Valdes, 2003a). Dialogical exchange helps determine whose rights should be included and what these rights should include (Majury, 2002; McIvor, 2004; Smith, 2005). Accordingly, the role of law and legislated inclusion is to encourage enhanced social receptivity and facilitate greater public discourse. Thus, the language of equal rights and the discussion engendered by such claims may be a useful space for AOP social workers from which to increase conscientization, begin the process of coalition building, and expand discourses of transformation and resistance.

COMPLEXITIES OF INTERSECTIONALITY

To complicate matters, even if equality rights do offer promise of redress, it is impossible to be reflected in the courts or in public policy as the "complex, compound, and internally diverse subjects that we are" (Brown, 2002, p. 429; Kelly, 2010). Law's preoccupation with *categories* of discrimination is a problematic one, as "the implication of membership of an individual in more than one category of disadvantage is not easily explained" (Stychin, 1995b, p. 52). Thus, the legal approach to social change is problematic from an anti-oppressive social work model as multiple oppressions "overlap, contest, undermine and/or reinforce one another" (Baines, 2007, p. 20). Ideas and concepts come to us through a plurality of experiences that relish diversity, difference, and a clash of multiple identities (Benhabib, 1993). Identity is too fluid to try and reconstruct as rights, as there are too many diverse and competing claims. Indeed, the disparity that exists in the multiple identities embodied in one individual can result in "unresolved dissonance" (Warner, 1999). Discrimination is multifaceted in character and calls attention to the intersectional nature of oppression. Because law is too rigid to recognize the intersectionality of its subjects, it is almost impossible to recognize subjects marked by more than one form of social power at a time (Crenshaw, 1994). In fact, the rights of a particular identity may actually be "oppressive for sub-groups that have cross-cutting allegiance" (Kennedy, 2002, p. 207). Rights skeptics reason, while the promise of equality holds appeal and may even offer immediate reprieve from intolerable conditions, the results gained on the premise of such action may only be temporary and illusory, as its potential to dismantle social hierarchy is limited and may even serve to perpetuate structural inequality.

IMPLICATIONS FOR ANTI-OPPRESSIVE PRACTICE

Individuals who identify under the LGBTQ umbrella have moved to both a new place of legitimacy and a new place of peril. While the legalization of same-sex marriage and increased access to equality rights paint a picture of social tolerance, inclusion, and equality, one need not look very far or deep to realize that discrimination and exclusion are still very much part of the social order (Onishenko & Caragata, 2010). However, there is the risk that the entrenchment of formal equality rights will be falsely equated with an end to marginalization for LGBTQ people. In the current context, since the advent of same-sex marriage, there has been an increase of LGBTQ visibility in popular culture and society. Concurrently, there has been an increased reporting of hate crimes (Allen, 2014), sexualized bullying (CBC, 2010), and an amplified contestation of public space represented in the struggle over Gay-Straight Alliances (GSA) wherein we witness queer youth and their allies battling with schools and school boards for space and recognition (Baluja & Hammer, 2011; Potts, 2014; Schwartz, 2012); this reality, in conjunction with claims and discussions that LGBTQ people are no longer socially excluded, point to the continued prevalence of socially sanctioned homophobia and heterosexism.[2]

It is imperative that practitioners be aware that rights do not directly transform embedded homophobic values, attitudes, and structures, factors that continue to directly impact LGBTQ people. Practitioners operating from an anti-oppressive framework need to be aware that as new rights such as marriage are secured for LGBTQ individuals, blatant acts of homophobia may be overshadowed by more insidious and less-recognizable acts of discrimination and oppression. Indeed, while equal rights and legislated inclusion may be beneficial for some LGBTQ individuals, sexual minorities who do not nicely fit within dominant, socially acceptable bodies (i.e., middle class, cis-normative, Euro-heteropatriarchal, able-bodied, white, citizen, etc.) may be further marginalized and/or rendered invisible (Murray, 2014).

How sexuality has been historically viewed, expressed, and characterized, both within the queer community and by society at large, is a concrete example of how access to equal rights and increased access to mainstream services and programs may further marginalize individuals who do not comply with dominant narratives. An illustration of this dichotomy is the recent debate regarding banning nudity at Toronto's annual gay Pride parade. Historically, Pride has been a countercultural demonstration of sexual difference, embracing—or at least tolerating—diverse expression and representation; Pride was an event for and by the queer community and was the public manifestation of a personal and heterogeneous lived reality (see Houston, 2014; Teitel, 2014a). However, as "queer has become mainstream," various sectors—both from within the LGBTQ community and society at large—feel entitled to weigh in and impose boundaries and restrictions on this expression; this is occurring to the extent that the Toronto District School Board, some city councillors, members of the public, and others are calling for anyone displaying public nudity at Pride to be arrested, provoking vitriolic public debate. Divergent expressions of sexuality have always defined, and likely will continue to define, queer identity. For many queer people, challenging sexual norms and situating themselves within a countercultural sexual movement is central to their identity and sexual expression such as drag, cruising, kink, burlesque, erotica, fetishism, and polyamory, while not embraced by all members of the LGBTQ community, remain a recognized part of queer identity. Thus, for social work practitioners to assume that sexuality within LGBTQ relationships can be defined or viewed through a heteronormative lens seriously risks further marginalizing sexual minority identity. It is imperative that social workers understand the unique role that sexuality plays for some in the LGBTQ community and that they do not impose restrictive views of sexuality on service users. For some practitioners, whether straight or queer, countercultural expressions of sexuality will challenge their own values and beliefs about how marriage should influence expressions of sexuality—expressions such as role division and monogamy. It is key to recognize that the LGBTQ community is not a homogeneous group and that this is particularly true as it is related to expressions of sexuality; for some, sexuality will more closely mirror practices within the heterosexual community, while for others it will continue to diverge from socially acceptable expressions. Indeed, social work practice occurs in a societal context where heteronormativity is all-pervasive. The situating of social work practice is important because, given the normalcy society places on heterosexual constructs, practitioners, regardless of their own sexuality, are at risk of viewing sexual minorities through a lens of heteronormativity, a risk that is magnified as equality is equated with sameness.

While it may be accurate to portray an ideological division among LGBTQ activists, failure to accommodate the voice of various factions falls into the trap of essentializing queer culture. It presumes that because there is no cohesive community perspective, there can be no common cause. As critical legal studies highlights, outsider groups need to recognize and acknowledge group differentiation and establish pedagogies of praxis that are grounded in the multiple and dissimilar lived experiences of oppressed people (Matsuda, 1995). In reality, there is no single voice of opposition; homogeneity must always be held suspect as a simultaneously divisive and normalizing arrangement (Crenshaw, 2002; Valdes, 2003b). Thus, the homogeneous nature of the language of equality rights, and certainly equal marriage, may work to privilege those of preferable ethno-racial, gender, ability, sexual identity, cis-normative, and socioeconomic standing. Aboriginal and racialized participants in this study reported a complicated relationship with the institution of marriage, as well as to the queer community itself. Access to marriage and the entitlements of marriage are still largely conferred on white, middle-class, gay men and disproportionately serve to benefit that demographic (Hunter, 2013; Hutchinson, 2001; Parks, 2010). While some participants chose marriage as a cultural norm, they found that marriage did not override their queerness. Still other participants reported that in the debate, all other aspects of their identities became subsumed in the privileging of sexual identity, to the point of rendering invisible the racism they encountered from within the queer community. In fact, the quest for equal marriage served to eradicate discussions of racism from the conversation of equality altogether (Hunter, 2013; Murray, 2014). An example of this is the discourse around immigration and the importance of equal marriage to that cause; in haste to utilize this line of argument to secure support for the equal marriage cause, any acknowledgement of a racist immigration system was avoided (Lahey, 2010; Onishenko, n.d.). In order to avoid essentializing the queer community, it must be understood as a cultural identity that loosely encompasses diverse and dissimilar members. While marriage may not be an appropriate or desired expression of relationship for some members of the queer community, that may not necessarily hold true for all LGBTQ individuals, and any politics of identity must allow for that within-group diversity.

In a racist, sexist, homophobic society that has despised and devalued certain groups, it is necessary and desirable for members of those groups to adhere with one another and celebrate a common culture, heritage, and experience. However, too strong a desire for unity can lead to repressing the differences within the group or forcing someone out (Young, 1996, p. 312).

Taking us forward in seeking recognition of diversity of experience and avoiding assimilationist pitfalls requires looking to emerging intersectional/multidimensional identity explorations, such as those provided by Black-queer, "queer-crip," and

Two-Spirited activists/theorists (e.g., Bailey, Kandaswamy, & Richardson, 2006; Carbado, 2002; Gilly, 2014; Hill Collins, 2000; Jindal, 2006; Kelly, 2010; McRuer, 2003; Sandahl, 2003). The exploration of intersectional oppression may assist the quest for a more integrated understanding of outsider critical praxis. These counter-countercultural discourses must be included in theorizing and developing the future of anti-oppressive practice.

The reliance on formal equality is an important consideration for anti-oppressive social work practice for, as the legal realm and a rights discourse have surfaced as the preferred means of social action and formal equality becomes the sole measure of inclusion, it becomes more complicated, but also more critical, to recognize and ferret out spaces of injustice (Reichert, 2011). Additionally, while we see the social service sector complying with this demand for formal inclusion, it may be that the neutral policies and programs implemented further marginalize "objectionable" populations and render invisible those already excluded within those populations. Thus, it is important that those engaged in anti-oppressive social work practice remain attuned to these impending outcomes and ready to support models of relationships that challenge oppression and traditional relations of power. This implies intense individual critical reflexivity, as well as a willingness to continue to challenge the standpoints from which we construct our social institutions and processes and so shape individual subjectivities.

CONCLUSION

The language of human rights is not an end in itself but rather a cultural frame by which to resist hegemony. The discourse of equality enables a repertoire of contention that serves to interrupt and irritate the boundaries of heteronormativity and challenge hegemonic ideologies and narratives. Equal marriage undermined cultural imperialism by colliding with prevailing beliefs and offering alternative discourses; certainly notions that portray queer marriage as a threat to heterosexual families, same-sex families as bad for children, and LGBTQ people as pedophiles and sexual predators have been challenged and shifted in the course of the equal marriage debate. The equal marriage court case served to challenge neoliberal, gendered, heteronormative citizenship, and as an example to and for making space for alternative voices—it is up to us, as anti-oppressive practitioners, to identify, encourage, foster, and ally with those alternative voices.

Additionally, as one area of oppression is exposed/reduced, space for other issues to surface and claim space is opened up. Therefore, one must begin to speculate about the impact of jurisgenerative praxis beyond the LGBTQ community and consider how other marginal and detested populations, who have recently used courts to seek inclusion and recognition, have fared in the process. Some examples include the lobby to have transgender identity added to the human rights code; the recent court challenge by sex-trade workers to have prostitution laws changed; the "Mad" movement's fight for self-determination; and the movement within the harm reduction community at the 2010 World AIDS symposium to have the city of Toronto sign the Vienna Convention, entrenching harm reduction as AIDS prevention strategy. Anti-oppressive practice must take into consideration that as one marginalized group attains equality rights via the courts, other, arguably more detested, populations feel entitled to seek remedy using human rights as a starting point. Consequently, the claiming of equal rights is an ever-growing, morphing, and expanding entity that challenges anti-oppressive practice to continually re-evaluate how power is being operationalized and who continues to be excluded.

NOTES

1. I am using "LGBTQ" recognizing that the language of equal rights does not appeal equally to all members subsumed within this acronym, nor is it a homogeneous community. Indeed, over the years we have seen many additional identities subsumed under this acronym (i.e., intersex, asexual, Two-Spirited, queer of colour, etc.); however, in general, within-group differences have been ignored largely in the quest for "equal" rights. Thus, while rights do not apply uniformly to all members who fall under the LGBTQ classification (Butler, 2004a; Lahey, 1999), they have been assimilated into one "resistance identity" (Lahey, 1999), and, as such, I will use the acronym without making the distinction of (or even exploring) who benefits from rights and which members may actually be further marginalized with the achievement of certain rights. To further complicate the matter, additional language has been taken up as either more descriptive or more inclusive. For example, *queer* has been reclaimed and often signifies a countercultural resistance identity (i.e., Butler, 2004a; Halberstam, 2005; Sycamore, 2008), and, in fact, has an entire theoretical corpus attached to it; similarly, gender and sexual minority (GSM) has been taken up as a more inclusive term that recognizes that not all individuals feel comfortable defining themselves by Western definitions and labels (*Pink News*, 2013). Regrettably, this discussion is beyond the scope of this chapter, and it will have to suffice to say that I have used this language interchangeably and with little attention to these very real and important discussions.
2. We can see in popular media that even within the LGBTQ community there exists a perception that with marriage comes the end of the need for activism and that we live in an era where it is no longer an issue to be queer (i.e., Fedosenko & Leong, 2011; Gilbert, 2015; Solleder, 2011; Tatchel, n.d.). However, equally prevalent are examples of the way in which homophobia/heteronormativity are entrenched in social values; one only need to look at the outcries related to the new 2015 Ontario school curriculum on sexuality, which faced significant objection in part related to inclusion of "discussions of gender identity and sexual orientation" (Brockman, 2015), to understand how issues of homophobia/ heteronormativity remain pertinent.

Section III

Engagement with Marginalized Populations

7 | Anti-Oppressive Social Work with Disabled People

Challenging Ourselves to Do Better

Judith Sandys, Associate Professor, School of Social Work, Ryerson University

Oppression and the disadvantage attached to it come in many, often intersecting forms, and disabled people[1] are certainly amongst the most disadvantaged in our society. The term *ableism* refers to the pervasive and systemic disadvantage imposed by society on people whose bodies and/or minds do not conform to what is considered typical or "normal" and who, as a result, experience marginalization and oppression (see, for example, Goodley, 2011; Linton, 2010; Mullaly, 2010; Pothier & Devlin, 2006; Withers, 2012). Mullaly (2010) relates disability oppression to the "combination of personal prejudices, cultural expressions and values, and the social forces that marginalize people with disabilities and portray them in a negative light" (p. 215).

Anti-oppression theories and the practice approaches (Baines, 2011; Carniol, 2010; Dominelli, 1996; Fook, 2012; Lundy, 2004; Morgaine & Capous-Desyllas, 2015; Mullaly, 2010) that follow from these have served to enhance our understanding of the processes by which certain groups become marginalized and oppressed and have helped us to think about how we might effectively respond to the resulting disadvantage. However, while what these and other scholars say has much relevance to disabled people, often there is little emphasis on the issues faced by this group. Within the AOP social work literature, discussions of race, gender, sexual orientation, and class predominate, with significantly less focus on disability. As a result, even social workers who have had a significant exposure to the AOP literature may never have fully considered how disability oppression is like, or unlike, other forms of oppression or the relevance of AOP to this population.

This chapter explores the application of anti-oppressive theory and practice—and critical and social justice approaches more broadly—to social work with disabled people. It provides a definition of disability, discusses societal responses to disability historically and today, and provides a brief overview of some of the major theoretical frameworks that shape current understandings of disability. In its final section, the chapter identifies practice issues as they relate to the application of AOP to social work with disabled people.

DEFINING DISABILITY

While impairments and disabilities are sometimes thought of as being one and the same, and we often use the terms interchangeably, it is helpful to make a clear conceptual distinction between the two. Impairments refer to specific conditions of the body, the senses, or the mind that contribute to functional limitations—including, but not limited to, one's ability to walk, see, hear, or speak; the loss of a limb; being of very small size; and so forth. Some, but not all, impairments are likely to result in a person being defined as disabled, particularly if the impairment extends over a long period. Whether or not a particular impairment is constructed as a disability is a complex matter and varies over time, place, and context.[2] Determinations of what degree of cognitive impairment constitutes an intellectual disability, what height determines whether one has dwarfism, what degree of vision impairment qualifies one as "legally" blind—all these are arbitrary and may vary from one place or time to another. To a large extent, impairments are constructed as disabilities when they are perceived by the dominant group(s) as significant enough to render a person unable to fulfill societally expected roles, or at least, to significantly interfere with the ability to do so. A chronic bad back is a "disability" when it interferes with a person's ability to hold a job; otherwise, it may be seen merely as an annoyance or inconvenience. The inability—real or perceived—to engage in relationships, to be a parent, to learn in typical ways, to take care of oneself, or to be employed, whether due to real or perceived impairments, all will lead to a person being defined as disabled. "Disability," as Withers (2012) notes, "is not a fixed category ... [but has] a fluid definition that depends not only on the context in which it is defined, but also who defines it" (p. 8).

RESPONSES TO DISABILITY, HISTORICALLY AND TODAY

Historically, people with impairments of the body or mind were seen as sick, helpless, often dangerous, a burden to society, and a threat to the social order. As a class, disabled people have endured countless generations of exclusion, segregation and congregation, institutionalization, rejection, violence, poverty, neglect, and being subjected to treatment that has caused or hastened their death (Wolfensberger, 1994, 2013). Drawing on eugenics theories developed in Europe and America, the Nazi Holocaust began with the extermination of disabled people, ultimately killing hundreds of thousands of disabled children and adults (Evans, 2004). Thousands of people with intellectual disabilities were subjected to forced sterilizations in the United States and Canada, a practice that was legal in Canada as recently as 1972 (Malacrida, 2015). The incarceration and often brutalization in large institutions of thousands of people with intellectual and psychiatric disabilities are recounted in many books, including those by Blatt (1974), Malacrida (2015), Reaume (2009), Trent (1994), and Wheatley

(2013). Despite fewer people being incarcerated today in large institutions and the passage of rights-based legislation—including, for example, the ADA in the United States, the Canadian and Ontario Human Rights Acts, and the AODA (Accessibility for Ontarians with Disabilities Act) in Ontario—disabled people here, and elsewhere, continue to be seriously marginalized.

Disabled people are far more likely to be unemployed, to be poor, and to lack postsecondary education (Crawford, 2013). They are more likely to be homeless (Mercer & Picard, 2011) or in prison (Ben Moshe, Chapman, & Allison, 2014). Disabled women are discouraged from becoming parents (e.g., Grue & Laerum, 2002; Malacrida, 2009) and, for those who do become parents, "losing custody of their children is an omnipresent fear" (Filax & Taylor, 2014, p. 1). Disabled people are often denied opportunities for sexual expression because they are perceived to be asexual or hypersexual, undesirable, or incapable of participating or taking pleasure in sexual activity (Liddiard, 2014; Shakespeare, 2006; Tepper, 2000).

OPPRESSION AND DISABILITY: THE SOCIAL MODEL AND BEYOND

While disabled people, as a group, have been and continue to be disadvantaged within society, there have been some changes in how disability is viewed, and these hold out possibilities for additional change over time. This section includes a brief—and necessarily incomplete—review of some of the theoretical issues pertaining to disability.

Until recently, the "problem" of disability was seen simply as an individual issue, a tragic mistake of nature or the result of illness or accident that left its victim considerably diminished. The prevailing wisdom was that disabled people needed treatments that might "fix" or "cure" them or, failing this, placement in an institution to protect them and society (Stienstra & Wight-Felske, 2003; Trent, 1994). Disability was equated with illness and the "treatment" of disabled people was considered largely within the purview of the medical establishment. The medical model—sometimes referred to as the individual tragedy model or the charity model—reflects the traditional view of disability, where it is assumed that a disability is simply what happens when an unfortunate tragedy befalls an individual—at birth or later in life—that results in an impairment that renders him or her unable to function effectively in society. Within this model, disability is medicalized; disabled people are seen as sick or damaged, and in need of being treated, fixed, or cured if they are to have any chance at all of participating in society. Those not able to be fixed or cured are seen largely as objects of pity and charity, to be cared for at public expense. Segregation and exclusion are hallmarks of the medical model.

Over time, this view of disability has been challenged. Much has been written about the need to move away from the "medical model" of disability and to adopt a "social model" (see, for example, Linton, 2010; Oliver, 1990; Wehbi, 2011b;

Withers, 2012). The social model draws a clear distinction between an *impairment* and a *disability*. While an impairment refers to a functional limitation of the body or mind, disability refers to the societally imposed restrictions on those who have or are perceived to have an impairment. The social model contends that the disadvantage experienced by disabled people is not the inevitable outcome of the "condition" (i.e., the impairment) that results in them being defined as disabled, but the outcome of the societal responses to that condition/impairment. Rather than being the result of impairments, the disadvantage experienced by disabled people results, it is argued, from the discriminatory attitudes, ideologies, and societal structures that surround them and keep them oppressed. They are "disabled" by a society that isolates them, excludes them, and denies them opportunities for full participation. Oliver (1990), one of the first to write extensively about the social model, presents a materialist theory that sees the oppression experienced by disabled people as rooted within the capitalist system. Change, he suggests, must come about through transforming the consciousness of disabled people so that they do not internalize their oppression, and through collective action to change the oppressive structures of society. Abberley (1987) and Charlton (1998) also relate the oppression of disabled people to our capitalist society. Charlton (1998) claims that the "logic of disability oppression closely parallels the oppression of other groups ... bound up with political economic needs and belief systems of domination" (p. 22).

The social model has played a key role in helping to change the way we think about disability and has served as a rallying point for the disability rights movement, bringing together people with different disabilities, and their allies, to work together to fight for change. But the social model is not without its critics (see, for example, Anastasiou & Kauffman, 2013; Crow, 1996; Morris, 2001; Shakespeare, 2010, Withers, 2012). They argue that by suggesting that the disadvantage that disabled people experience is rooted entirely in societal structures, the social model denies or trivializes the impact of an impairment, fails to represent the experiences of people with intellectual disabilities or mental health issues, and may be interpreted as rejecting any kind of medical intervention designed to prevent or ameliorate impairments.

Another perspective on oppression comes from Wolfensberger (2013), who uses the term *devaluation* to mean the attaching of negative value by one entity to another. Devaluation is enacted on those whose characteristics are perceived to be both different and negative, characteristics that reflect the opposite of what the perceiver values most highly. At the individual level, we may devalue a person or group of people (e.g., a politician or a political party) because of a characteristic that we see as negative, and we may respond in any number of ways (e.g., avoidance, speaking out against the individual or group). Within any organization there is a value system and the way people are viewed and treated within that organization will be influenced by the extent to which they manifest those characteristics that the organization values. In these instances, the people who are devalued are not necessarily members of an oppressed group. However, as Wolfensberger (2013) notes,

> devaluation of people also take[s] place on the level of a social collectivity and even an entire society, where entire classes of people are judged negatively by an entire collectivity, society, or majority thereof. It is this second type of devaluation that is the most devastating, because it creates and maintains societally devalued classes who systematically receive poor treatment at the hands of their fellows in society and at the hands of societal structures—including formal organized human services. (p. 22)

When devaluation takes place at a societal level, the devaluation is systemic and the result is oppression. A society that places a very high value on health, productivity, and independence will devalue and oppress those groups or classes of people that are *perceived* to be sick, non-productive, and/or dependent. People who are oppressed within their society will be devalued, and the widespread and systemic devaluation of whole classes of people constitutes oppression. The more people are oppressed and devalued, the worse they will be treated. At the societal level, devaluation and oppression are sustained by societal belief systems and ideologies and are played out in societal structures. Institutionalization, segregation, rejection, isolation, poverty, lack of opportunities to work or engage in other meaningful activity, being subjected to regimentation and control by others, being seen and treated as a menace, object of ridicule, forever child, object of pity, burden, and so forth—all these are manifestations of very deep devaluation and oppression (Wolfensberger, 2000, 2013).

A more recent theoretical perspective is critical disability studies (CDS). CDS is not a single unified theory but a theoretical approach that undertakes to challenge the way we think about disability, to question the processes and ideologies through which we have come to think about it as we do. Like the social model, CDS sees the disadvantage experienced by disabled people as rooted in oppression. However, within this framework, the roots of oppression are seen as broader than the materialist explanations articulated by Abberley (1987), Charlton (1998), and Oliver (1990). Shildrick (2012) contends that CDS has

> added new force to the theoretical impetus already at the heart of the social model, taking it in innovative directions that challenge not simply existing *doxa* about the nature of disability, but questions of embodiment, identity and agency as they affect all living beings. (p. 30)

A central focus of critical disability theory is "a challenge to normativity, of what is good and bad or right or wrong" (Vehmas & Watson, 2014, p. 640). Impairment is not assumed to be a negative; it is not something that should be treated, cured, fixed, or prevented. Disability is seen as part of the human condition, one more form of diversity, and like other diverse groups within society, disabled people are seen to have much to contribute that is enriching to everyone. Rather than seeing disability as a disadvantage, CDS celebrates disability as a valued aspect of the human condition.

Critical disability studies also has its critics. Vehmas and Watson (2014) contend that CDS seems to argue against efforts to prevent disability and provides little basis on which to make decisions as to what is right or fair. They note that societal attitudes and responses to disability continue to reflect considerable ambivalence. At the same time as we decry the ableist attitudes that keep disabled people oppressed and marginalized, our society seems often to question the inherent value of disabled lives. While critical disability theorists may argue that there is nothing inherently negative about having a disability, that disability merely constitutes a *difference*, neither good nor bad, it is rarely thought of as such in the broader society. Giving birth to a disabled child is, for many people, seen as tragic—the mother perhaps deemed neglectful of her societal duty if she could have had an abortion and did not. An accident that renders a person disabled is usually viewed—at least initially—by the person and those closest to the person as a tragedy. These views of disability are so deeply rooted in our society that they are often "taken for granted."

Efforts to eliminate disabled people through genetics or abortion reflect this very deep-seated devaluation. The current debate on assisted suicide includes an implicit assumption on the part of many people that to have a disability is to "suffer" and that a disabled life is not worth living (see, for example, Frazee, 2014; Longmore, 2003; McBride-Johnson, 2003). Parents who kill their disabled children may be cast into the role of "hero" for ending their child's suffering or "victims" who simply can no longer bear the "burden" of having a disabled child (e.g., Lucardie & Sobsey, 2005). Barnes (2014) contends that while it would be unethical to knowingly cause someone to become disabled, this does not mean that the lives of disabled people are without value or that all disabled people are unsatisfied with their lives and want to be "cured" of their disabling conditions. CDS forces us to confront and challenge common assumptions about what is "normal," acceptable, good, and beautiful, and serves to enhance our understandings of society well beyond issues pertaining only to disability.

Critical disability studies also makes linkages between different forms of oppression, noting that the historical roots and contemporary stereotypes surrounding other marginalized groups share common features with those surrounding disabled people (e.g., Baynton, 2013; Ferri & Connor, 2014; Goodley, 2011; Liasidou, 2014). Thus, along with disability being seen to justify the poor treatment of disabled people, Baynton (2013) argues that "the concept of disability has been used to justify discrimination against other groups by attributing disability to them" (p. 17). Ideological assumptions that certain groups—women, immigrants, poor people, racialized people—are somehow less capable, less responsible, less productive, or even less than fully human have been reflected in societal responses designed to control, incarcerate, exploit, or even eliminate members of these groups.

Some disabilities have relatively little relationship to one's race, gender, class, sexual orientation, and so forth, occurring more or less at random. But people may become disabled at any point in their lives. Illness, accidents, violence, poverty, environmental conditions, and isolation—all these may contribute to a person becoming disabled or, if already disabled, becoming more disabled. To the extent that being a member of a particular marginalized group increases the likelihood of these conditions occurring, the greater is the risk that people in these groups will be or become (more) disabled. It is important to be very clear about this; it is certainly not that members of particular oppressed groups are inherently less capable than any other group. The issue is that one of the impacts of oppression is that it may create conditions that are, in and of themselves, disabling. Ferri and Connor (2014) explore how "race, economic disadvantage and dis/ability work to justify exclusion and inequality" (p. 472) in the context of schools. These authors emphasize the need to avoid what they refer to as "single axis analyses." They say:

> To focus exclusively on dis/ability discrimination to the exclusion of other aspects of disadvantage, benefits those disabled people who are most privileged in terms of race, class, nation, sexuality and gender ... [and] further marginalizes those individuals who experience multiple forms of oppression. (p. 479)

DISABILITY DISADVANTAGE

As the foregoing discussion suggests, the interrelationships between disability oppression and other sources of oppression are complex and often difficult to disentangle. Oppression by definition is systemic and without a doubt, much of the disadvantage experienced by disabled people is related to disability oppression, as it intersects with other sources of oppression.

Some disabling conditions may be directly caused or exacerbated by the poor life conditions that are the hallmark of oppression. But as our discussion of the critiques of the social model suggests, we cannot assume that *all* the disadvantage experienced by disabled people is rooted in oppression. It is not difficult to identify the systemic barriers that keep some disabled people excluded and oppressed. For example, for many people with physical disabilities who are often unemployed, it may be quite clear that if we could change the physical and attitudinal barriers that have often kept them excluded, they could get jobs. If parents and teachers all had high expectations and provided good learning opportunities, if people had access to postsecondary education, if places to engage in learning and work and leisure were accessible, if assistive devices and needed accommodations were routinely available, if employers were committed to hiring a diverse workforce, and so forth, there is a good likelihood that many more people with physical disabilities would be employed. While physically disabled people do encounter barriers to employment, we can at least imagine how things could be different, particularly if other sources of oppression were also adequately addressed. In other life areas, as well, we can identify ableist attitudes and discriminatory structures that create barriers for disabled people. Disabled people, as has been noted, are often perceived as unable to parent effectively (Filax & Taylor, 2014; Malacrida, 2009). This disableist attitude is a barrier in and of itself, discouraging disabled people from becoming parents and, if they do become parents, subjecting them to a system that may be more likely to provide surveillance than support (Malone, 2014). Nevertheless, one cannot assume that the exclusion of disabled people from paid employment is *always* related to societal barriers. Nor can we assume that every disabled person can effectively parent, if supports are available.

In addition to the extrinsic, societally imposed disadvantage that disabled people often encounter, there is also often an intrinsic disadvantage related to the impairment that has led one to being defined as disabled. There are some disabled people, those with very severe physical disabilities; with conditions associated with chronic pain; with very severe disabilities of the mind—rather than of the body—including, but not necessarily limited to, very severe intellectual disabilities, brain trauma, and various forms of dementia, where the disabling condition itself creates enormous disadvantage. It is hard to imagine a society where people with very severe disabilities would not, overall, experience significant disadvantage in at least some areas of life.

However, while it is important to acknowledge that an impairment may well create some inherent or intrinsic limitation or disadvantage apart from the societal responses to that impairment, it is even more important to recognize that regardless of the nature or the severity of this limitation, it is invariably the societally created disadvantage that does the most damage. The more impaired a person is perceived to be, the more vulnerable the person is to the effects of devaluation and oppression. By and large, the worst atrocities have been inflicted on the people with the most severe disabilities. We may not be able to imagine a world in which some severely impaired people did not experience some disadvantage, but surely we can imagine a world in which they would experience far less.

APPLYING AOP TO SOCIAL WORK WITH DISABLED PEOPLE

As Baines (2011) notes, anti-oppressive practice is not a single approach but

> an integrated model drawing on a number of social justice-oriented approaches. ... It attempts to analyze how power works to oppress and marginalize people as well as how power can be used to liberate and empower them across a wide range of social settings, relations, environments and systems. (p. 26)

Without a doubt, disabled people are an oppressed group within society, and AOP has much to offer that is of benefit to this population. However, in applying anti-oppressive practice to disabled people, we cannot ignore the impairment itself in terms of its impact on the life of the person or group we are supporting. The discussion that follows explores some of the core themes of AOP—critical reflectivity, empowerment and autonomy, and the interrelationships among different levels of action. The concept of valued social roles is introduced and related to these themes.

Critical Self-Reflection

A central tenet of anti-oppressive and other social justice approaches to social work is that it is essential that social workers engage in critical self-reflection (e.g., Baines, 2011; Fook, 2012; Morgaine & Capous-Desyllas, 2015; Mullaly, 2010). Critical self-reflection, writes Mullaly (2010), "is a form of 'internal criticism,' a never-ending questioning of our social, economic, political and cultural beliefs, assumptions and actions" (p. 277). Through this process, we attempt to uncover—as much as possible—and challenge the inevitable unconscious biases that we all hold. Negative perceptions about disabled people are so deeply embedded in the ideological structures of our society that it is impossible not to be influenced by them at least to some extent. The thought of becoming disabled is frightening to most people, perhaps because we are reminded of our own vulnerability, since becoming disabled is an ever-present possibility, indeed a likelihood if we live long enough. This may make the process of critical self-reflection challenging and, for that reason, all the more important.

Being an anti-oppressive social worker requires that we continue to develop a critical consciousness of various manifestations of oppression. As with other forms of oppression, we need to become ever more conscious of our own privilege as non-disabled people—if that is our identity—and to understand how each of us—seldom intentionally—contributes to disability oppression. It is important to develop a greater awareness of the dire life circumstances of so many people with disabilities by getting to know disabled people and hearing their stories. In some situations, disabled people cannot tell us their stories in the usual manner, and in those situations we must seek out alternate means of developing our understanding, using our powers of observation and being sensitive to non-verbal cues.

Empowerment and Autonomy

Empowerment is a much-loved, frequently used—but not always clearly defined—term that plays a central role within the AOP literature. Adams (2008) defines empowerment as

the capacity of individuals, groups and/or communities to take control of their circumstances, exercise power, and achieve their own goals, and the process by which individually and collectively they are able to help themselves and others to maximize the quality of their lives. (p. 182)

Appreciating the inevitable complexities and contradictions involved, Fook (2012) identifies power as dynamic, expressed in different ways in different contexts. She stresses the need to develop a process of empowerment that takes into account "many different viewpoints and positions" (p. 63) and notes that it is often personal rather than structural. "'Being given' power," she notes, "may not be experienced as empowering, but in fact may have disempowering effects" (p. 50).

Without a doubt, we want to enable disabled people to become empowered. However, discussions of empowerment often focus on people having the opportunity to make their own choices and decisions. We cling to the notion that the decisions people make about how they want to live their lives are usually in their own best interests and that, anyway, people have the "right" to make decisions, even when they are harmful ones. We may worry about what to do when people make decisions that seem to deepen their oppression. But trying to influence the decisions of the people we are supporting may be seen as disrespectful. We know that disabled people are very often controlled by others, and we worry about exerting power over someone or trying to make people conform to our—or society's—values, and so forth. Because we are fearful—as we should well be—of furthering the oppression of the people we are wanting to support and empower, there is the risk that we become so afraid to take action that we do nothing.

Traditional perceptions of empowerment and independence often do not "work" for people who are very devalued, including, but not limited to, a good many disabled people. Most of us have a range of relationships with people we can count on for support and advice, for encouragement, for assistance in hard times. Particularly when we are making important decisions, we will look to those we know and trust for their input. We hope that the people we count on would step in to stop us if we were going to do something that would really harm us. And if we think that someone we care about is going to do something that is really not in their best interest, we will go to considerable lengths to try to stop them. All this increases the likelihood—although, does not guarantee—that we will usually make good decisions, or at least not too many awful ones. And for the most part, we make reasonably good decisions most of the time.

Many disabled people—as well as many members of other deeply devalued groups—are very isolated, poor, and experience-deprived. They lack this web of supportive relationships; they have no one around to help them make good decisions or prevent them from making bad ones. Further, they are likely to have often been subjected to the control of others, surrounded by those who hold low expectations and cannot even imagine that the disabled person's life could be different or better. In these situations, the person will have had little experience making decisions about anything very significant. Adding to the complexity is the fact that some disabled people do have competency limitations that will impede their capacity, to some extent, to participate fully in all the decisions that affect their lives.

It is essential to support disabled people to be involved in decisions about their own lives. But in promoting such involvement it is important to recognize that some people may need a great deal of support in this regard. As Fook (2012) notes,

> there are still some people caught in situations where the actions of a more powerful person might assist in more beneficial ways. In short, there may still be a need for advocates, a need for people more articulate or more powerful to act on behalf of those who cannot. (p. 172)

No one is ever empowered in isolation, but within a social context that includes people to teach, support, mentor, advise, and care about us. Further, to make decisions implies that one is choosing between, or among, alternatives. If there are no choices to be made, then there is nothing to be decided. Empowerment is not simply about *making* choices; it is about *having* a range of meaningful choices, along with the support required to, as much as possible, make good choices.

The Importance of Valued Social Roles

A number of people have discussed the importance of promoting valued social roles for people with disabilities (see, for example, Barnartt, 2001; Lemay, 1999; Osburn, 2006; Race, 1999; Wolfensberger, 2000, 2013). They argue that when people are devalued, they will be treated poorly, and contend that one way to address this devaluation is to promote socially valued roles for people in their society. When people have roles that are valued within their society, it is more probable that they will be treated better and have greater access to the "good things of life" (Wolfensberger, Thomas, & Caruso, 1996). Most of us will have a good many valued roles, along with perhaps some that are not. These roles, together, define our lives and shape our identities. Devalued people have few roles, and those they do have are much more likely to be negative.

The kinds of barriers that the social model and AOP seek to address are highly congruent with a focus on social roles. We seek to address barriers to education and to paid employment. We want to challenge those ideologies that keep people oppressed, the ones that exclude people by casting them into roles as helpless, dependent, a burden of care, asexual (or hypersexual), childlike, a menace, an object of pity, and so forth. We want to challenge societal barriers so that disabled people have access to the roles of student, worker, lover, parent, family member, friend, taxpayer, citizen, neighbour, teacher, athlete, artist, singer, volunteer, and so forth. Of course, one cannot impose a role on a person; a valued social role must be by definition authentic, reflecting the interests and gifts of the person.

Working at All Levels

One of the many binaries that social work creates is between working at the individual level versus working at a community or societal level. AOP does address this, claiming that we must work at all levels and that these levels are often interconnected. So too it is with promoting valued roles. Supporting a person to acquire work-related skills or to dress appropriately for a job interview may be the very issues that enable him or her to become employed. It may well be true that one reason why a disabled person is unable to get a job is due, in good part, to ableist attitudes. But each time we provide the support that enables a disabled person to get and keep paid employment, we challenge the stereotype that suggests disabled people cannot be employed. And we make it just a little bit easier for the next disabled person. Because oppression and devaluation are sustained through societal ideologies that define certain groups as being of little or no worth, every action that challenges or disrupts these ideologies is an act of resistance. Of course, not all disabled people can or should work, nor should we assume that this is the only valued role that disabled people need or want. It is important to explore other valued roles that might be available to the person, some of which have been noted above.

People who are deeply oppressed over a long period of time are likely to lose hope and to no longer have the ability to even imagine a better future. If we, too, can think of nothing better for them than their current situation, it is unlikely that anything will ever change. While not wanting to minimize the challenges involved, one way to empower people is to work with them to enable them to acquire valued social roles. People in valued roles likely have more control over their own lives and more opportunities to make decisions, to be more empowered.

Wehbi (2011b) describes anti-oppressive community organizing in Lebanon that involved disabled people as active partners in the process of change. Without a doubt, for both the disabled and non-disabled people involved, this was an empowering experience; being seen "as leaders in change" (p. 144) was clearly a valued social role, and it undoubtedly changed how the disabled people viewed themselves. But many disabled people, particularly those with significant disabilities, spend their days not in empowering environments or engaged in empowering activities but in programs that reflect their devalued position in society. We talk about building inclusive communities, but provide services for disabled people that are overwhelmingly segregated. We talk about everyone's need to engage in work or other meaningful activity, but most often surround disabled people with activities that lack meaning or challenge, or sometimes leave them with nothing to do at all except "hang around." Many social workers come to believe that an adult with an intellectual disability "needs" to live in a group home or that it is in the natural order of things that frail, elderly, disabled people should live out their last days in long-term care facilities; as long as disabled people have a place to go to, it doesn't much matter what they do when they are there.

We know that oppression is sustained through ideologies, which serve to rationalize the way oppressed groups are treated. Services for many disabled people continue to surround them with images that perpetuate their devaluation. When adults with intellectual disabilities or elderly people are engaged in childish activities or when their program settings are decorated with childish pictures, we reinforce the societal perception that they should be treated as children. With such expectations, we increase the likelihood that they will behave childishly, thereby reinforcing the original perception. We may—and certainly we should—do what we can to make these environments as good as possible for those who are dependent on such services. But we should not convince ourselves that these settings are good or good enough.

While we cannot deny the reality of impairments and the limitations that these may create, people's lives should not be defined by their impairments. Regardless of the impairments that people have, everyone needs and benefits from opportunities for growth and development, meaningful activities, relationships—or at least the opportunity to develop them. Systemic responses that deny people these opportunities invariably diminish their capacities far more than did the original impairment. Further, they contribute to the societal perceptions that disabled people don't belong, that they invariably lack competency, and so forth, thereby contributing to the barriers encountered by other disabled people.

While it is easy to be aware of the barriers that keep people oppressed, it is more difficult to understand how these are reflected in the supports and services that have been developed ostensibly to meet the needs of disabled people and to appreciate how these reinforce and replicate disability oppression. Some disabled people have never experienced anything better than they have now or may even have been in far worse situations in the past. A person who has experienced a lifetime of deep devaluation may not be able to imagine that anything could ever be different or better than it is now. Such a person needs strong and committed allies to help develop a personal vision for a better future, allies who truly believe that a better future is possible. This may mean actively encouraging the person to seek out and explore new challenges, even when much support and encouragement is needed to do so.

CONCLUSION

Working with disabled people requires that AOP social workers bring their activist orientation to the fore, regardless of whether they are working to assist particular individuals or advocating for better services or greater access. Disability oppression is deeply embedded in our society and is unlikely to change greatly in the foreseeable future. At the same time, as we work toward systemic change, we should be doing all we can to improve life conditions for individual disabled people and to challenge oppression whenever and wherever we can. We cannot "give" anyone a valued social role or empowerment. But by working at all levels we can help to create the contexts in which these are more likely to occur. Each time we enable a disabled person to have a more valued role, there is a ripple effect that has an impact well beyond that person. Each time we create positive change, we are challenging and disrupting societal stereotypes and creating change one person at a time. In order to do this effectively, we ourselves must be able to imagine a better life for disabled people.

NOTES

1. There is continuing controversy over whether it is preferable to use people-first language—as in people with disabilities—or identity-first language—as in disabled people. Mullaly (2010) suggests that the phrase "disabled people" is ableist and results in "disability becoming the person's master status" and claims that "people with disabilities" is "the term preferred by persons oppressed by ableism" (p. 215). However, others disagree. Linton (2010) explains:

   > since the early 90s, disabled people has been increasingly used in disability studies and disability rights circles. ... Rather than maintaining disability as a secondary characteristic, disabled has become a marker of the identity that the individual and the group wishes to highlight and call attention to. (pp. 225–226)

   See Pothier and Devlin (2006), and Titchkosky (2003, 2007) for further discussion on this topic. Both expressions are used in this chapter.
2. For example, a person who wears glasses to correct a vision impairment is not likely to be defined as disabled. By contrast, wearing a hearing aid—particularly if one is young—to correct a hearing impairment is more likely to be associated with having a disability. The impairment created through the historical practice of binding feet in China would today be seen as a disability, but at that time was a mark of status (Ping, 2000). Groce (1985), in her aptly titled book *Everyone Here Spoke Sign Language*, writes about a small community in New England in the early part of the 20th century, where, due to the genetic makeup of this isolated community, some 15 percent of the population was profoundly deaf. Within this community, sign language was widely known and utilized. Deafness was considered a characteristic, rather than an impairment, and deaf people were not considered disabled; those who did not know sign language were the ones who were disadvantaged.

8 | When the Suffering Is Compounded

Toward Anti-Black Sanism

Idil Abdillahi, Assistant Professor, School of Social Work, Ryerson University

Sonia Meerai, Research Consultant

Jennifer Poole, Associate Professor, School of Social Work, Ryerson University

Sanism or mentalism[1] is a particular form of oppression experienced by millions of people living with issues that fall under the categories of "psychiatric diagnosis," "mental illness," and "mental disorder." Sanism is pernicious, pervasive, and penalizing, presenting itself in a myriad of obvious and subtle ways. Sanism may manifest as blatant discrimination, lost work or housing, low expectations, or hate language—such as flippant use of the word "psycho" (Chamberlin, 1990; Perlin, 1992). Yet few are aware of the term, its history, and the literature that has grown up around it. Similarly, few are aware that sanism creates a particular kind of suffering, the kind that has been normalized and sanctioned by many as "good" clinical practice.

We three authors know sanism all too well. We experience it almost daily, we chart its consequences (Reid & Poole, 2013), and we try to ease the pain it causes for us. We are part of a growing Mad studies (LeFrancois, Menzies, & Reaume, 2013) community that seeks to name, chronicle, and work against sanism and its effects, and, as social workers, we do this from an expressly anti-oppressive stance. By *Mad*,

> we are referring to a term reclaimed by those who have been pathologized and psychiatrized as "mentally ill," and a way of taking back language that has been used to oppress. …We are referring to a movement, an identity, a stance, an act of resistance, a theoretical approach and a burgeoning field of study. (Poole & Ward, 2013, p. 96)

By Mad Studies we mean an interdisciplinary, multi-vocal, critical project of inquiry, knowledge production, and political action devoted to the critique and transcendence of psy-centred ways of thinking, behaving, relating, and being (LeFrancois, Menzies, & Reaume, 2013, p. 13).

And yet, for all these critiques, there continues to be less comment on the kind of suffering experienced by the millions of people who are not only categorized as mentally ill but who are also racialized and colonized (Mills, 2014; Tam, 2013). In this space where the suffering is compounded lie long-silenced hurts and harms, born of institutionalized white supremacy[2] (Smith, 2006). Indeed, racial oppression may be sustained through people's encounters with psychiatry/psychology/social work (Tam, 2013), as well as their encounters with the Mad movement. Both sanist systems and those that work against this oppression are themselves carved from and perpetuate whiteness. As Mills (2014) argues, the time has come to decolonize mental health and madness.

Of particular concern for us in this chapter are the experiences of racialized people who identify as Black, African, or of African descent, because our lead author is both Black and African and our second author is racialized. In addition, we have in horror noted an anti-Black trend in mental health "care." For instance, young Black men are diagnosed with schizophrenia more than any other group (Fernando, 2012). Black children are being psychiatrized and medicated at higher rates than other children, pushing them directly into the "prison pipeline" (Contenta & Rankin, 2009), and in our experience on the frontline in Toronto, more Black and African identified patients are being held against their will in hospitals. Is what we are seeing here a kind of sanism, a particular form of racism, or something intersecting that has, of yet, no name? Tentatively, and with respect, we three authors have begun to call what we are seeing, reading about, and experiencing *anti-Black sanism*.

Before we introduce what we understand as *anti-Black sanism*, in this chapter we will first situate ourselves, and explain how we understand sanism generally and then the kind of racism known as anti-Black racism. We will take up the work of others thinking through these issues in and out of social work and Mad Studies and review some of the research that supports our concerns with this horrifying anti-Black trend in mental health and madness. We will argue that anti-Black sanism builds on scholarly work in the areas of anti-oppressive practice, sanism, Mad Studies, anti-racism, and anti-Black racism by providing a space, both theoretically and practically, to begin to discuss issues faced by Black and African peoples within the mental health system. In a direct attempt to de-centre the whiteness so common both in "psy" sciences and Mad politics (Gorman, 2013), we believe that the experiences of Black and African peoples with "mental health" need particular attention and focus. In short, we seek to begin to language the suffering long compounded by sanism and anti-Black racism and to start a response.

ABOUT US

We are all doing social work of various kinds, Jennifer and Sonia are users of the mental health system, and we are involuntary students of sanism. We have been influenced by anti-oppressive practice (AOP; Baines, 2011), by the burgeoning field of Mad Studies, by histories of madness and the long-standing work of psychiatric survivor movements worldwide (Starkman, 2013). Theoretically, we also hold tight to our copies of Foucault, Butler, Fanon, and Ahmed. With these and other lenses, we seek to understand what has happened to us and our peers, where the gaps in knowledge are, and what we can do to address them.

We are also not innocent in the complex roles that we occupy as authors, practitioners, scholars, and educators. We too are implicated in our present and past roles within institutions in advancing agendas that are awash in sanism and practices that sustain white supremacy. "In retrospect, [we] also think [we] have hoped that finding a site of innocence could take away the pain of [our] contradictory relationship to the state" (Rossiter, 2001, p. 201). And take away the pain of our contradictory relationship to each other, for there is an important difference between us, one that has also pushed us to talk about anti-Black sanism in these pages. Specifically, two of us are racialized and one of us is white, and that changes everything when it comes to our conversations about naming, resisting, and writing about sanism. Others are also aware of this difference, for along with Gorman (2013) and Tam (2013):

> In the Canadian context, Mad Studies scholars drawing on transnational and postcolonial Feminist critiques of multiculturalism ... have produced important concepts that can help us think critically about the co-organization of colonialism and psychiatry. Roman et al. (2009) develop tools for thinking about "medicalized colonialism," while Howell (2007) traces the expansive regimes of ruling implicated in the narration of the racialized "terrorist." (Gorman, 2013, p. 271)

But before we add to those concepts and delve deep into what we are now calling anti-Black sanism, we want to move into a discussion of sanism generally.

ABOUT SANISM

Sanism is the belief system that makes it "normal" to pick on, make fun of, discriminate, reject, silence, incarcerate, shoot at, and commit other forms of violence against people who are othered through mental "illness" diagnosis, opinion, and experience (Poole, 2013). The practice of sanism is ages old and centuries deep, has taken many forms (i.e., witch hunts), and has become decidedly more entrenched since the so-called Enlightenment and the rise of science and reason. The term, however, is generally credited to Morton Birnbaum, an American doctor and graduate of Columbia Law School (Ingram, 2011). Influenced by the civil rights work of Black legal scholar Florynce Kennedy, in 1958 Birnbaum began to argue that patients in American mental hospitals should have "adequate" care. He first outlined and used the term *sanism* in his piece for the American Bar Association, entitled *The Right to Treatment* (Birnbaum, 1960).

American advocate Judi Chamberlin (1990) also took up the cause, working with the terms *mentalism* or *sane chauvinism*. Writing about the ex-mental health patients' movement, in which she was a central figure from the 1970s until her recent death, Chamberlin argued mentalism was a set of negative assumptions that most people, including health care providers and ex-patients themselves, held about "mental patients." More recently, Kalinowski and Risser (2005) have explained mentalism as the systematic subjugation of people who have received mental health diagnoses or treatment.

And then there is Michael Perlin, a professor at New York Law School who has written most extensively about sanism. In one of the first of his influential papers, Perlin (1992) defines sanism as "a form of bigotry that respectable people can express in public" (p. 375). Sanism, he writes, creates the conditions in which those with "mental 'illness' have been made largely invisible and without power, institutionalized, deprived of the right to vote or the right to be parents" (p. 392). In the absence of an alternative, Perlin (1992) cites a list of sanist myths that have been allowed to flourish about people with mental health issues. One such myth is that such individuals are different, weak, frightening, and unable to make decisions about their own care. Another is that what is depicted in the media is the truth, and finally, that using pejorative labels to describe such people, including psycho or insane, is not as "bad" as other recognized hateful terms.

However, as the myths have flourished, in recent years so have the critiques, especially from the fields of critical disability studies and Mad Studies. For Mad scholar Fabris (2011), the kind of sanism we see today is "the division of persons into 'mad' and 'sound,' especially based on an interpretation of ill logic, reason, or wisdom, such as in 'delusion'" (p. ix). For Hamer (2011), we also need to broaden this notion to include "state sanism" and "institutional sanism."

Additionally, many are making clear the distinction between stigma and sanism and the need to focus our attention on the latter. The Coalition against Sanist Attitudes (CASA, 2011) explains that the focus must be on sanism, because it is sanism that makes possible and gives rise to stigma. Similarly, Thornicroft (2006) and Sayce (1998) argue that a focus on stigma perpetuates medical conceptions/language around mental health, and minimizes the reality of widespread rights abuse and oppression— or sanism—experienced by mad individuals. Large and Ryan (2012) have argued the same with respect to the sanist belief in the dangerousness of mad people. Finally, in Holley, Stromwall, and Bashor's (2012) review of stigma and anti-oppressive social work practice, the authors find the term stigma to be grossly inadequate, arguing that stigma is often "the tip of the iceberg ... and has frequently served as a means of giving short-shrift to powerful social inequalities ... that are much harder to identify and conceptualize" (Holley et al., 2012, p. 54).

Given this, as well as the dominance of the medical model and widespread social investment in sanist myths, it follows that seldom is sanism acknowledged in social work. With few exceptions (see LeFrancois, 2011; Poole et al., 2012), it is often the case that in social work "offensive and injurious practices are integrated into everyday procedures to the point where we no longer recognize them as discrimination" (Kalinowski & Risser, 2005, p. 2). It follows that there has been no outcry around studies that claim social work needs to be protected from "dangerous" practices by students with mental health issues or that degree program acceptance be delayed for these individuals (see Poole et al., 2012, for more). It is rare that social workers are aware and supportive of the international Mad Pride movement, challenging conceptions of normal and "well" while celebrating madness through writing, research, annual festivals, marches, lectures, and art shows around the world (see www.torontomadpride.com). It appears that social work has a good deal of catching up to do when it comes to understanding sanism and rooting it out in the academy, in practice, and in the literature.

ABOUT ANTI-BLACK RACISM

The same can be said of anti-Black racism, an oppression with malign, pervasive, and penalizing effects. As stated by Walcott (2003), "writing blackness is difficult work" (p. 25), so we begin this section on anti-Black racism with the conceptualization that Black peoples are diverse and unique even within the shared identity of "Black" as a category. Indeed, our use of the terms Black and African peoples is an effort to speak to the complexity of Blackness as an identity and to further acknowledge that within these terms there is space for individuals to place and shift themselves on the continuum of Blackness as an occupied space rather than a fixed category.

We also begin with Fanon (1952/1991), who wrote about the issue that haunts us today. He described how many of his Black patients seeking help with mental health issues were bent on striving to be white. He wrote that the Black identity seemed to be up against a system where only "one race" is visible, accepted, and valued. That Black identity is colonized, instructed institutionally to perform in a manner of whiteness, and it is often the psychiatric system that perpetuates this construction. This happens through language and its erasure as well as through fear. In sum, according to his work, racism is equated to "pro-white, anti-Black paranoia" (Butts, 1979, p. 1016).

To this, Benjamin (2003) adds that like whiteness, Black and Blackness must also be seen as a system that is more than observable characteristics, traits, attributes, or tied to concepts embedded in identity. Blackness must be seen to represent a system of marginality, powerlessness, and subordination, one that is often experienced at the institutional level through systemic policies, processes, and practices (Benjamin, 2003). The term *anti-Black racism* provides an entry point to unfolding the manifestations of systemic racism toward Black and African peoples in different institutional settings (Benjamin, 2003), such as prisons and the education system.

Anti-Black racism (ABR) is thus the understanding of how racism is experienced in Canada affecting Black and African peoples. Connected to Garveyism, Black nationalism, anti-colonial, and anti-imperial theories (James et al., 2010), ABR is entrenched at all levels of Canadian society, functioning to preserve systems of whiteness and power and dominance based on a false perception of white superiority (Henry & Tator, 2010). Starting in Toronto in the 1990s, anti-Black racism materialized as a "term and concept," made by "grass-roots and working class intellectuals" who were a part of the Black community (Benjamin, 2003, p. 61). Anti-Black racism was a direct focal point to address the impact of police violence, brutalities, and gun violence, while simultaneously addressing the historical implications of policies and practices that were "perpetuated upon Black peoples by the police and criminal justice system" (Benjamin, 2003, p. 61; James et al., 2010). Benjamin (2003) states,

> The concept of anti-Black racism emerged as an analytical weapon in the struggles against racism in policing by the Black community. This concept became a lightning rod that gave specific focus to the issues of police violence, harassment, and shootings impacting the Black community in Toronto. (p. 60)

Benjamin (2003) explains that the concept of anti-Black racism emphasizes both the severity and particularity of racism experienced by Black peoples in Canada, a situation that Smith, Lawson, Chen, Parsons, and Scott (2002) attribute predominantly to two factors:

1. The particular history of anti-Black racism which traces itself back to slavery in Canada and its legacy as determined through specific laws and practices enforcing segregation in education, residential accommodation, employment and other economic opportunities; and
2. The impact of anti-Black racism today as distinct from the racism experienced by other subjugated groups and evidenced in the differential treatment experienced by peoples of African descent in immigration, education, employment, the justice system and in Canadian mass media and culture. (as cited in Warner, 2006, p. 15)

Clearly, race has not lost its power as a key signifier in structuring all aspects of life in the Western world. We may believe our societies to be culturally diverse. We may have already agreed that there is no biological basis for distinguishing human groups based on "race" (Omi & Winant, 1994, as cited in Fernando, 2012), but "race thinking" and specifically anti-Black race thinking continues. Our principle concern is how this kind of thinking permeates mental health.

ANTI-BLACK RACISM AND RESEARCH ON MENTAL HEALTH

The over-pathologization, over-diagnosis—especially with respect to severe mental illness—and overrepresentation of Black and African peoples in the mental health system is well documented, both in Canada and around the world (see Fernando, 2012). In the literature, Xanthos (2008) documents the over-diagnosis of schizophrenia amongst British African-Caribbean populations. Xanthos (2008) draws on research that concludes schizophrenia "affects only one percent of any given population. However, there is a six to eighteen-fold elevated rate of diagnosed schizophrenia in the UK African-Caribbean population compared to whites" (Hickling, 2005, as cited in Xanthos, 2008, p. 1). Xanthos (2008) also documents research conducted in the 1980s by Bell and Mehta (1980, 1981), which indicates overrepresentation of diagnosing Black clients with schizophrenia and minimal diagnosis of depression.

Mfoafo-M'Carthy (2010) cited a study conducted in England surveying 32,023 patients in the mental health system, where 21 percent of respondents identified being of Black descent despite only accounting for around 7 percent of the population. With respect to admission to psychiatric institutions, there are also alarming disparities between white groups and Black and African peoples, where Black peoples and mixed race peoples are admitted involuntarily at a 19 to 39 percent higher rate than white groups (Mfoafo-M'Carthy, 2010). In addition, the author cites studies indicating that Blacks experiencing mental health issues are more likely to be prescribed antipsychotic medication and less likely to be offered psychotherapy as a form of intervention. Other studies cited by the author indicate drop-out rates or "non-compliance" in regards to mental health interventions, which are highly related to cultural incompetence in service provision, and negative/opposing experience within the mental health system.

Lack of access, coordination, and differential treatment is documented in a review by Shavers and Shavers (2006) where racial discrimination, association of behaviours, and negative stereotypical attitudes create immense disparities with Black peoples accessing mental health services, often through force and involuntarily and often misdiagnosed. The discrimination does not work in isolation, as Shavers and Shavers (2006) discuss how discrimination toward Black peoples is documented through housing, employment, health care services, and the criminal justice system.

According to the Afrikan Canadian Prisoner Advocacy Coalition (ACPAC, 2012), African-Canadian inmates within the provincial and federal criminal justice institutions who are living with mental health issues require immediate action to address their mental health needs. The Mental Health Court of Toronto found that 85.5 percent of immigrants were diagnosed with schizophrenia (Dinshaw, 2010). Within the broader 85.5 percent of immigrants seen through the Mental Health Court, there still remains a disproportionate representation of African and Caribbean peoples (Dinshaw, 2010).

"African Canadians make up only 2.5 per cent of Canada's population. However, in 2010–2011, the proportion of African Canadian offenders in federal prison was 9 per cent. This represented a 52 per cent leap from just a decade earlier" (African Canadian Legal Clinic, 2012, p. 25). We also know Black men are more likely to be "streamlined" into the justice system rather than the health care system (Social Planning Council of Peel, 2007). This can also be connected to how Black masculinities are interpreted and problematized. Schools often encourage Black parents to put their children on medication to "control" their "bad" behaviour (Contenta & Rankin, 2009). Indeed, Black children make up 12 percent of high school students in the Toronto public school board, yet account for more than 31 percent of all suspensions (Rankin, Rushowy, & Brown, 2013). This overrepresentation is paralleled in the criminal justice system, demonstrating the early pathologization, psychiatrization, and ostracization of young Black children. This system creates "push outs" (Contenta & Rankin, 2009), a process embedded in white supremacy from the underrepresentation of Black and African teachers and to the erasure of Black and African identities within the mainstream curriculum. This does not address the loss of identity or problematizing of the Black body, and it often functions as a "prison pipeline" (Contenta & Rankin, 2009) without ever accounting for the systemic hurts caused by the micro-aggressions of racism within the educational institution, which manifest in the context of mental illness (James et al., 2010).

In short, if we can identify anti-Black racism by differential treatment experienced by peoples of Black and African descent in immigration, education, employment, the justice system, and in Canadian mass media and culture (Benjamin, 2003, p. 15; James et al., 2010), the research above suggests we can add mental health to the list. Black peoples and people of African descent are often misdiagnosed, over-diagnosed, over-hospitalized, over-medicated, and under–cared for. And this situation exists across the board in Western systems that rely on white, colonizing psychiatric tools and categories. Colonizing mental health practices name people's "experience in alien and alienating technical terms that deny personal or social meaningfulness, labelling people as 'irrational'… and subjecting people to forced treatment and involuntary detention" (Mills, 2014, p. 6). Is it not time to decolonize this by subverting this practice through a different kind of naming? Is it time to decolonize mental health by naming what we see as anti-Black sanism?

ANTI-BLACK SANISM

But why anti-Black sanism? Along with the work we cite above, "users, survivors, Mad people, and their allies" have already attempted to "discuss the significance of race, racism and racialization for Mad people's oppression through using various frameworks for analysis, including analogy, intersectionality and trauma"

(Tam, 2013, p. 281). All of this work has proven very valuable to us, as has the transnational and postcolonial writing of Gorman (2013) and Tam's (2013) work on conviviality. Elsewhere, one of us has also helped to take up an anti-colonial lens to deconstruct the recovery movement with respect to Indigenous Peoples in Canada (Lavallée & Poole, 2010).

But here, we are specifically concerned with Blackness and its psychiatric pathologization, and believe that by naming it as anti-Black sanism, we can begin to address issues of overrepresentation, misdiagnosis, and inadequate intervention in mental health practice today. As we have noted, there has long been a co-organization of colonialism and psychiatry. Born of so-called progressive and enlightened pursuits, both seek to "make white" by making strange that which is local or Indigenous or in any way different to northern European/American behaviours, emotions, and ways of being. These colonizing practices not only give rise to a sanist construction of Blackness, to what Fanon calls anti-Black paranoia, but the ongoing pathologization and maltreatment of Blacks and Africans both inside and outside of the mental health, educational, and criminal justice systems. Although individuals might have agency by engaging in self-definitional notions of Blackness, medical colonization will always determine, categorize, and interpret identity beyond self-report and self-disclosure.

This kind of sanism, which is both centuries old and yet newly named, reminds us of Pon's (2009) reference to "new racism":

> racial discrimination that involves a shift away from racial exclusionary practices based on biology to practices based on culture (Goldberg, 1993) … new racism is difficult to recognize as racism because racist discourses are interwoven with discourses about social cohesion, cultural preservation, and nationalism, which discriminate without actually using the word race …. (p.61)

And because this kind of sanism is as slippery, as difficult to recognize, and, indeed, interwoven with new forms of racism, we believe we need to respond to it with as much agility and versatility as possible. Anti-Black sanism is an opportunity to place emphasis on alternative explanations in order to provide a response to "the problem of the twentieth century, the problem of the color-line" (Du Bois, 1903, p. 34). Along with all the concepts and approaches we have noted thus far, we see anti-Black sanism offering another, complementary way to see and name the suffering that has always been felt.

But what else can we say about anti-Black sanism? Although our ideas are in the genesis stage, with respect to mental health, we do know our anti-Black sanism focus is particularly concerned with some specific points of analysis. The first is discourse and language. In mental health, we have often noted an anti-Black trend in "professional" forms of communication. The linguistic disconnect often experienced by Black and African peoples has usually been met with attempts at "cultural competence," poorly translated flyers or professional attempts to manipulate "other" languages, styles, and ways of communicating to better fit with English phrases, grammatical rules, and parlance, including those in the DSM-5. Importantly, we experienced this while writing and editing this chapter. Questions such as who edits what, why, and how began conversations about colonizing. What is an editor really doing who seeks to "correct" style and grammar according to pre-established—white—rules (i.e., APA)? Who benefits from manipulating language in this way? Is the often untroubled act of "improving" an academic piece a colonizing act of violence?

If translation is needed, it is often incorrect or not direct, and if not needed, the cultural nuances are often missed, marring the possibility for meaningful interaction and intervention. Very rare is the individual professional who acknowledges that his or her notions of "illness," "wellness," and "diagnosis" are understood, named, assessed, and treated from a white, medical model perspective that is embedded in relations and exchanges of power. These relations will often make it impossible for non-white people to construct and position themselves within medical institutions, within the Mad movement, and within academic publications.

This inability to name, understand, and language within the context of white supremacy directly impacts how Black and African peoples are understood by practitioners and advocates alike. When asked to speak to "your illness or diagnosis" by a practitioner, it is an attempt to ascertain your "insight." Practitioners infer if you agree with, can live with, or "accept" your illness. This inadvertently also speaks to an individual's compliance, cooperativeness, and treatment plan. However, there is no discussion of the power of language and its use as a "tool" for assimilation, or as a "barrier" into dominant culture (Fanon, 1952/1991).

Similarly, we have noticed anti-Black sanism when mental health professionals regard behaviour and decide what counts as "good," "normal," or "compliant" (Fernando, 2012). For instance, a "good" client, patient, or program participant understands their illness and limitations and works toward accepting this label. A good client is not loud or angry that they are being "formed" involuntarily or injected with an unknown substance to "calm them down." A good client is well kept and as little "hassle" as possible. While treated, a good client accepts what is happening, for acceptance is often celebrated as a badge of honour on the road to "recovery" (Poole, 2011). This is done without consideration for the parts of one's identity and ways of being with others that have to be negotiated, sold, or denied in order to be released from hospital or to avoid restraints and community-based treatment. Speaking literally, in order for someone to express wellness, one must adopt white language and behaviour to be released from the shackles of psychiatry, or—as the story illustrates below—to avoid them in the first place.

A Case Example[3]

A 25-year-old woman of Black Caribbean descent was brought into a busy Toronto emergency room department after eating at a local restaurant and being unable to pay her bill. When confronted by the waitress, the woman reported that she was really hungry and had no money. She asked if there was any way that she could come back at the end of the month and pay? The waitress informed her that was not an option and either she paid or the waitress would have to call the police. The waitress called the police. According to the police and emergency services report, the patron attempted to plead with the waitress, becoming loud, aggressive, and potentially violent. She spoke quickly, appeared "manic," and "ranted" about poverty and large corporations. When the police spoke to the patron, she asked for a ticket or court date, so she could pay. She pleaded that she did not have the money right now and asked why they were all against her. She said she could have run, but did not. She told the truth.

She was subsequently placed on a Form 1 and deemed a threat to herself and others due to her loud, aggressive, and potentially violent behaviour in the restaurant, although the woman did not assault anyone. She was described as a tall, Black woman with a boyish haircut, extremely "unkempt" with a severe body odour. Based on the report that police provided, she continued to show "oppositional behaviour" and was placed in restraints, although she never displayed such behaviour in the hospital. Many of the attending hospital staff—doctors, nurses, personal aides, and others—wore protective gear such as facemasks and gloves to separate themselves from her unkemptness and odour. Staff continued to fear her due to her height and size, making comments about how big she was. She made many requests for sanitary napkins when she arrived in hospital, but was ignored. Forty-eight hours later, hospital staff complained about her odour publicly, and hosed her down with a handheld device in an open concept shower.

Highlighting anti-Black sanism, and how bodies, language, and behaviour are "read" and pathologized, the story above narrates just one case of many we have seen. It also stands as an example of what we are most concerned with in this chapter. Why did the waitress have to call the police? Why did the police have to use a Form 1? Why did staff fear this woman so much? Why the inhumane response? This is what anti-Black sanism looks like, this is what happens when the suffering is compounded, when anti-Black racism and sanism collide. And this collision not only results in the above kinds of "treatment" but, in some circumstances, death by police shooting.

A recent inquiry into police shootings of individuals with mental health issues was damning of how our "protectors of the peace" see and deal with people experiencing distress (see *Toronto Star*, 2012).

Fuelled by fear of anti-Blackness and sanism, these protectors do not usually seek to calm or comfort. Fuelled by anti-Black sanism, the capturing and, at times, murdering of Black bodies under the guise of public safety or "good care" has become the norm and fear of many Black and African peoples alike. For instance, on August 29, 2010, a Toronto police officer murdered a 25-year-old Black man by the name of Reyal Jensen Jardine-Douglas. Despite being aware of Jardine-Douglas' mental health status, the police shot him multiple times.[4] Similarly, on February 3, 2012, Michael Eligon, a 29-year-old Black man, was shot to death by police after a psychiatric evaluation at a Toronto hospital. In both cases, the Special Investigations Unit cleared the officers and the Toronto Police Services of any wrongdoing. Clearly, anti-Black sanism is an issue of life and death.

It follows that we believe not only officers but white mental health practitioners need "to be able to tolerate the knowledge that they will be dangerous to people of colour all their lives" (Rossiter, 2001, p. 207). In mental health care and practice, whiteness needs to be de-centred and the hierarchy and elitism of white supremacy acknowledged. Like others (e.g., Gorman, 2013), we argue the same needs to happen in the Mad Movement.

An anti-Black sanism approach highlights how many Mad advocates/Mad movements "forget," deny, or plain refuse to provide space for Black and African peoples at the centre of the work. From where we stand, everyone should want to understand our particular histories, "without jumping to innocence in the form of these absurd cultural competence models ... or a crash course in anti-racist social work" (Rossiter, 2001, p. 207). We need to acknowledge the consequences of what Dei (2000) says when he argues that white people—even solidly anti-sanist, progressive Mad people—often do not want to talk about race.

And the consequences are many. In part because of anti-Black sanism and the silence around it, the current Mad movement in Toronto is dominated by people who do not identify as Black or African. Like colonialism, anti-Black sanism contributes to the reason why many well-paying, peer-based positions are occupied by white bodies. Further, it is why discussions regarding difference may be based on diagnostic criteria and not the lived experiences of racism. The denigration of African-centred healing traditions as "unscientific," illegitimate, and not clinical has also led to the reason why many communities continue to suffer in the face of failing white supremacist, evidence-based clinical practices (Bracken et al., 2012). If in fact Western psychiatry looked at African and global South interventions regarding people that are Mad-identified, some would argue that African societies are far more progressive in addressing people holistically (Fernando, 2012; Watters, 2011). For example, in some of these societies, it is ensured those who are living with mental health issues are still part of the economic and social fabric, that they contribute to the community in a way that is meaningful, much-needed, and does not other their contributions based on their diagnosis/point of difference.

Rossiter (2001) thinks about,

questioning how we can tell the difference between helping people who are trapped by historical and social circumstances, and pathologizing them. It means trying to understand the difference between inspecting people for flaws and getting to know them. It means understanding the difference between power and domination. (p. 207)

Within our well-intentioned capacities to "help," it is imperative that we recognize the inherent white supremacist, colonial, pathologizing nature attached to many of the mental health professions. Relieving ourselves as practitioners from the effects of imperialism and colonialism will in fact have a much greater impact on Black and African peoples. Thus, when we speak to healing, we need to understand that the work must not leave out the histories of peoples still attempting to recover socially and politically from the impacts of colonialism and degradation (Lavallée & Poole, 2010).

CONCLUSION

Obviously, we have only scratched the surface in our thinking about anti-Black sanism. We know there is so much more to be done. We wanted, however, to name what has not, for us, been named before. We wanted to highlight the "evidence" of this decidedly anti-Black trend, and we wanted to do this in a way that adds to the existing work being done to decolonize mental health and ease the suffering that it has created in the name of "care" and "safety." We deeply admire and respect those thinkers and advocates that are working against sanism and against racism. However, because of anti-Black sanism, because of the whiteness of mental health work and advocacy, because of the shootings and the lock-ups we see day in and day out, we want those advocates working and thinking together.

Coming back to Benjamin (2003), she states:

issues of race and racism are not to be overshadowed or eclipsed by a focus on other oppressions. As often the case, issues of race often disappear when other forms of oppression are raised. Conversely, other forms of oppression can also be eclipsed by the over determination of race. A theory of anti-Black racism that pays attention to ways in which race is interlocked and intersected with other forms of oppression, strategically and creatively works towards keeping in balance these different forms of oppression while seeking to accomplish the common goal of eradicating all forms of oppression. Inspired by this, we seek not to eclipse other forms of oppression. We seek not to silence. Instead, in this short piece, we offer a new way of exploring how race is always "interlocked and intersected" with sanism. Through our focus on the research literature, on the importance of language, on behaviour and on acknowledging the danger of silence or denial around this anti-Black trend, we are attempting a more creative and honest response. (p. 80)

We suggest anti-Black sanism speaks specifically to the violence experienced by Black and African Canadians in mental health care with respect to communication, diagnosis, hospitalization, treatment, intervention, and the involvement of the criminal justice system. We recommend the deployment of anti-Black sanism as a tool in the ongoing response to fundamental gaps, poor treatment, and lack of health care for many non-white bodies and minds. Let us continue the mobilization and radicalization of a "critical mass" for change beyond those currently invested in the well-being of Black and African Canadians.

NOTES

1. The terms *sanism* (Perlin, 1992) and *mentalism* (Chamberlin, 1990) are sometimes used interchangeably, but not always. We have chosen to use the term *sanism* in this chapter because it is recognized in the fields of law and human rights (Poole et al., 2012).
2. According to Smith (2006), white supremacy is not enacted in a "singular fashion" but through such processes as slavery, genocide, and capitalism (p. 67). We therefore understand it as a system that privileges whiteness in all aspects of life including laws, norms, control of power and material resources, behaviour, expression of emotion, and notions of rationality.
3. This case is taken from our first-hand practice experience and has been anonymized.
4. See Nangwaya (2013) for more, as well as Kennedy (2010).

9 | "It's Like a Tattoo"

Rethinking Dominant Discourses on Grief[1]

Robyn L. Ord, Learning and Organizational Development Specialist, Toronto Central Community Care Access Centre

> All that is gold does not glitter;
> All that is old does not wither;
> Not all that is over is past;
> Not all those who wander are lost ...
> (Tolkien, 1954, p. 224)

The universality of death is accompanied by unique experiences of grief that are worthy of exploration. In Western society, grief is studied by many disciplines and has become a highly contested discursive terrain, affecting definitions, perceptions, and conceptualizations about what it means to experience loss. Dominant discourses on grief have made "normal" the practices of pathologizing, othering, and essentializing those living with loss. Upon reflection, I recognize that many of my experiences with loss—both personally and as a social worker—have been informed by dominant discourses on grief or resistance to them. However, I believe that there are many ways to experience and cope with grief and to resist the "normalizing" gaze of these discourses. As a means of coping and healing, I have embodied my experience and pain with tattooing.

I begin this discussion with a deconstruction, applying Foucauldian/Foucauldian-inspired poststructural ideas about discourse, power, and resistance to the experience of loss and grief. I call into question the medical model's dominance, control over, and discipline of "grief work" and theory. I resist and challenge these constructions by drawing on ideas from Judith Butler and queer theory—including normativity, the body, and performativity. I argue that the body can be an instrument for resistance to dominant discourses on grief, and that there are many ways to experience loss. In particular, I explore tattooing as an embodied resistance to the medical model, as a means of performing one's grief, and as an alternative discourse on grief. I then discuss implications for social work practice. Overall, I attempt to reimagine the way in which grief, as a whole, is constructed.

DECONSTRUCTION

Poststructuralism challenges us to raise "questions about knowledge, power, truth, difference, and the constitution of the self" (Strega, 2005, p. 215). Fook (2002) asserts that deconstruction is the first stage involved in the critical reconstruction process, and that the act of deconstruction involves a process of uncovering and questioning dominant discourses. As "forms of practice and forms of knowledge ... often converge in their consequences" (Chambon, 1999, p. 57), it is important to uncover the structures of discourse that are operating with and through us in our practices. Foucault believed, while not everything is "bad," everything has the potential to be dangerous if accepted uncritically (Fook, 2002). He believed that discourses are largely implicated in discussions of truth, knowledge, and power in relation to grief and have real and often damaging effects on those experiencing loss (Breen & O'Connor, 2007; Reimer, 2003; Valentine, 2006).

Death may occur in a variety of settings. However—excluding deaths resulting from colonialism, wars, and other violence—in contemporary Western society, death occurs overwhelmingly in hospitals, giving medicine a prominent role. Today, grief is often viewed as a psychological problem resulting in a need for professional intervention. Bereavement services have emerged as a psychological solution for managing grief. While many people do benefit from psychological intervention and research in this area, no discipline is completely benevolent, and thus there is a great need to problematize and question the dominant discourses and constructions of grief that have become self-evident.

Psychology has always been closely tied to medicine, with its roots as a colonial, patriarchal invention utilizing positivist notions of linearity and reason to shape the construction of "mental illness," which Burstow (1992) asserts is a social construction that has been entrenched in our society due to its uncritical acceptance. The medical model discourse through which psychology predominantly operates is implicated in how bereavement is conceptualized and managed. The sites of professional grief activities and the epistemologies that underpin them are derived from the Enlightenment era (Kellehear, 2007).[2] These modernist assumptions seek rational truth and are constructed in binaries, with little consideration of the grey spaces in between (Strega, 2005). Since modernist thinking constrains both the creation of knowledge and participation in the creation of knowledge, modernist discourse is largely implicated in conceptualizing grief, thus controlling knowledge about the grieving process (Brown & Strega, 2005). Grief has been medicalized by professional expertise, and dominant discourses on grief have focused on practices of pathologizing, othering, and essentializing those living with loss. Through these discourses, grievers are produced as objects of professional knowledge *and* as subjects for themselves (Foote & Frank, 1999).

These constructions of grief are institutionalized in state-controlled grieving practices such as the length of time one allots to grief and the type of mourning that can be displayed in public. "Even during the most intense periods of grieving, mourners are expected to restrain their displays of grieving to appropriate times and places" (Foote & Frank, 1999, p. 172). As a means of keeping grief out of the "public eye," services for sanitizing and suppressing grief—into invisibility—have emerged. Grief counselling has become an institutionalized part of Western society, and grief has become a site of disciplinary power within these institutions (Foote & Frank, 1999).

Institutionalized grief work has resulted in the need to be more effective and the emergence of assessment and measurement tools. Many have proposed "best practices" with which to address grief. Stages from which to progress have been developed and have evolved within a "one-size-fits-all" agenda to normalize and pathologize grief. Hadad (2008) describes many stage-or-phase-based models that have emerged, with descriptions of what normal grief is supposed to entail. One of the most influential is Kubler-Ross's model for dying and bereavement, in which individuals follow a trajectory from stages of denial to acceptance. As cited in Hadad (2008), Parkes, Worden, Rando, as well as Stroebe and Schut propose models that describe tasks, phases, and a broad description of how one can achieve successful grief. While many were left out of Hadad's (2008) overview, the above-mentioned have been the most influential within the area of grief work. Central to these approaches is an attempt to get to the essence of, and define, a universalized grief—one that can be better managed and controlled.

Grief is expected to be an ordered, limited process that moves by identifiable steps toward "recovery" (Doss, 2002; Foote & Frank, 1999). These technologies and the institutionalization of grief therapy "have attempted to empower dying and grieving people but have at the same time made their own presence a precondition for that empowerment" (Kellehear, 2007, p. 73). Bereavement is thus constructed as an individual problem and has become a professionalized specialty (Garavaglia, 2007; Valentine, 2006).

The medicalization of grief has become a contested issue within social science disciplines. Medicalization can be defined as a process by which health or behavioural conditions come to be defined and treated as medical issues (Breen & O'Connor, 2007; Burstow, 1992; Conrad, 1992; Garavaglia, 2007). It enables aspects of everyday life to become accessible to and permeable by medical engagement, study, and treatment. The medicalization of grief is problematic because it assumes that grieving is a condition or illness necessitating a treatment or cure. It can result in individuals believing that there is something wrong with them when they are not conforming to what is considered normal grieving.

The release of the fifth edition of the *Diagnostic and Statistical Manual of Mental Disorders* (DSM-5) by the American Psychiatric Association (2013) actualized the looming possibility that "abnormal" or "complicated" grief would be included. The

DSM-5 includes two changes that address grief: Firstly, the bereavement exclusion criteria for major depression disorder has been eliminated, rendering those who are grieving as possible targets for this diagnosis; and secondly, a new category entitled "persistent complex bereavement-related disorder" has been added. Wakefield (2013) asserts that the latter was included in order to pathologize those who do not have the normal trajectory of adaptation to a loss and sets out to capture when "normal grief has failed" (p. 151). While representatives of the DSM-5 suggest that a "heightened risk of serious adverse outcomes" is a legitimate reason to include these entities, the concern of pathologizing and labelling the grief experience is considered by many to be more troublesome and dangerous (Breen & O'Connor, 2007; Conway, 2007; Howarth, 2000).

The medicalization of grief also involves an element of social control (Foote & Frank, 1999; Hart, Sainsbury, & Short, 1998; Kellehear, 2007). Discourses of grief seek to discipline and control it by creating boundaries between normality and abnormality (Howarth, 2000; Reimer, 2003). Disciplinary power is an instrument of modernity used to control our consciousness and is deeply entrenched in society (Moffatt, 1999). Foucault (1977) asserts that disciplinary power operates by normalizing. To discipline grief is to police the border between life and death, and medicalization has become a tool for such surveillance (Conway, 2007; Foote & Frank, 1999; Hart et al., 1998; Valentine, 2006; Walter, 2000). Grief work, then, also becomes an instrument of surveillance, a site of power, and an agent of social control. It is constructed as a tool for seeking the "truth" and essence behind grief. Neimeyer (2005/2006) refers to these "truths" as diagnostic labels of grief that are socially constructed and reified in discourse. Truth becomes a form of power precisely because it is accepted as self-evident (Foote & Frank, 1999; Kellehear, 2007). "Grief, like sexuality, is a rich site for power because anyone becomes a potential subject for disciplined grief" (Foote & Frank, 1999, p. 167). Within grief work, "experts" diagnose "problems" and prescribe "treatments" to direct "assessment" toward "what is wrong" with someone living with loss. These discourses label individuals as objects of professional knowledge, transforming people into patients, consumers, and objects of discipline (Conway, 2007; Foote & Frank, 1999).

The medical construction of grief is problematic because it attempts to universalize an experience that is incredibly personal, diverse, and often indescribable (Breen & O'Connor, 2007; Hart et al., 1998; Kellehear, 2007; Valentine, 2006; Walter, 1996). Both loss and grief are embedded in social and relational contexts, and dominant constructions of grief lack an acknowledgement of this variability (Breen & O'Connor, 2007; Gilbert, 1996). Within grief literature, there is a paradoxical trend of recognizing the variability that exists in the grieving process while also trying to define what constitutes "normal" and "abnormal" (Breen & O'Connor, 2007; Howarth, 2000). The use of theories that discuss abnormal and "complicated" grief imply a predetermined definition of appropriate grief and place an emphasis on the individual to recover in a predetermined manner (Howarth, 2000; Goldsworthy, 2005; Reimer, 2003; Valentine, 2006). While these models may provide insights into the grieving process that some people experience, they can also be dangerous because not everyone can or will "recover" from loss, nor will they do so in a specific way.

Irving (1994) states, "the real logic behind Enlightenment rationality [is] a logic of domination and oppression" (p. 24). Medical constructions of grief often neglect and exclude the social locations of grievers, resulting in further marginalization of those disadvantaged by these identities (Bevan & Thompson, 2003). Since constructions of grief are disciplined by Enlightenment thought, resistance can involve the refusal to participate in these constructions (Fook, 2002). We must exercise our power to unlearn, disbelieve, and unsettle. As Fook (2002) asserts, "The very process of deconstruction is in itself an act of resistance" (p. 95).

Chambon (1994) states, "The ways in which we define social problems are closely connected to the dominant assumptions and values of our own professional field" (p. 62). Thus, we decide what is possible and what is a "problem." Since all knowledge is socially constructed, we must question what version of reality is being produced, for whom, and by whom (Brown, 1994). The ways in which we construct knowledge are always tied to relations of power. Fook (2002) encourages us to look at knowledge as being contestable, contradictory, and socially constructed: "The strength of dominant discourses is at the same time their very weakness. They are powerful often because they are unquestioned ... [and] uncritically accept[ed]. In this sense, their power lies in the degree to which they are unquestioned" (p. 89).

RESISTING, CHALLENGING, AND RECONSTRUCTING GRIEF

Discourses of grief can easily be reduced to their negative effects. Yet, for those experiencing loss, they can be quite alluring. There is a reason these discourses are so effective: They can be comforting and reassuring. They can, and do, help people feel as though their grief is manageable, controllable, and shared. The idea of being able to manage something so difficult and complicated is seductive. The feeling that one is not alone or that what one is experiencing is normal cannot be underestimated. Sometimes, this is exactly what we need. While these discourses must be challenged, and while I feel that the comfort they provide can be both illusory and self-regulatory, I acknowledge that there is more to the story.

Examining both the positive and negative effects of discourses of grief provides an opportune platform from which to reconstruct and reclaim. Since grief and loss are also social experiences, we need to (re)imagine a different way to make sense of death (Fowler, 2008; Kellehear, 2007; Reimer, 2003; Walter, 1996). "The point is not that institutionalized death work and grief aid are not necessary or helpful for mourners"

(Winkel, 2001, p. 75), but that they can be dangerous and are not benign (Conway, 2007; Walter, 1996). Rather than dismissing problematic models of grief, we can critically build upon them (Chambon, 1999). Ultimately, there are critical possibilities for reconstructing and reclaiming grief work as a form of discursive resistance (Foote & Frank, 1999; Guilfoyle, 2005; Kellehear, 2007). By refusing to accept these discourses, one is engaging in resistance. Thus, we must challenge the ways in which we have been taught to "know."

"The strong desire of mourners to tell their own story, unedited and un-policed by others, is in part driven by resistance to medicalization" (Walter, 2000, p. 110). Actively engaging with one's grief does not have to entail pathology, abnormality, or linear progression; it can take the form of difference, diversity, and uniqueness (Espiritu, 2006). I am personally concerned with how the construction of knowledge is implicated in grief, in difference, and ultimately in the embodiment of experience. To further explore this, I draw on queer theory.

Queer theory is a tool for reframing approaches and practices, a method for imaging difference on its own terms, and a discipline that refuses to be disciplined (Ford, 2004; Sullivan, 2003). It is a model that contests binary oppositions and critiques self-evident cultural and social institutions that seek to normalize, essentialize, and define us through normative categories and hierarchies (Ford, 2004; herising, 2005). It re-evaluates notions of identity that have been used unproblematically and uncritically in everyday life (Eng, 1997).

Queer theory faces criticism for being "male-centred, anti-feminist, and race-blind" (Sullivan, 2003, p. 48). However, I feel that it offers potential to explore intersectionality and recognition of how numerous systems of oppression interact to inform how we experience grief and the prevailing systems of power/knowledge at work (Sullivan, 2003). Grief, in whatever way a griever experiences it, is universal and intersects all social locations, regardless of power and privilege. Yet, while experiences of domination and marginalization are structural and systemic, they are also personally experienced (Fook, 2002). Thus, is it not also possible that individuals who identify with similar social locations may experience entirely different grief? As stated above, queer theory aims to re-evaluate problematic and uncritical notions of identity (Eng, 1997) and is concerned with social change and explicating power relations and normative ideology (Bird, 2004; Walker, 2004). Therefore, I do believe it is an ideal platform to re-imagine grief across difference. It allows us to "understand practice strategies as being based on curiosity rather than expertise" (Ford, 2004, p. 17). Thus, we become more aware of the power dynamics inherent in the work and call into question the idea of "expertise" altogether. We can then consider those experiencing grief as the experts of their grief, whatever their social locations. Ultimately, it is concerned with rethinking, remaking, and reclaiming.

Queer theory includes ideas of the body and how it "performs" in everyday life. This can be expanded into a discussion of how the body experiences, embodies, and even performs grief. The body plays a crucial role in how we experience and respond to everyday life. The body, like grief, has been constructed through dominant discourses as an object of medicine, discipline, and social control (Lyon & Barbalet, 1994). The medical model operates with the understanding that the practitioner must be in hegemonic control of the body (Lyon & Barbalet, 1994). This implies that we do not embody our feelings and experiences.

In stark contrast, sociologists Nettleton and Watson (1998) assert that every aspect of our lives is embodied. "Via discourse, physical sensations produced by our bodies ... are interpreted as emotions" (Lupton, 1998, p. 83). If we are embodied social agents, then we must also embody grief. Often it is too difficult to express grief, and "indeed, language can frequently fail our needs when we try to articulate our feelings" (Lupton, 1998, p. 83). The body can be a powerful medium through which to express our experiences.

The body is not only a site for subjugation or expression; it is also a site of resistance. Can we not actively resist the medical model's dominance over grief as well as over the body? Many scholars, including Butler and Foucault, discuss the importance of the body as a site of resistance. Foucault saw the body as a product of discourse and site of discipline (Turner, 1994). "For Foucault, the body is the text upon which the power of society is inscribed" (Lyon & Barbalet, 1994, p. 48). Yet Foucault also said that where there is power, there is resistance. Can resistance not also be inscribed upon the text of our bodies? "The body implies mortality, vulnerability, agency: the skin and the flesh expose us to the gaze of others, but also to touch, and to violence, and bodies put us at risk of becoming the agency and instrument of all these as well" (Butler, 2004b, p. 26). I am particularly interested in the body as resistance, and what implications this resistance entails. I will further examine this by looking at Judith Butler's ideas about the body.

Butler's contributions to queer and poststructural theory have resulted in an embodied examination and celebration of difference. A significant contribution is her concept of performativity. For Butler, performativity is the discursive vehicle through which ontological effects are produced (Sullivan, 2003). She distinguishes between performing and performativity, and asserts that "there is a difference between the embodying or performing of ... norms and the performative use of discourse" (Butler, 1993, p. 231). Performativity is not something that is done, but is a process through which one is constituted. It is not voluntary; it is done automatically and repetitively, to appear as truth. Performance, on the other hand, is voluntary and intentional. Both performance and performativity can be modes of discursive production; however, Butler (1993) asserts that the former embraces this production, while the latter precludes it (Sullivan, 2003). She suggests that we perform in ways that we are taught from birth and often do not question our performances (Butler, 1993; Sullivan, 2003). We replicate and reproduce dominant norms, constructions, and discourse. Norms operate by requiring the embodiment of certain ideals. "If the power of discourse to produce that which it names is linked with the question of performativity, then the performative is one domain in which power acts *as* discourse" (Butler, 1993, p. 225). We are always implicated in the production of meaning, and our performances should be understood as a mode of discursive production (Sullivan, 2003).

Performativity is a discursive act of subversion (Watson, 2005). The many ways in which grief is embodied can be interpreted as being ambiguous. Since some embodiments are often interpreted as problems, I ask, "For whom is this a problem?" Perhaps grief is not a problem requiring clinical or pathological solutions. Perhaps the tears, the sorrow, the pain, and the other ways that grief embodies us can be reframed as resistance to these prescribed solutions. If these interventions truly made us feel better or healed, then would we not be rid of the lifelong pain? Should we not, rather, problematize the discourses that have created conditions in which we feel as though we are a problem? There is no "one way" to grieve, and yet we have been socialized to feel that we must grieve in specific ways or risk becoming pathological or abnormal. In a sense, we are engaging in performativity, and grieving the way in which we have been socialized.

The ways in which we grieve are performative. We do what we think we should, often automatically, and are rewarded with positive feedback. If we behave in this prescribed way, we will get better and we will "be over" our grief. We perform our grief by engaging in grief-appropriate behaviour and reinforce the dominant discourses on grief without intention or awareness. I do not wish to place blame or additional burden on those who are experiencing loss; I am simply bringing awareness to the additional vulnerability that is inherently placed on grievers merely as a result of their being in a position of grieving.

RE-IMAGING GRIEF

After deconstructing and challenging the ways in which grief has been dominantly constructed in Western society, I now ask how we can reframe our performances as resistance and resilience. While performativity is not voluntary, performance is, and it can be a means of challenging dominant constructions of grief (Butler, 1993). Practices of pathologizing, othering, and essentializing are performative; these practices are an effect of discourse. Being aware of the performative and actively engaging in resistive performance is a way in which the body can be an instrument of resistance.

Our performances will always be ambiguous and subjective, and some may interpret our grief as being a problem. However, what if we choose to perform and embody our experiences as an intentional act of resistance? By embodying our experiences, we are performing in ways that resist the idea that we must act in specified manners. Those daring to ask for whom their grief is a problem have found alternative possibilities. Should their grief not be recognized? For those who have felt pathologized, marginalized, and silenced; for those who wish to contest the way in which they have been socialized to perform, perhaps this discussion is for you. Grief is not simply the presence or absence of suffering: It is the grey spaces in between.

"IT'S LIKE A TATTOO"

Tattoos are often thought to represent a subversive resistance to the dominant culture because they are still frequently thought of as being taboo (Mifflin, 1997). Historically, tattoos represented rebellion and still hold negative connotations (Mifflin, 1997). Yet many who get tattoos do so as a means of personal expression. To this end, many people get tattoos as emblems of grief and memorial and as a means of telling their story (Mifflin, 1997).

> When my mom passed away I went through a really tough time. I needed something to remind me of her that I could have with me all the time. Roses were my mother's favourite flower, so getting a rose tattoo on my foot was a way for me to have her with me all the time. (L. Scott, personal communication, April 20, 2009)[3]

The use of symbolism can be very powerful in helping to make sense of death (Hedtke, 2003; Valentine, 2006). "Tattoos can be a disconcerting performance ... [that] help people reclaim their physical bodies; being tattooed is ... a performance of the self" (Modesti, 2008, p. 209).

Since loss and grief have profoundly shaped my life, I speak from a place of personal experience. I have several tattoos that help me express my grief. Tattoos are a way in which grief can be embodied on the skin. Tattooing one's grief can be an act of resistance to the notion that grief can or should be cured. Tattoos are counter-hegemonic and challenge dominant notions about the body and how it is supposed to be used (DeMello, 1995). Tattoos particularly challenge discourses of professionalism and medicalization, which seek to keep grief confined to a tidy office couch accompanied by a box of tissues and a compulsory confession. "Tattooing is one form of the many, micro-political acts a body can perform" (Maccormack, 2006, p. 72). By putting tattoos on my body as a symbol of my grief, I am using my body as a site and instrument of resistance. Ultimately, I am breaking the normative, disciplined performance of grief and performing differently and freely. I am creating an alternative discourse through which to grieve and experience loss and reframing it as resistance.

Like a tattoo, grief may begin to fade over time, becoming less visible or profound in our lives, but it will always be present. The very act of tattooing suggests that grief is permanent, lifelong, visible, and always present. And like a tattoo, grief has traditionally had a way of making people feel uncomfortable, uneasy, and forbidden.

We are expected to cover it up, tidy it up, sanitize it, and make it fit into the right box. However, embodying grief on the skin makes it visible and permanent. It is a way of asserting that it is okay that grief is messy, visible, and beautiful. Tattoos are a powerful way of performing grief.

Tattooing may not be available to all individuals, for various reasons. However, grief can be embodied by all of our senses, including touch, and through symbolism. Some people experiencing loss have indicated that receiving a hug or a pat on the back—actions that are forbidden by discourses of professionalism—was a source of comfort for them (Hadad, 2008). Individuals occupying professional positions often refrain from "getting too close" to their "clients" and are bound by professional ethics, standards, and regulations. The power of physical touch is often dismissed. Additionally, the use of artwork and symbolism can also be a helpful way of making experiences with loss meaningful, while also challenging the dominant discourses (Doss, 2002; Grainger, 1998; Winkel, 2001). Some find it helpful to travel to places that remind them of someone they have lost. Some may even create their own "temporary tattoos" in the form of artifacts that have symbolic meaning. Perhaps it is a ring, a watch, or even a lock of hair that becomes particularly meaningful to them. They may draw strength from having this physical object with them at all times (J. Poole, personal communication, May 2, 2009).

CONCLUSION

There are many ways for people to engage with and embody grief. What these engagements have in common is that they are considered "alternative" and often discouraged. Western society does not adequately recognize the diverse ways in which people grieve, and thus does not readily facilitate alternative ways of grieving. This is indicated in labour laws and policies that allow individuals to take only minimal time off from employment without consequence following a death. Additionally, those already disadvantaged by their social location become further marginalized by a society that privileges this dominant view, imposing a set of expectations and perceptions upon different types of grievers. For example, a white mother who has lost a child to war or a random act of violence may experience vastly different support than a Black mother who has lost a child to gun violence, especially if it is perceived that this child may have been in contact with the law. In addition to experiencing an unfathomable loss, this mother may also feel marginalized by the type of loss and associated perceptions and expectations imposed upon her by a society that privileges a certain type of "acceptable" grief, while subjugating grief labelled as "other." This shows a clear lack of recognition of the unique experiences every individual has with loss and serves to reinforce dominant discursive constructions of grief. It also reinforces the great need to ask questions and apply an anti-oppression lens in order to be critical when thinking about grief.

It is a daunting task to "take on" dominant discourses on grief and propose alternatives. In terms of social work practice, grief is something we all encounter; regardless of where we work. While I do not suggest there is one good or better way to engage with grief, I do suggest that we all have a responsibility to be critical with respect to what we have come to "know" about it. As stated earlier, structures of discourse can be dangerous if we do not question the ways in which they are operating through our practices. These structures can also be inherently oppressive and marginalizing in their effects to those living with loss. I strongly urge that we be careful and critical of the potential effects these discourses may have and be open to rethinking and re-imaging new possibilities. We must recognize the diversity that exists in the ways people grieve and reflect upon the ways we ourselves experience, perceive, and even embody grief. We must also be mindful of and acknowledge the vastly different expectations our society imposes upon different types of grievers and the marginalization grievers may experience as a result.

Individuals grieve, cope with, and experience loss in many ways, and these experiences are worthy of exploration and reimagination. Sometimes grief does not look the way we feel it should. Sometimes it is colourful. Sometimes we can taste it, smell it, hear it. Sometimes it can be permanent. Sometimes we can feel others' grief just by looking at them—their bodies, their photos, their artwork, their artifacts. Maybe it is in their eyes. Maybe they wear it like a coat. Maybe it is found in the ink imprinted upon their passport. Maybe it is found in the ink upon their body. Maybe they do not need to be fixed, helped, or changed—for maybe they are just wandering, not needing to be found.

NOTES

1. This chapter reports on a study that was undertaken in partial fulfillment of the MSW Major Research Paper degree requirements. A modified version of this chapter was first published as Ord, R. (2009). "It's like a tattoo." *Canadian Social Work Review, 26*(2), 195–211. Winner of the Student Manuscript Competition. Reprinted here with permission.

2. "The Enlightenment is the period in European thought when the demarcation between science and non-science was established, and when 'science' and 'knowledge' began to have the same meaning" (Strega, 2005, p. 202). The Enlightenment marked the beginning of the "modern era," and "Enlightenment epistemology is the foundation for three major methodologies in the social sciences: positivism, qualitative methodology, and critical social science. ... Positivism ... is positioned not only as the best way but also the only way to discover social science 'truth'" (Strega, 2005, p. 205).

3. In citing "personal communication," what is meant is that these insights and quotes resulted from personal, informal communication with these two individuals. These conversations were initiated based on mutual interest in the subject, but not part of a research project or formal interview.

Section IV

Anti-Oppression as a Frame for Transformation

10 | Building Anti-Oppressive Organizations

Thoughts from a Multi-Dimensionally Informed Journey

Lisa Barnoff, Associate Professor, School of Social Work, and Dean, Faculty of Community Services, Ryerson University

Idil Abdillahi, Assistant Professor, School of Social Work, Ryerson University

Beth Jordan, Principal, Adobe Consulting Services

This chapter outlines a suggested framework for anti-oppressive (AOP) organizational development in social service agencies. This framework identifies key areas for intervention when designing and implementing AOP organizational development. We propose a "3-P" model for AOP organizational development, consisting of three broad categories—policies, people, and practices—with ten areas of intervention, each of which represents a broad area for intervention. We argue that organizations seeking to continually improve their organizational practices in relation to AOP need to elaborate a systematic, organization-wide, ongoing plan that simultaneously addresses each one of these ten broad areas. In this chapter, we draw heavily on our own previous work, both academic and practice oriented. We have spent more than 25 years engaged in the work of anti-oppression organizational practice, beginning not as academics, researchers, or authors but as practitioners working in the very organizations we are writing about now.

ANTI-OPPRESSIVE PRACTICE IN ORGANIZATIONS

While AOP has received much attention in social work theory, education, and direct practice, other than our own publications and that of a few others (Barnoff, 2001, 2002, 2011; Barnoff, George, & Coleman, 2006; Barnoff & Moffatt, 2007; Hyde, 2003, 2004; Jordan, 2006; Karabanow, 2004; Moffatt, Barnoff, George, & Coleman, 2009; Yee, Hackbusch, & Wong, 2015), very little has been written about anti-oppression as it applies to organizations. Yet the implementation of anti-oppressive practices "demands deep changes in the organizational structure and institutional culture of social services" (Strier & Binyamin, 2010, p. 1911). We know from our professional experiences that some organizations are attempting and succeeding at this in various ways, although often not without tremendous struggle. Barnoff (2011) has defined an "AOP agency" as:

> one that operates in accordance with an anti-oppression theoretical framework and in ways that promote anti-oppression principles. AOP agencies have a social justice oriented mission and constantly work toward all of the following: the eradication of all oppressions and discriminatory practices; continual reflection on and evaluation of their organizational processes and outcomes; wide participation and inclusion in the organization; responsiveness to a reflection of the communities in which they are situated; the fostering of alliances across diverse groups; and engagement in social justice oriented activities "beyond the walls" of the agency. (p. 179)

In defining an "AOP organization," we are describing what sociologists would call an "ideal type" and therefore outlining a *model* that does not necessarily exist in reality. It may be more appropriate to think about an organization as always engaged in a process of *becoming* anti-oppressive, rather than believing any organization can be completely, perfectly AOP. In fact, in our experience, we find that most AOP agencies can be doing well in some aspects of AOP, while simultaneously being greatly challenged by other important respects.

For our purposes here, we propose that an "AOP organization" is one that does all of the following: promotes and reflects an anti-oppression analysis/approach; has a social justice/social change–oriented mission (i.e., views itself as having a larger political purpose rather than simply service); explores and seeks to eradicate oppressive power relations and discriminatory practices in its every organizational system, policy, program, and process; ensures the ways in which *all* forms of power are exercised is addressed; ensures that anti-oppression is *core* to its functioning and can never be set aside nor removed (i.e., it is always central to everything the agency does); continually reflects on and evaluates its processes and outcomes; enables wide participation and inclusion in the agency; is responsive to and reflective of the communities in which it is situated; fosters alliances across diverse groups; engages in social justice–oriented activities outside the agency; has clear, defined, measurable goals in relation to AOP; and is continually engaged in a planned, systematic process of AOP organizational development, including ongoing evaluation of these efforts.

ANTI-OPPRESSIVE ORGANIZATIONAL DEVELOPMENT

Organizational development is not *ad hoc* nor random. It is a systematic process that is well-planned, monitored, and evaluated. Goals must be clearly identified, change must be measured, and accountability processes must be implemented. As organizations lay out a clear map for their work in this regard, they must constantly collect information to be able to periodically assess whether their efforts are having the desired impact.

Jordan (2006) notes three important components of a solid organizational development endeavour:

> (i) the work is *planned*, meaning that organizations "intentionally set out to do or achieve something and put forethought and resources into achieving a desired outcome"; (ii) organizational development models are *participatory*, and draw on "the skill sets available within [the] organization from all structural levels and from external sources"; and (iii) the organization is fundamentally focused on *systemic change*. (p. 143)

In Jordan's (2006) words,

> the change you are seeking is not superficial. It will significantly change the way your organization operates and this is indeed the goal. You will work with the systems and structures, policies and procedures, employment practices, programs and services within your organization and ensure that everything operates within a feminist antiracist anti-oppression framework. The goal of systemic change is to positively impact those who are most oppressed within your organization and to measure your success in relation to their experience. (p. 143)

Jordan (2006) further suggests that every well-developed organizational growth plan will share some commonalities, such as details on projected outcomes, identification of critical steps to reach these outcomes, clear timelines, and appropriate resource allocation to be successful in the work. Kerman, Freundlich, Lee, and Brenner (2012) emphasize the importance of ongoing learning and adapting through this change process. Hyde (2012) reminds us that this work must always begin with a common vision, which is clearly articulated. She notes, "Without a vision that can be translated into a clarity of purpose relevant to practice, can inspire participation, and can point to fundamental change, human service agencies are likely to experience problems, failures, and backlash" (p. 452) when engaging in this work. All those involved with the organization must understand where the organization is headed and what they are expected to contribute in this development process (Hyde, 2012; Kerman et al., 2012; Lopes & Thomas, 2006). Being guided by an analysis of power and oppression is key to AOP organizational development. As Lopes and Thomas (2006) argue in their book about anti-racist organizational change,

> anti-racism change work is transformative—it aims to change the organization at its core. To succeed, it requires a thorough understanding of how power operates in the

organization: the values that are considered essential, how decisions are made and how they are carried out, the ways in which people learn about what is important and what is peripheral, and how people are formally and informally rewarded or punished. Power is at the root of all these systems. The systemic analysis of racism and other forms of discrimination reduces the tendency to blame individual people for organizational inequities and demonstrates how regular organizational systems reinforce power inequities. (p. 111)

In the remainder of this chapter, we outline a framework for anti-oppressive organizational development. Our underlying assumption is that AOP is always work *in progress*. As Pender-Greene (2007) notes, this process is best described as "a journey and not a destination" (p. 16). This is why we avoid the concept "organizational change" and instead favour the language of "organizational development"—the former implies an endpoint whereas the latter suggests an emphasis on continual engagement.

A FRAMEWORK FOR ANTI-OPPRESSIVE ORGANIZATIONAL DEVELOPMENT

To be successful, AOP must be integrated into all aspects of an organization and must involve all stakeholders. We propose a 3P model for AOP organizational development, consisting of three broad categories—policies, people, and practices—with ten areas of intervention, each of which represents a broad area for intervention. We argue that organizations seeking to continually improve their organizational practices in relation to AOP need to elaborate an ongoing, systematic, organization-wide plan that simultaneously addresses each of these ten broad areas. As we elaborate the three "Ps" and their ten subthemes, note that the scope of this chapter allows us only to identify *areas* for organizational development, rather than discuss the processes or concrete strategies for engaging in such.

In putting our model together, we must acknowledge that we draw from previous works including, for example, Barnoff (2001, 2002), Doyle (1990), Fong and Gibbs (1995), Ferguson (1996), Gutierrez and Nagda (1996), Hyde (2003, 2004), Jackson and Holvino (1988), Johnson (1996), Minors (1996), San Martin and Barnoff (2004), Thomas (1987), and the United Way of Greater Toronto (1991).

Category One: Policies

The category "policies" is composed of three areas of intervention: (1) organizational purpose, (2) organizational structure, and (3) organizational policy documents.

Table 10.1: 3P Model for AOP Organizational Development

Category	Area of Intervention
Policies	Organizational Purpose
	Organizational Structure
	Organizational Policy Documents
People	Organizational Composition
	Organizational Culture
	Organizational Internal Processes
	Organizational Learning
Practices	Organizational Programs and Services
	Organizational Connections with Local Communities
	Organizational Action in Working for Social Change

Organizational Purpose

Most importantly, organizations need to reflect on their purpose or aim. It is inherent that anti-oppressive organizations have a political purpose. Understanding that people's needs and issues are rooted in larger social problems, anti-oppressive organizations are always fully conscious of their dual purpose, being both service-oriented and social change–oriented. Such fundamental and foundational aspects of an organization should be reflected in its mission, vision, and core values, which should then provide the motivation, impetus, and guiding force for everything that the organization does (Barnoff, 2001). Hence, AOP organizations need to examine their foundational documents. Jordan (2006) explains,

> foundation documents are the most important or fundamental pieces of papers required to incorporate and define your organization. They confirm the purpose, mandate, beliefs and aims, and guiding principles of the organization. Foundation documents include the letters patent, bylaws, mandate/mission statement, and statement of beliefs and aims or statement of principles for your agency. (p. 3)

An organization's mission, vision, and core values guide everything. Being clear from the outset that an organization is committed to anti-oppression practice, social justice, and social change means that the organization is then required to evaluate whether or not these principles are being upheld as it engages in its work, and, where this is not happening, the organization can be held accountable. Making these commitments visible also helps ensure that as new members get involved, they understand the kind of organization they are joining and their responsibilities therein.

Organizational Structure

AOP organizations do not have to be completely nonhierarchical nor governed collectively; however, democratic and participatory processes are key to AOP organizational practice. Board, management, staff, service users, and community members need to work together as a team to determine the ways in which the organization will operate. Board members should be familiar with the frontline work— whether it is service provision, advocacy, or activism—and have a solid understanding of the work, how it's conducted, and to what ends. For example, in an AOP woman's shelter we know, board members are expected to work one shift in the shelter each month in order that they be kept abreast of the realities of daily frontline work in the agency and the needs and issues of the women using the service.

Transparent and democratic decision-making processes are necessary in AOP organizations (Strier & Binyamin, 2010), since "an environment of participation" is important:

> The challenge is to acknowledge the value of diverse views and incorporate them into the organizational culture, clinical practice, administration, and policy decision-making. This can be achieved only if these diverse voices are consistently and prominently present at each of these tables. (Pender-Greene, 2007, p. 13)

AOP organizations understand that the best decisions are those made after careful reflection of multiple subject positions. Therefore, organizational committees should have representation from all stakeholder groups, including service users, and information and communication should flow between all of the various stakeholder groups in an open and transparent manner. All stakeholder groups should feel a sense of ownership of the organization.

Organizational Policies

There are two different, but interrelated approaches to thinking about AOP policy. The first is the development of stand-alone policies that focus specifically on AOP; the second is a review of all organizational policy through an AOP lens (Barnoff, 2011).

Stand-alone anti-oppression policies are important in that they clearly state the organization's understanding of and commitment to AOP. The best AOP policies will also articulate what is expected of organizational members in relation to AOP, how people will be held accountable to these expectations, and what the consequences will be if and when this does not occur. AOP policies should clearly define for all organizational members exactly what AOP means in their specific organizational context. Clear expectations and consequences help organizational members to understand and, therefore, to be able to implement the policy (Barnoff, 2011).

Bringing an "AOP lens" to bear on every organizational policy—whether or not the policy seems to have anything to do with AOP—is a second area for intervention. Every organizational policy should reflect the organization's commitment to AOP and should specify how the enactment of this policy will further the agency's AOP goals (Barnoff, 2011). One example is to explore an agency's financial policies, which may seem irrelevant to AOP considerations, but are not. Financial policies might specify, for example, where an agency banks or invests surplus funds. Who makes decisions about financial matters and the allocation of agency resources? Another example is personnel policies. How is individual performance evaluated? Is feedback gathered from a variety of perspectives? Is the person's ability to enact and uphold AOP part of the evaluation? Organizational members must constantly ask how the enactment of each organizational policy promotes the agency's overall anti-oppression goals. No policy should be considered neutral or excluded from the organization's AOP goals.

When writing or reviewing policy from an AOP standpoint, it is critical that agencies "focus on implementation" and be sure that implementation is "everyone's work" (Lopes & Thomas, 2006, pp. 112–113). In other words, it is not enough to specify what *should* happen or what *could* happen; instead, what *will* happen and who *will* be held responsible must be declared. All too often excellent policies are written, but not followed. An AOP organizational development plan should address how policies are followed—or not—and, if they are not followed, it is important to ask why and to take steps to correct the situation. As Lopes and Thomas (2006) argue, "organizational change acknowledges that policies, procedures, and protocols are support instruments for change. Policies are not an end in themselves, nor do they implement change" (p. 173). It is people who make change happen. This leads us to the second "P" in our three-category framework, and that is "people."

Category Two: People

This category, "people," is composed of four areas of intervention: (1) organizational composition, (2) organizational culture, (3) organizational internal processes, and (4) organizational learning.

Organizational Composition

Anti-oppressive organizations are inclusive and diversity can be found at every level of the organization.

> If the diversity of the community is not represented in an agency, there are probably institutional barriers preventing certain groups from accessing the agency, or perhaps even worse, making them not *want* to access the agency. Equity and inclusion for all

groups in terms of access, decision-making, and service delivery systems is important in AOP agencies. (Barnoff, 2011, p. 178)

An AOP organizational development plan should consider who is represented in the agency and who is not. Strategies must ensure that every stakeholder group—board, management, full-time staff, relief staff, volunteers, service users, students, and so forth—has diverse representation (Barnoff, 2001). By "diverse," we do not mean just in terms of social identity, although that is a priority. Diversity is also about skills, perspectives, and life experiences. And by "representation," we note that is not enough just to have particular bodies present, with particular skills. Rather, diversity has to be infused and privileged throughout all of the organization's practices and not be a token gesture. As Hyde and Hopkins (2004) argue, an organization needs to have "considerable demographic diversity, integrated throughout the organization ... [so that the] benefits of diversity are supported or nourished through various organizational practices embedded in the organization's culture" (p. 27). This means that multiple identities, voices, ideas, and perspectives are included in all aspects of an AOP organization. AOP organizations constantly evaluate how various groups of people are integrated—or not—throughout the organization's core operations (Barnoff, 2011; Hyde, 2003; Hyde & Hopkins, 2004).

Another aspect of organizational composition for an AOP perspective is that people involved in the organization need to understand and be committed to an AOP perspective. It is not enough to bring people in just because they "represent" a particular group or particular skill set or viewpoint. Organizational members need to be committed to an anti-oppression perspective even if they do not necessarily know how to practise from this approach in significant depth (Barnoff, 2005). New skills can be taught and learned, but an overall attitude that is predisposed toward AOP must be pre-existing. Baines (2011) suggests that as a social justice–oriented approach to practice, an AOP perspective is a political perspective. It is one in which attention is always being paid to the larger context of oppressive policies and practices, even as we consider what might seem to be "personal" issues and situations. Everybody who is involved in an AOP organization must understand that they will be expected to continually struggle to challenge problematic power relations both within and outside the organization. This includes looking not only at how power is *experienced* but also how it is actively *exercised* by each organizational member—including themselves. Individuals within AOP organizations can expect to be held accountable for their individual behaviour at the same time that they also have a responsibility to focus on the practices of others.

A sustained focus of attention on the organization's leadership is another important aspect of AOP organizational development. Organizational leaders set the tone, they role model desired behaviour, and they, therefore, require solid AOP knowledge and skills (Hyde, 2012). We often consider board members and senior administrators as organizational leaders. Kerman and colleagues (2012) remind us that middle managers also play an important role:

> Well prepared middle managers and supervisors facilitate organizational change. Comprehensive preparation strengthens the capacity to both do and lead. Supervisors must be compelling spokespeople for the rationale and goals, active and effective models of new practices, and able to reward changes and confront resistance among their supervisees. Accomplishing these important functions requires training and support because of the daunting challenge of learning and supervising simultaneously. (p. 252)

Results of a study by Barnoff (2005) confirm this: Where frontline workers did not see their managers actively engaged in promoting AOP, they did not have the desire to engage in this difficult work themselves. They also wanted managers to be consistent in applying policy and careful to always follow through with accountability measures in a swift and fair manner.

Organizational Culture

By organizational culture, we mean the overall atmosphere or "feel" of an agency, its tone and tenor, and the unspoken norms or rules guiding language, attitudes, and behaviours of organizational members (Galambos, Dulmus, & Wodarski, 2005; Glisson, 2007). Certain features of an organization's culture are conducive to promoting AOP. Cultural norms that value ongoing learning help facilitate an AOP approach in organizations (Barnoff, 2011). Since AOP is a process, AOP practitioners are always engaged in furthering their learning and improving their practices. We are never "experts," but are always engaging in learning processes. Based on this understanding, AOP organizations work hard to foster a culture where openness to ongoing learning is valued and rewarded and where multiple opportunities for learning exist, although not always as formal training. For instance,

> a board might decide to begin each board meeting by discussing a current issue relevant to the agency's work so they can learn from each other's perspectives. Alternatively, a staff team might decide to set aside the first 20 minutes of every staff meeting to share knowledge ... [or] practic[e] their skills in giving and receiving feedback in respectful ways, or discussing a social policy of relevance to service users so they can all be better informed. The opportunities for engaging in ongoing learning are endless. (Barnoff, 2011, p. 188)

In an organizational culture where ongoing learning is valued, members are rewarded for taking risks and trying new practices, even if they make mistakes or their efforts do not bring about the desired results immediately (Barnoff, 2011; Nybell & Gray, 2004). The idea is that people are trying new things and are open to the challenge. Kerman et al. (2012) discuss the importance of supporting "good risk taking." They argue

> change involves deviating from established practice and expectations, which can be risky. Mistakes while learning are inherent to change and can lead to improvement provided there are candid and timely feedback loops. Supervisors and managers need to tolerate the discomfort that arises when their staff tries new practices. (p. 252)

A culture of fear and silencing, where people are humiliated when they make mistakes and are expected to be "AOP experts" all the time, is unhealthy and will only stifle, rather than promote AOP (Benjamin, 2007). People will be willing to take risks when they are in an organizational context where ongoing learning is valued and rewarded.

Further, it is key to an organization's AOP development plan to promote an organizational culture that values honest, open, respectful communication, but also recognizes that challenge, debate, and sometimes even conflict are integral to the ongoing learning process. In an organization where ongoing learning is required, there should be no expectation of "safety," because AOP education is difficult and often unsettling. As critical social work scholars Campbell and Baikie (2012) suggest, "Educational processes (pedagogy) that are congruent with critical social work may be unfamiliar and initially uncomfortable as they require active engagement from learners: mentally, emotionally, spiritually, and physically" (p. 69).

Organizational members need to understand that they will be personally challenged and are likely to experience discomfort at times. These moments of discomfort should be valued for providing evidence that learning is taking place. In AOP organizations, it is important for people to come together "in good faith," meaning that members need to respect each other and be prepared to give each other the benefit of the doubt in difficult and sometimes "heated" moments of debate, challenge, or struggle.

Regarding her organization's attempts to engage in anti-racist organizational development, Pender-Greene (2007) notes that managers have a particular role to play in these processes:

> The organization's leadership must consistently demonstrate its commitment to the process to all employees by setting the tone for honest discourse by openly acknowledging tensions. Friction must be resolved respectfully and swiftly when possible, and staff must be helped to accept a degree of uncertainty and discomfort. (p. 12)

Managers need to be responsible for setting "a tone of non-judgment, no guilt tripping, no attacking" (Pender-Greene, 2007, p. 14). If people are prepared to start from the premise that everyone has work to do and that all are committed to doing it, they are likely to be able to be more patient with each other's learning processes. Effective teamwork requires that staff learn how to resolve conflict, respect one another's differences, and be ready to work cooperatively.

A note of caution regarding openness: Lopes and Thomas (2006) argue that it is important to "create both a learning context and a compliance context," by which they mean:

> the organization can and should regulate the behavior of workers and service recipients who are in contact with other service users and with staff to ensure compliance. The change outcomes need to be behavior based and breaches of the required behavior must have clear consequences. (p. 115)

At some point people should be held accountable to particular standards of expected behaviour. Organizational members need to be allowed to make mistakes and to be supported in their efforts to try something new, but they also need to demonstrate that when they make mistakes, they are learning from them and improving their future practice.

Organizational Internal Processes

By the phrase *organizational internal processes*, we include the various ways in which things actually happen in the organization. While this theme is closely related to two themes already reviewed above, by distinguishing it here we aim to draw specific attention to the need for organizations to continually examine the actual everyday processes of how they are doing their work. As opposed to what might be *stated* about how the organization does its work, what might be *preferred* about how the organization does its work, or what might be *communicated* about how the organization does its work, we want to examine what *actually* happens.

AOP organizations need to engage in an ongoing process of looking honestly and deeply at their day-to-day, on-the-ground practices and asking how closely these match the stated organizational goals, communications, and policies. Where a match does not exist, serious efforts need to be made to bring the actual and stated practices closer in line. Depending on the area in which the mismatches occur, a variety of different techniques and strategies can be used to bring the practice more in line with the preference. As part of this process, organizations need to be continually soliciting feedback—and taking this feedback very seriously—from every stakeholder group. In particular, organizations must solicit feedback on internal processes from those who are likely to be the most marginalized within the organization, by asking questions such as: How do the staff experience their managers?; How do service users experience the staff?; How does information flow?; and

Who has access to what information? An AOP organizational development plan should include processes that will specify how, and how often, the organization will evaluate its internal processes and make attempts to continually improve.

Organizational Learning

We noted above how important it is to create a culture that values ongoing learning. In this category, we focus on some of the practices AOP organizations can adopt to provide ample and useful opportunities for organizational members to engage in both formal training and informal learning. Too often we have seen "AOP training"—where organizations bring in an outside consultant to do a workshop—as the *only* area of intervention. Even worse, far too often we see "one-off" AOP workshops as the only strategy for change being used. Opportunities for AOP learning, education, and training should be mandatory, continuous, and viewed as just *one aspect*—albeit an important one—of an agency's AOP organizational development plan (Hyde, 2003; Hyde & Hopkins, 2004; Martinez, Green, & Sanudo, 2004; Mederos & Woldeguiorguis, 2003).

For agencies initiating their AOP organizational development journey, it is important to bring together all organizational members for training that lays some of the foundational groundwork (Barnoff, 2011). This kind of training should focus on defining AOP and why it is important, and should outline some key principles and guiding practices within the particular organizational context to establish a baseline of knowledge about AOP practice among organizational members. This preliminary training can be used to make sure that everyone in the organization understands what it means to be an AOP agency, the overall goals of this work, and how they will be expected to participate. Because new members are always being added, this first-level training needs to be periodically repeated. Once the basic groundwork has been set, organizations can move into specific topic areas related to the particular area of service they provide and/or their particular service user groups. Organizations can provide different kinds of training for different stakeholder groups, as appropriate. For example, a training session could be organized specifically for managers to help them understand how to integrate AOP principles into their everyday management practices. Frontline workers, on the other hand, could focus on AOP-oriented direct service strategies.

It is important to develop knowledge not just for its own sake but to use these opportunities to develop peoples' abilities to *apply* this new knowledge (Bernard & Hamilton-Hinch, 2006). Ask questions such as "'At a program level, how does our service provision need to change, in light of this new knowledge we have gained today?' and 'How will I practice differently, given this new information?'" (Barnoff, 2011, p. 185).

AOP education helps people learn the skills they need to be aware of the dynamics of oppression and to confront problematic power relations. This includes the skills that all organizational members need to develop so that they will be better prepared to be open to challenging each other and to engage respectfully in difficult conversations, in those moments when oppressive incidents occur or when power is unfairly exercised. These are always difficult, but they can be made easier if people have had the opportunity to practise these skills in circumstances that are not "heated" or "real," by role-playing specific types of scenarios and practising how people could best respond to hypothetical situations—"What would you say if you heard or saw ... ?" or "How would you confront your colleague when ... ?"—when they are relatively calm. This can assist them in being better able to deal with those situations when they actually happen and when emotions are running high. Teaching people to expect that these types of difficult situations *will* happen—and that when they do, it does not mean that the organization is in trouble or that the individuals are being blamed—should be part of the preparatory work that people do in AOP training.

Another related skill important for AOP engagement in organizations is that of critical reflexivity. Critical reflexivity is about being able to question our own practice, behaviours, and actions; to understand how power relations are inherent in these; and to learn to take action and change based on these reflections. This skill is fundamental to AOP (Baldwin, 2008; Burke & Harrison, 2002; Heron, 2005; Morley, 2008; Sakamoto & Pitner, 2005; Strier & Binyamin, 2010). In fact, as Danso (2009) argues, this is "a necessity, not an option" in AOP practice (p. 563). The above are just a few illustrative examples, not an exhaustive list, of potential curriculum areas for AOP training. Each agency needs to reflect on its own context and the issues that are relevant in particular moments in time in order to best plan their unique AOP training strategy.

Category Three: Practices

This category, "practices," is composed of three areas of intervention: (1) organizational programs and services, (2) organizational connections with local communities, and (3) organizational action in working for social change.

Organizational Programs and Services

We could write an entire paper about AOP practice at a program or direct service level— and have done so in other publications (see, for example, Barnoff & Coleman, 2007). Space limitations do not allow us to delve into this aspect here. Instead, we refer the reader to some key literature that describes what AOP practice can look like at a program and service level. Excellent examples include: Clarke and Wan (2011) on settlement work; Curry-Stevens (2011) on advocacy work; Danso (2009) and Sakamoto (2007) on work with immigrants/refugees; Corneau and Stergiopoulos (2012) and Larson (2008) on mental health; Hines (2012) and Langley (2001) on queer communities; Pollack (2004) on women in prison; and Strier and Binyamin (2010) on poverty issues.

For our purposes here, we simply note that in any AOP organizational development plan, the agency should focus its efforts and attention on its direct practices, programs, and services, and how power relations may be evident as these programs are carried out. Using the literature noted above as a guide to what is important when working from an AOP perspective, organizations need to ask whether or not and/or how their direct practices fit the key tenets of AOP social work practice, and how well their programs meet their stated mission and the identified needs of people in their surrounding communities. Further, organizations need to reflect on whether they are engaged only in service provision or to what extent they are also taking action at a more systemic level by engaging in advocacy and activism work to promote broader change.

Organizational Connections with Local Communities

An anti-oppression organizational development plan needs to attend to how the organization connects with its local communities as vital partners, involving them in the internal operations of the organization (Gutierrez & Nagda, 1996; Jackson & Holvino, 1988; Jordan, 2006; Thomas, 1987; United Way of Greater Toronto, 1991). As Minors (1996) suggests, "members of the larger community [should] participate at all levels and help make decisions that shape the organization and influence its direction ... [and the organization should see] itself as part of the broader community" (p. 204). Anti-oppression organizations reflect the diversity of the communities in which they are situated, and those diverse communities are represented within the organization at all levels.

Organizations should periodically solicit evaluative feedback from their local communities to ensure that their actions meet local community needs, as defined by the community itself, and, if necessary, develop a plan to better engage with the community and ascertain how the community can become more involved in the organization. Ultimately, anti-oppression organizations do not view themselves as separate from their local communities, and actively recognize that they are accountable to those communities. Some do this by establishing community advisory committees, which can be a useful strategy, but is far from enough. Communities should not just be "advising" organizations; rather, they should be actively integrated into the actual decision-making structures of the organization. Community involvement in the organization should be meaningful and significant, with community members playing active roles at all organizational levels (e.g., as members on the agency's Board of Directors).

Organizational Action in Working for Social Change

Anti-oppression is an approach to practice that recognizes the social roots of people's needs and issues and that social change is required to adequately resolve them (Clarke

& Wan, 2011; Corneau & Stergiopoulos, 2012; Hines, 2012; Sakamoto, 2007; Strier & Binyamin, 2010). Therefore, AOP organizations cannot only focus on their internal organizational processes and external partnerships and connections. They must actively engage in social action work (Barnoff, 2011; Karabanow, 2004).

Social service organizations that operate from an AOP approach recognize that they have a dual purpose of social care and social change. They must never forget that they are not in existence simply to perpetuate themselves. Ultimately, the overriding goal of an anti-oppression organization is to work itself out of business, that is, to bring about a social environment in which the organization itself is no longer needed (Adams, 2008). An anti-oppression organizational development plan, therefore, should address how the organization is engaging in social action. What is being done? Who is involved or not involved? What are the outcomes of the organization's efforts in this regard? What else can the organization do to further its social change goals?

CONCLUSION

In the current neoliberal and neo-managerial context, with steady withdrawal of state support and funds for the social service sector, agencies are increasingly struggling in "survival mode" (Barnoff, George, & Coleman, 2006), pushed to compete with each other for time-limited funding, suppressed by advocacy "chill," and impaired in their ability to stay focused on AOP organizational development. As Shaheen Shaikh (2012, pp. 72–74) argues, this hostile context for social service work, and the restructuring of the nonprofit sector

> has affected the viability and overall health of nonprofit and voluntary sector organizations, particularly since the 1990s. ... [D]espite the gains made by anti-racists, feminists, and other social justice advocates in highlighting and addressing inequity and oppression, this space for social and organizational change is becoming more limited. ... Nonprofit organizations have had to focus their energy and resources on their very existence. On the other hand, community and social service organizations offer concrete spaces of struggle against racism, sexism, and other relations of oppression.

While it is beyond the scope of this chapter to detail the mechanisms and strategies agencies use to engage in this work, it is clear that many agencies continue to do so quite successfully, in spite of everything that seeks to stand in their way. Yes, the implementation of AOP organizational practice in the current context is difficult, but it is definitely still achievable and perhaps it is more important than ever.

11 | Trade Unions and Social Work

Toward New Convergences Against Austerity[1]

Winnie Ng, Unifor-Sam Gindin Chair in Social Justice and Democracy, Ryerson University

Globally, trade unions, public services, and the public at large are bearing the brunt of the deep cuts in social spending, job reduction, and outsourcing in the name of deficit reduction. In this gloves-off economy (Bernhardt, Boushey, Bresser, & Tilly, 2008), where managerial flexibility and corporate profit margins trump any rights and respect for working people, the global labour market restructuring has had a devastating impact on workers, their families, and their communities (Berberoglu, 2011).

The dominant political narrative of the austerity agenda has been a "blame game"—blaming the victims, blaming others who are more vulnerable, and blaming anyone (such as union members and environmentalists) who can be construed as demanding too much and making business less "efficient." At the same time, the serious funding reduction in social services has ushered in a new era of commodification of services (Dominelli, 2004). Social work services are increasingly under threat and undermined. As a result, people in poverty end up having less access to public services. In the context of a genderized and colour-coded labour market (Galabuzi & Block, 2011), the intersectionality of race, class, gender, and other forms of systemic oppression is clearly reflected in who bears the burden of this global race to the bottom.

Given the adverse impact of the austerity agenda on both the labour movement and social work, this chapter explores what trade unions and social work share and reimagines the conditions for possible convergences between the two. Finally, this chapter considers the strategies that social workers, in the dual roles of social work practitioners and trade union activists, can carry out to create a collective narrative of resistance.

In 1975, I began working as a community worker at University Settlement House located right in the heart of Chinatown in Toronto. Working closely with immigrant workers from diverse backgrounds led me to recognize that a case-by-case approach, and even occasional advocacy support, was not powerful enough to penetrate the factory walls to address the systemic practices of workplace discrimination and exploitation. I realized then that workers need a collective presence to challenge unequal power relations, and this prompted me to join the International Ladies Garment Workers

Union (ILGWU) as a union organizer in 1977. Ever since then, the labour movement has been my site of activism. In a sense I have come full circle in my current role of teaching community organizing at Ryerson University, where I share learnings from social movement activism with social work students.

This chapter is very much grounded in my experiences in the Canadian context. Furthermore, it is important to note that this chapter does not speak to trade unions or social work practice that does not subscribe to transformative social change. The reimagining of a potential partnership between trade unions and social work can only take place when it is grounded in progressive core values of economic, social, and racial justice for all.

THE NEED FOR RENEWAL AND CONVERGENCE BETWEEN IMPACTS ON TRADE UNIONS AND SOCIAL WORK PRACTICE

Within the Trade Union Context

There has been a massive erosion of public sector employment. In Canada alone, the federal government as an employer has eliminated 26,000 jobs over the past three years and is on track to reach its target of 35,000 by 2017 (May, 2014). The other pressing challenge is the growing presence of precarious employment as the new norm in workplaces. *Still Working on the Edge*, a recent report by the Workers Action Centre (Gellatly, 2015), showed that in comparison to its 2007 study, the employment situation in Ontario has worsened. Not only has the number of part-time jobs risen much faster than that of full-time jobs, workers are increasingly working longer hours and are subjected to more exploitative working conditions as they juggle work and family responsibilities.

Over the last two decades, with the decline in union density, labour scholars have urged unions to give priority in organizing the growing ranks of marginalized, contingent workers who are predominantly women, youth, and racialized and immigrant workers (Fairbrother & Yates, 2003; Fletcher & Gapasin, 2008; Kumar & Schenk, 2006). Feminist and anti-racist scholars have emphasized the centrality of an equity agenda as prerequisite to labour renewal in Canada (Briskin, 2009; Das Gupta, 2009; Foley & Baker, 2009; Ng, 2012). Yet a study by Briskin, Genge, McPhail, and Pollack (2013) reveals that equality issues have still not moved into the mainstream of union culture. In fact, there is now a decline in women's participation in leadership, fewer resources for equity organizing, and, in some cases, outright attacks on advocates. This means the road to equality within the labour movement for workers of colour and, more recently, Aboriginal workers continues to be too long with far too many detours (Wall, 2009).

Trade unions—as a microcosm of a society where colonialism, sexism, racism, and other forms of systemic discrimination are reflected as part of everyday practice—are no different from any other institution with their subscription to the dominant narrative and their own share of structural challenges. The labour movement continues to wrestle and attempt to mitigate the rift between union principles of solidarity and the actions of union members and leaders.

Within the Social Work Context

The austerity agenda has social workers caught juggling the ideal of social justice inclusion with the harsh realities of funding. Government funders have imposed and restricted the level and amount of advocacy work that agencies can do. Such restrictions on mobilizing have prompted agencies to become highly sensitive to self-censorship, while others have opted to retreat totally from advocacy work, which is now deemed too political (Carniol, 2010).

The new approach of service provision means clients are "case managed" and social workers "micro-managed." Not unlike the piece-work system in the manufacturing sector, frontline service providers are pressured to "process" more cases as part of their performance measure, to thereby justify their social agency funding. At the end of the helping process, the clients, or service users, are never engaged as subjects who feel empowered to exercise their own autonomy or agency.

Very often, the clients of service providers are workers who have lost their jobs due to plant closure and are now seeking help through this traumatic period of transition. Not only is there a total erasure of former identities and experiences as employees, union members, and/or activists, there is a glaring absence of collective work that will probe into the root cause of the problem and the question of who benefits from their job losses. Fisher and Shragge (2008) have been critical of such social work practice and urge community organizations to embrace the model of social action organizing that will deal with underlying issues, create opposition, and challenge the status quo.

On the other hand, a client could be an immigrant worker, who has been exploited by the employer, seeking some form of redress. One wonders how many social workers will identify with Baines's (2011) stance that unions are an effective vehicle for anti-oppressive resistance and suggest union organizing to their clients as a possible course of action.

Edward Scanlon and Scott Harding (2005) suggest the potential for social work to "reconnect" with organized labour, based on shared fundamental values and the history of the early days of social work. The social work profession needs a political ally if it is to be successful in advancing the historical progressive vision of the profession and protect social programs from current cuts or threats.

THE DEEP HISTORICAL ROOTS OF COLLABORATION AND SHARED VALUES

The labour movement has always acknowledged the unequal power relations in the workplace and in broader society, and has recognized that power comes from organizing, mobilizing, and agitating. Employers have never willingly relinquished or shared their control and power in their workplaces. In North American labour history, worker-oriented legislation and social programs were won as a result of protest, civil disobedience, and working-class solidarity.

May 1st, International Workers Day, originated as a way to commemorate the workers killed in protest for an eight-hour work day in Chicago in May 1886. In Canada, the Winnipeg General Strike of 1919 is a testimony to workers' courage, as skilled trade workers protested about unemployment after World War I. The On-to-Ottawa Trek in the 1930s was initiated by unemployed workers as a desperate response to the intolerable conditions in work camps set up by the federal government during the Great Depression. As a result, unemployment insurance benefits were legislated in 1936. Through the years, other key social reforms such as pensions, worker's compensation, universal health care, occupational health and safety, and employment standards have all come into being as a result of labour and community mobilizing.

Social justice–oriented social work has deep historical roots in mobilizing and organizing against oppressive forces (Benjamin, 2011). Throughout these milestones in workers' struggles, social workers walked side by side with organized labour as community advocates. During the Depression era in the United States, the emergence of the social work rank-and-file movement, with its members swelling to 15,000 in 1936, was a force to be reckoned with (Fisher, 1980). Rooted in Marxist class analysis, these rank-and-filers identified themselves as white-collar workers and were strong supporters of workers' rights to organize unions. The founders of the Settlement House movement, such as Jane Addams, Lillian Wald, and Florence Kelley, established the National Women's Trade Union League and worked closely with organized labour in advocating for strong social public policy and services. As a result of this formidable alliance and mobilizing, far-reaching social and labour legislations—the Social Security Act and the National Labor Relations Act—were passed during this period (Scanlon & Harding, 2005).

However, after the post–World War II era, the relationship became more tenuous as unions lost some of their activism during the period of McCarthyism. For fear of being targeted politically, social workers retreated from identifying themselves with the working-class labour movement. Some social workers moved to the path of professionalization, "cultivating" a middle-class and professional identity. Instead of pursuing union organizing strategies, priorities were placed on the professionalization of social work, such as advanced clinical training, the development of professional journals, and the formation of professional associations of social workers (Walkowitz, 1999).

Today, the majority of social workers have become more engaged in the mainstreaming of the social work profession and have left the notion of the "worker" in social work behind. Others have retained a social justice orientation and become involved in civil rights activism, the women's movement, anti-war protests, and, more recently, environmentalism and the movement for marriage equality and LGBTQ rights.

Similar to trade unions, the social and human services system is also fraught with the chasm between ideals and practices that often reflect the dominant narrative and unequal power relations. The Sixties Scoop, a phrase coined in Johnston's (1983) report on the adoption of Aboriginal children, refers to a period between 1960 and the mid-1980s when thousands of Aboriginal children were "scooped" from their birth families without knowledge or consent, and placed in non-Indigenous families for adoption. Such mass removal of children from their birth families and communities is a glaring reminder of the complicity of social and child welfare agencies and practitioners in implementing policies with little recognition of the historical context of colonial policies of assimilation. Sinclair (2007) forcefully argues that

> such child welfare intervention follow[s] upon the heels of the residential school system, which included, as by-products of an assimilationist agenda, the deliberate destruction of traditional family, social and political systems, intergenerational abuse, and social pathology in many communities. (p. 68)

These are issues that require all of us to reflect critically on social work practice from a decolonizing framework and to strategize for change.

COMMUNITY–LABOUR ALLIANCES AND BEST PRACTICES IN THE MOBILIZATION FOR SOCIAL JUSTICE

For the past three decades, some of the more progressive trade unions have recognized the need to build broad-based community coalitions as part of the fight against the neoliberal agenda. Coalitions are able to provide a shield for community agencies participating on broader shared goals, to avoid being targeted or run the risk of losing funding. Peter Leonard refers to such coalitions as "confederation of diversity," where the politics of difference are incorporated with the politics of solidarity (Leonard, 1994; Mullaly, 2002). Four such examples of successful coalition-building are discussed below: the women's movement's involvement in trade unionism; mobilizing for employment equity legislation; the minimum wage campaign; and the Toronto Public Library workers' strike.

One key example of community–labour alliance has been women as bridge builders, traversing between labour and the feminist movement. The influx of women members in the public sector in the 1970s enabled activists in the women's movement to use their trade unions as another site to challenge the systemic gender discrimination in workplaces, unions, and the broader society. As a result of their commitment and mobilizing support on the union convention floor, creating self-organizing space such as women caucuses, progressive and inclusive policies such as childcare, pay equity, and initiatives to end violence against women have been instituted, initially at the bargaining table and later legislated as part of broader social change.

The late 1980s in Ontario witnessed the coming together of trade unionists with women's organizations, people of colour, people with disabilities, and Indigenous Peoples under the broad umbrella of Alliance for Employment Equity—to address systemic and discriminatory barriers in employment. This was a proud example of coalition building that led to the passing of the historic mandatory employment equity legislation in Ontario in 1993, an act immediately repealed after the Conservative Harris government came to power in 1995.

The successful mobilizing of the minimum wage campaign in Ontario is an example of community mobilizing and political bargaining. The Toronto Workers Action Centre (WAC), a community-based agency providing advocacy services for low-wage, non-unionized workers, began the initial mobilizing and campaigning for a minimum wage raise after a ten-year freeze under a Conservative regime. The campaign was strengthened by a targeted lobbying effort by the Toronto and York Region Labour Council in forging a broad-based coalition and a groundswell of support. The minimum wage was increased to $10 per hour in 2007.

The second wave of the minimum wage campaign came after the minimum wage had been frozen for three years. In that period, food and transit costs soared, while inflation drove down minimum wage earnings to 19 percent below the poverty line (Khosla, 2014). The WAC provided leadership and worked closely with the Common Front, a newly founded labour community coalition supported by the Ontario Federation of Labour, to coordinate to an intensive, province-wide campaign. At the launch in March 2013, community groups across Ontario delivered a block of ice to their MPPs' constituency offices, driving home the message that it was time to thaw the freeze on minimum wages (Khosla, 2014). Under the banner of Raising the Minimum Wage to $14, highly visible and creative actions were held on the 14th of every month thereafter to sustain media attention and to build community support and, in particular, support from the low-wage workers themselves. The intensive campaign led to the appointment of a task force by the Ontario government in the summer of 2013 and an announcement by the premier of Ontario, upon the release of the task force report in January 2014, of an increase of the hourly minimum wage to $11, with annual adjustment based on the cost of living. In anchoring the campaign on the lived experiences and voices of the minimum-wage workers from diverse communities, WAC has been able to harness the leadership potential of the workers most directly affected and to build capacity for a worker-centred movement for the long haul.

The above examples of community–labour collaboration speak to the power of numbers. They underscore the importance of moving from the traditional practices of electoral politics to building broad-based coalitions where the inclusion of marginalized groups is meaningful and real. These activities allow deeper relationship building and thereby build trust and commitment based on shared community interests and values. Community mobilizing in support of the 11-day Toronto Public Library (TPL) workers' strike is one exemplary campaign against the austerity agenda of the Toronto City Council and cutbacks on public library services.

Over half of the Toronto Public Library Workers Union/Canadian Union of Public Employees (CUPE) Local 4948 members are part-time workers, three-quarters of them are women, and most have few or no benefits. In 2012, Toronto's Ford administration attempted to impose a 10 percent cut across the board on public services and set an unreasonably high threshold of 15 years of seniority for part-time workers to obtain full-time status (M. Smith, 2012). There was no option for the union but to prepare for the strike in defence of part-time workers' rights and job security. What ensued was a public campaign brilliantly executed with a key message: "What My Library Means to Me." Against the backdrop of the anti-library and anti-reading stance of local politicians, the campaign enlisted the support of everyone from renowned authors to schoolchildren, who shared their personal experiences as library users and emphasized the importance of public libraries as community hubs and places of learning. The strike by the library workers evolved into a broader citizen campaign to save the public library system and public services more generally. The picket line became a gathering place for community members, who came with their favourite books and stood in solidarity with the TPL strikers. The strike was successful in engaging the public in challenging the austerity agenda. The campaign achieved some victories in pushing back the 10 percent cut to 3.9 percent and reducing the seniority period from 15 to 11 years to qualify as a full-time worker. Such action speaks to what Mullaly (2002) has referred to as a political strategy to "re-legitimate the state" and "build more rather than less government involvement in social, economic and human affairs" (p. 202).

While the efforts of coalition building can be uplifting, working across sectors and boundaries is not without its challenges and tensions. Sometimes, partners come to the table merely for the optics, while others making financial contributions can be overzealous in taking up space and claiming credit. With different organizational cultures, structures, and practices, coalition partners have to step outside of their respective comfort zones and challenge each other. These moments of tension, if handled with mutual respect, are instructive in working across differences and building equal partnership. The immigration reform movement south of the border provides important lessons on diversity of organizing strategies for a unified purpose.

Lessons from Los Angeles Immigrant Labour Activism

The successful collaboration between labour and community can be best demonstrated by the mobilizing of Latino immigrants in Los Angeles (LA) County. Due to the deep organizing over the last 15 years, LA has gained over 60,000 new members of predominantly Latino workers, bringing new energy and vision to a troubled American labour movement (Milkman, 2012). Milkman's (2012) study argues that their success is underpinned by the overlap of three distinct strands of organizing. The first involves traditional trade union organizing. Several leading US unions have organized Latino immigrants employed in low-wage janitorial, retail, and hospitality work. The Justice for Janitors campaign launched by Service Employees International Union (SEIU) has been a prime example of a more innovative organizing approach combining direct action and sectoral initiative, rather than a movement restricted to a single workplace.

The second strand within immigrant labour activism is the advocacy and organizing efforts of labour-oriented NGOs—known in the US as worker centres, which number well over 100 and are scattered across the country. They provide advocacy support and mobilize workers in precarious employment or in the informal sector. Finally, the third strand is the broader immigrant and migrant rights movement organizing. This broad-based coalition includes partners from churches, ethnic organizations, community agencies, and organized labour. Foregrounded by a vision of human rights, the coalition has worked for legal status as the panacea to improve immigrant workers' employment and working conditions.

The synergy of the three strands of mobilizing has radicalized immigrant workers into a cohesive group with a class identity grounded in their common experiences of exploitation and exclusion. It has dispelled the myth commonly held by unions that immigrant workers are "unorganizable" (Tattersall, 2009). This mobilizing has also politicized workers and transformed members of the Latino community into a powerful voting bloc that American political parties have taken notice of. In the re-election of Obama in 2012, over 75 percent of Latino Americans voted for the Democratic Party. One of the most instructive lessons from the LA mobilization for immigration reform is the harnessing of the tenacity and the commitment to deep organizing within one particular community.

SOCIAL WORKERS AS PROFESSIONALS AND UNION MEMBERS

The ideal of social work practice as a caring profession that fosters social justice has been greatly undermined by the rise of new managerialism, under which the service standardization and performance management models typical in retail sales are repackaged and introduced into the social services sector as New Public Management (NPM; Baines, 2011; see also Smith, this volume). Contending with multitasking and case overload, social workers employed by the City of Toronto are either pushed to have more qualifications or experience deskilling and devaluing of their work, according to David Kidd, Chief Shop Steward with the Canadian Union of Public Employees (CUPE Local 75; personal communication, March 6, 2013).

Unionization provides an alternate forum for social workers to exercise their commitment to not only improving their own working conditions but also to advocating broad public policy change. Collective bargaining has been effective in countering the pace of restructuring in the social services sector. For example, one community agency in Toronto has secured a no-contracting-out clause in their collective agreement and has set a precedent in the sector.

Others have used the contract negotiation process to raise work-restructuring issues that are detrimental to the quality of care and wellbeing of their clients. La Rose's (2009) study of the strike of a child welfare agency describes how the workers, who were members of CUPE, went on strike for six weeks after management refused to address the issue of caseloads and high levels of stress experienced by their members. Through the bargaining and strike process, workers developed a strong bond, exercised their collective power as union members, challenged state managerial policies, and created positive social change (La Rose, 2009). Hard-won gains such as caps on caseloads, and improved workload and contract language have set a precedent for child welfare agencies across Ontario (Baines, 2011).

Another successful example of collective resistance comes from a group of social workers who are employed by a social service agency in Toronto and belong to the Ontario Public Services Employees Union (OPSEU). Carniol (2010) provides a vivid account of how Lisa Quarta, a clinical social worker, and the president of her local organized to stop management from laying off housekeeping and clerical staff, who were predominantly racialized women, in order to cut costs. Quarta first called a union meeting where all the affected workers shared their stories and reactions about the pending layoffs with other union members, who were mainly white professionals. As a result, staff members showed up to the subsequent meeting with management wearing black as a method of protest. Two days later, management backed off the restructuring scheme. Not only did the collective action succeeded in saving jobs, it also built solidarity and bridged the divide between racialized members who were in lower, entry-level positions and white professional members (Carniol, 2010).

The challenges for trade unions representing social workers are twofold. Firstly, as social work is a female-dominated sector, how can unions engage more social workers when women social workers are often juggling the responsibility of caring for their families with overloaded case files? Secondly, there is great need for rank-and-file membership to experience transformative union moments at the local level, which will instill a lasting sense of belonging and being part of the union family (Bernard, 2006). In my 30 years of organizing, I have realized there is nothing more magical and inspiring than hearing labour or community members switch from using "I" to saying "We." Organizing does not stop when workers sign their union cards. The notion of organizing the organized enables members to be more engaged and moves them from "member" to "activist."

TRANSLATING PROGRESSIVE CORE VALUES INTO MEANINGFUL PRACTICE

The community mobilizing initiated by TPL workers to challenge the austerity agenda, the immigration reform movement, and social workers' use of the collective bargaining process to resist some austerity measures, all illustrated above, are inspiring tales of resistance and the potential of strong community–labour alliances.

The progressive core values that trade unions and social work share are grounded on a critical analysis of the multiple ways social structures, power, dominance, and privilege are constructed. It is about asking who benefits. It is also about finding courage, creativity, and new ways to challenge these unjust social relations (Carniol & Del Valle, 2010) and transform them into equitable processes based on economic, political, environmental, and social justice (Baines, 2007; Benjamin, 2011; Carniol & Del Valle, 2010). The emergence of the vibrant and diverse Occupy Movement, with its iconic "We are the 99%" slogan, is one such moment of clarity in challenging some of the structural inequalities. In reimagining possible new convergences to resist the austerity agenda, it is critical to translate some of the progressive core values into meaningful practice. For further collaboration and bridging between trade unions and social work, I offer the following three ideas for consideration.

First, some advice for trade unions in handling complaints and grievances. Very often, in the name of expediency in the face of limited time and resources, union representatives end up resorting to the shortest route to resolve or mediate individual cases, without making deeper connections between the incidents and the larger structural context. I am deeply moved by a case documented by Carniol and Del Valle (2010) that vividly illustrates the respect and care of the structural social work counselling approach, which moves from a conventional, top-down therapeutic relationship to more power-sharing practice between the social worker and the client. Such transformative relationship-building and critical consciousness–raising power dynamics allowed an immigrant woman to break her silence, to file a complaint against her husband on domestic abuse, and to finally testify in court. Not only did the immigrant woman feel empowered and supported by the social worker, but she was also able, through her own journey, to inspire her daughter to find her own voice at school. Along with her social worker, she is currently co-facilitating a support group for abused, Spanish-speaking women. This is an inspiring story of personal transformation to collective agency that trade unions can learn and benefit from.

Potential cases of harassment and/or differential treatment based on sexism, racism, and other grounds of discrimination are often more complicated and harder to prove. These cases require empathy, skills, and time for the local leadership to take such complaints seriously and respectfully. For a union member from one of the equity-seeking groups who has finally mustered enough courage to step forward, the support and encouragement offered by a shop steward will make a world of difference and bring them closer to the union family. These can be powerful and transformative moments of union building.

Second is a recommendation for the social work profession to reinforce the clarity of social justice, and put the notion of "worker" back into social work. The primary entry point for this transformation is through social work education—by integrating social action organizing as a major element of the curriculum, and having a stronger presence of workers' struggles and trade unions in shaping progressive social policy change. I would argue that social work student placements in unions should be expanded, to create a critical mass of such students, dispel some of the myths about unions, and facilitate deeper understanding and relationship building for future collaborative projects.

Last but not least is the need to glean lessons from past community–labour collaboration. The conditions to deepen the roots of these community–labour alliances lie in more horizontal, democratic practices that are from the bottom up; a transformative leadership that has the political will and courage to challenge the status quo and has commitment to empowerment; and mobilizing strategies that will move people from the comfort of their own silos to the larger space of "We."

It is in the vision of rebuilding the "We" that we need to probe deeper into the nuanced notion of community unionism and the complexity of movement building for social justice. If the end goal for community unionism is premised on broadening unions' reach to potential membership and the strategic decision to "rebrand" the image of unions, such positioning will be fraught with self-interest and competition. Trade unions, in social movements, need to go beyond a narrow, economic focus and define themselves by demonstrating their capacity to connect with life experiences under capitalism (Fairbrother, 2008).

In the new norm of workplaces with precarious and informal labour, where workers are no longer confined to a traditional workplace setting, it is important to build a repertoire of practice that will reach out to these marginalized workers. Chang's (2012) study on the organizing efforts of workers in precarious employment in four East Asian countries proposes an alternate vision of the labour social movement, where the anchoring is shifted from unions, as the site of growth, to a community where precarious and marginalized workers, regardless of status and workplace, come together as a united force to be reckoned with. In these community settings, social work practitioners can play a pivotal role in mobilizing as a way to overcome fragmentation in the social sector. They can potentially represent a different path of coalition building that offers more genuine partnership and solidarity.

In closing, the stark realities of structural inequalities and the increasing fragmentation within the social service sector has compelled Benjamin (2011) to call for social workers to rekindle the proud history of resistance and to be at the forefront of struggle again. We cannot afford to deny the ongoing colonization project in Aboriginal communities in Canada; nor can we watch in silence the injustices experienced by migrant workers, racialized immigrants, and refugees, and the violence of anti-Black racism. Benjamin (2011) calls on us to "keep marching, keep expanding and deepening equity and services required to address such systemic gaps" (p. 295). It is in such a spirit of social justice and solidarity that we will continue to reimagine, to engage in new collaborations and practices of resistance, and to march together.

NOTE

1. Part of this chapter is reprinted from *International Encyclopedia of the Social & Behavioral Sciences*, Vol. 24, 2nd edition (J. D. Wright, Editor-in-Chief), "Trade Unions and Social Work: Lessons from Canada," by Winnie Ng, pp. 491–496, Copyright (2015), with permission from Elsevier. The author wishes to thank Ben Carniol, Deena Ladd, Judy Chow, Akua Benjamin, and David Kidd for their invaluable insights for the writing of this paper.

12 | The Professional Portfolio

Bridging the Classroom–Practice Divide in Social Work Education

Jennifer Clarke, Assistant Professor, School of Social Work, Ryerson University

Susan Preston, Associate Professor, School of Social Work, Ryerson University

Jennifer Ajandi, Contract Lecturer, School of Social Work, Ryerson University

Students entering social work programs are increasingly diverse in terms of age, class, experience, education, race, ethnic background, and family responsibilities (Razack, 2002; Timberlake, Farber, & Sabatino, 2002). Social work programs are being challenged to provide culturally relevant pedagogy and teaching approaches that respond to diverse student needs. Schools of social work have forged various relationships with social work practitioners in community-based agencies and human services organizations to provide students with valuable field practica experiences. These linkages are established to take the educational experience beyond the walls of university classrooms and into practice settings. Both formal and informal structures and processes have been put in place to facilitate students' learning and lay the groundwork for practice. These linkages also attempt to address historic tensions between social work education and practice (Davis, 1994; Goldstein, 1990; Leonard, 1994). Recently, there has been a renewed call for creative alternatives to traditional field practica, "which provides the bridge for theory and practice" (Razack, 2002, p. 17). The professional portfolio is a creative alternative that aims to bridge the classroom–practice divide in social work.

Adult learners who are returning to university have many strengths and competencies, such as formal, paid and unpaid, practice experience and life experience (Razack, 2002). On the one hand, mature students are looking for flexibility in the curriculum in order to be successful in meeting learning objectives and credential standards. These learners, many of whom have extensive paid human services–related experiences, often find it challenging to balance full-time jobs, family, and school responsibilities (Razack, 2002). Coser (1974) examines the phenomenon of the "greedy institution" in terms of restrictions and demands. In the university context, students are pushed and pulled in various directions and most often it is the family space that feels the brunt of time constraints and energy. Some students also find it difficult to integrate new ways of thinking and approaches into their current practice (Ruland & Ahern, 2007; Penna, 2004; Razack, 2002). Others do not "readily see the relevance of course content to their current practice" (Asselin, 2011, p. 125) and may resist new knowledge that could improve it. Many argue that the theories being taught in the classroom are not easily transferred to complex practice settings (Benner, Sutphen, Leonard, & Day, 2010; Corlett, 2000).

The challenge of integrating theory and practice is long-standing in social work (Fook, 2002; Gould & Harris, 1996; Payne, 2005; Penna, 2004; Winter & Maisch, 1996). It presents a sort of "classroom–practice divide" or what Schön (1983) has famously termed "the gap between '*the high ground of academic rigour and the swampy lowlands of practice*'" (as cited in Halton, Murphy, & Dempsey, 2007, p. 513, emphasis in original). Furthermore, because of their extensive work experience, some adult learners find the quality of field practica instruction and supervision very limited (Razack, 2002). As mature students with previous education and work experiences (re-)enter university, traditional pedagogical processes and social work field practica become a *fait accompli*. Of significance for schools of social work is to find new ways of bridging the gap between professional knowledge and professional practice so that what happens in the classroom connects with students' realities in various practice settings (Baines, 2006, 2011; Fook, 2002; Razack, 2002).

In response to these concerns, students and faculty in the Ryerson School of Social Work have engaged in dialogue and debates about alternative, innovative models for designing and delivering the field education curriculum. Effective organizing and advocacy by many of our mature students, school council representatives, and faculty led to the development and implementation of a portfolio course as a creative alternative to traditional field practica and a continuing commitment to integrating anti-oppressive practice and pedagogy in the classroom.

This chapter highlights the authors' reflections on and analyses of the development and implementation of the portfolio course for both on- and off-campus third- and fourth-year undergraduate students in our program. Our intent in this chapter is to offer the professional portfolio course as a creative and critical pedagogical alternative to traditional field practica. We contend that this course exemplifies a critical, creative, self-directed, and learner-centred approach that facilitates students' engagement in reflective practice (Osterman, Asselin, & Cullen, 2009; Ruland & Ahern, 2007; Weimer, 2002). The chapter begins with a brief review of the literature on the uses of portfolios in social work education, and then moves to discussing the development and implementation of the portfolio course in the school of social work. In this section, the aim is to highlight the salient theoretical underpinnings that guided course design, content, and delivery. The authors then reflect on their own teaching–learning experiences in developing and delivering the course to Aboriginal and non-Aboriginal undergraduate students. The chapter concludes with implications for social work field education.

PROFESSIONAL PORTFOLIOS IN SOCIAL WORK EDUCATION

The literature on professional portfolios across disciplines and curricula in higher education is extensive (Alvarez & Moxley, 2004; Coleman, Rogers, & King, 2002; Jones, 2010; Schatz, 2004; Sidell, 2003; Swigonski, Ward, Mama, Rodgers, & Belicose, 2006; Taylor, Thomas, & Sage, 1999). Meanings and purposes of portfolios are conferred through acts of interpretation in the many professional programs such as nursing, education, and social work that have embraced their use (Alvarez & Moxley, 2004; Coleman, Rogers, & King, 2002; Jones, 2010). The portfolio documents a student's learning, through critical self-reflection, regarding their past and present practice. Alvarez and Moxley (2004) note that portfolios may consist of seven sections: introduction, philosophical orientation to the concentration (social work), domain of practice, evaluation of learning experience, practice competencies, professional development plan, and conclusion. Elliott (2003) defines *portfolio* as "a creative process of developing and recording practice over time" (p. 328). Pierson and Kumari (2000) view the portfolio as a document or product that "addresses questions specifically posed by the faculty that are intended to guide students to synthesize understanding of theory and practice" (as cited in Swigonski et al., 2006, p. 817). Like Coleman, Rogers, and King (2002), we view the portfolio as both a process and a product for teaching and learning.

The literature consistently shows that portfolios are widely used for the foremost purpose of assessing student learning (Coleman, Rogers, & King, 2002; Johnston, 2004; Sidell, 2003; Swigonski et al., 2006; Taylor, Thomas, & Sage, 1999). As an assessment tool, portfolios help educators to determine students' progress and identify their strengths, weaknesses, and future learning needs. Educators and students are also using portfolios to assess and improve their own teaching and learning (Pearson & Heywood, 2004; Wolfe & Miller, 1997). Alvarez and Moxley (2004) and Coleman, Rogers, and King (2002) argue that portfolios have intrinsic value, and are excellent assessment tools that challenge traditional, rigid, and standardized assessment methods by allowing greater flexibility in the assessment process.

Portfolios are used to develop, demonstrate, and enhance students' knowledge, skills, values, and competencies in social work education (Coleman, Rogers, & King, 2002; Elliott, 2003; Swigonski et al., 2006; Taylor, Thomas, & Sage, 1999). As a documentary product, portfolios are used to stimulate students' creativity as expressed in works selected for reflection, the ways in which students convey the meanings of their work (e.g., through visual, digital, and print formats), analyses, and demonstration in the final product. Many studies support the use of portfolios for skills development, specifically critical thinking, self-reflection, use of self, and introspection (Coleman, Rogers, & King, 2002; Elliott, 2003; Graham & Megarry, 2005; Haffner, 2001; Lockwood, Walker, & Tilley, 2009; Ruth-Sahd, 2003; Schramm-Pate & Lussier, 2003–2004; Swigonski et al., 2006; Taylor, Thomas, & Sage, 1999; Wilding, 2008). Coleman, Rogers, and King (2002) and Schramm-Pate and Lussier (2003–2004) argue that portfolios enhance students' critical thinking skills, particularly around issues of power, privilege, and oppression. Phillips (2009) found that critical thinking and reflection in portfolio can reveal hidden agendas and gender stereotypes in educational institutions. Through critical thinking and reflection, students develop self-knowledge, critical consciousness, and action for challenging oppression and promoting social justice in society (Carpenter-Aeby & Aeby, 2009; Coleman, Rogers, & King, 2002; Loughran, 2002).

Like Graham and Megarry (2005) and Coleman, Rogers, and King (2002), we contend that the reflexive portfolio is a valuable tool in helping to facilitate a connection between classroom theory and field practice experiences. We believe, along with many others, that "portfolios are ideally suited to assist students to integrate their practice with coursework" (Coleman, Rogers, & King, 2002, p. 586). Through reflection-in-action, reflection-on-action, and reflection-for-action, students learn to integrate theories into practice and build new theories to improve practice (Fejes, 2008; Schön, 1983). Pierson and Kumari (2000) and Swigonski et al. (2006) also note that portfolios offer opportunities for students to learn how to synthesize and integrate theory and practice by forging linkages between academic knowledge and practical field experiences. As a pedagogical approach, the portfolio course requires students to be critical, reflective thinkers who question prior learning and integrate new knowledge into current and future practice in order to develop a well-integrated theoretical and conceptual framework to inform their practice.

As popular as professional portfolios have become in social work education, we contend, particularly among critical pedagogues, that our usage of portfolio is different. Perhaps our use may be considered more as a critical, political, anti-oppressive act of resistance to a long-standing barrier in field education with respect to mature students and the unique challenges they face in returning to school to meet credential standards or retrain and re-equip themselves with new knowledge and skills to compete in the global marketplace. In our usage, the portfolio course challenges traditional field practica in community-based agencies and human services organizations by offering an alternative, pedagogically sound way for adult learners to use their prior professional knowledge in the new learning environment. This creative alternative to teaching and learning in social work field education is, to our knowledge, a distinct feature of our portfolio course.

THEORETICAL UNDERPINNINGS

The theoretical underpinnings that inform the portfolio course evolve from three strands in the research literature: (1) adult education/self-directed learning, (2) critical thinking, and (3) reflection. The critical theories of anti-colonialism, anti-racism, and anti-oppression also guided our thinking and action in the development of the portfolio course. As social work educators, our teachings have been strongly influenced by scholars such as Baines (2006); Baskin (2008); Dei (2008); Dewey (1933, 1938); Ellsworth (2005); Freire (1985, 1993, 2001); Fook (2002); hooks (1994); James (2005); Knowles (1980); Kolb (1984); Kolb and Kolb (2005, 2006); LaRocque (2001); and Schön (1983), to name a few. Their writings highlight the importance of grounding teaching in critical theories and pedagogical approaches that facilitate both teaching and learning for students and instructors.

Adult Learning/Self-Directed Learning

Central theoretical foundations of the portfolio course are the importance of adult learning and self-directed learning. Portfolios are most successful when students, as self-directed learners, take responsibility for their own learning goals and needs (Kear & Bear, 2007; Knowles, 1978, 1980; McMullan et al., 2003). Knowles (1975) defines self-directed learning as "a process in which individuals take the initiative, with or without the help of others, in diagnosing their learning needs, formulating learning goals, identifying human material resources for learning, choosing and implementing appropriate learning strategies, and evaluating learning outcomes" (p. 18). Other theorists argue that when students are self-directed, they are also motivated to assess learning gaps, evaluate, reflect, and think critically about their knowledge and practice (Brockett & Hiemstra, 1991; Kear & Bear, 2007; McMullan et al., 2003; Stanton & Grant, 1999). Given the many complex settings in which social work occurs, students must be proactive, motivated, and self-directed learners if they are to grow professionally.

Students' direct practice experiences with individuals, families, groups, and communities provide significant opportunities for reflection and critical thinking in the classroom. However, some adult learners are challenged in linking new course knowledge with practice experiences. Through guidance and support from instructors and peers, as well as classroom discussions, email follow-up, and phone conversations, students enhance their capacity to be self-directed learners and critical thinkers who are motivated in the learning process. Grounded in theories of adult learning, students are encouraged to creatively and freely express their reflections and perspectives on the learning journey in a self-directed manner (Mezirow, 1991). The portfolio course is not only a personal, student-driven, and self-directed process, it is intensely personal and creative, and honours different ways of knowing and expressing learning through such things as painting, poetry, quilting, song, dance, interviews, journals, displays, and presentations.

Critical Thinking

The portfolio course is also grounded in theories of critical thinking. Critical thinking is a purposeful, goal-directed process that involves critical questioning and analysis (Alafaro-LeFevre, 1995; Patterson, Crooks, & Lunyk-Child, 2002). For Wenzel, Briggs, and Puryear (1998), "critical thinking is a rational process in which students demonstrate skills in analysis, research, or clinical decision making" (p. 210). Garrison (1992) emphasizes that critical thinking and self-directed learning are intricately linked. The two complement each other in a student's learning journey. These ideas fit well with the portfolio course objectives that require students' "use of research, policy, advocacy and mobilization in strategic and transformative change" (SWP 51 A/B, n.p.) and "to apply a critical understanding of existing social, economic and political forces and their implications for policy and practice within a field practicum setting" (SWP 36A/B, n.p.). In our courses, we also emphasize the need to identify and deconstruct dominant discourses in society that serve to stigmatize and marginalize voices and bodies, which strengthens our understanding of critical thinking. Callister's (1993) argument that critical thinking helps to link classroom theory and field work practice is also important for our course, as students are expected to understand the link between the content discussed in the classroom and field practice situations.

Critical Reflection

Critical reflection is increasingly being advanced in the portfolio literature as a strategy for developing reflective practitioners (Asselin, 2011; D'Cruz, Gillingham, & Mendez, 2007; Halton, Murphy, & Dempsey, 2007; Johns, 2007; Kear & Bear, 2007; Ruth-Sahd, 2003; Wong, Wong, & Kan, 1997). In many disciplines, such as nursing, education, and social work, reflection is viewed as a key and desirable element of professional practice (D'Cruz et al., 2007; Fejes, 2008; Fook, 2003; Gustafsson & Fagerberg, 2004; Thompson & Burns, 2008). Jones (2010) defines reflection as "a process of critically examining one's past and present practice as a means of building one's knowledge and understanding in order to improve practice" (p. 593). We also made use of Fook's (2002) work on reflection, specifically to enhance self-knowledge, build theories, and improve social work practice to help bridge the gap between theory and practice. Some scholars used the terms *reflection, critical reflection,* and *reflexivity* interchangeably (Potter & East, 2000; Ruch 2000, 2002), while others differentiate the terms (Deacon, 2000; Fook, 2002; Powell, 2002). D'Cruz, Gillingham, and Mendez (2007) define critical reflection as an approach to practice that requires the social worker to take a critical stance on self-evaluation, reflection on action, practice wisdom, and how knowledge/ power and theory are generated in order to challenge existing power relations. These "emancipatory elements" of critical reflection fit well with our portfolio course because students are expected to engage in ongoing critical reflection of their own practices and values over the two-semester course.

Schön's (1983, 1991) seminal work *The Reflective Practitioner* is instrumental to the reflective approach adopted in many disciplines and to the development of this portfolio course. His theory of reflection-in-action and reflection-on-action influenced the content, process, and structure of our portfolio course. Dewey's (1933) work on the centrality of reflective thinking and reflective approach to teaching and learning in adult education has also been central to the course design. Reflective thinking, according to Dewey (1933), is a "kind of thinking that consists of turning a subject over in the mind and giving it serious and constructive consideration" (p. 3). Reflective learning has also been put forward as both an inward and active thought process of looking back on what has been done "in terms of theory and practice and interaction with clients and colleagues" (Halton, Murphy, & Dempsey, 2007, p. 516). According to Kolb (1984; Kolb & Kolb, 2005, 2006), reflection is what forms the link between service and learning. Brazilian educator Paulo Freire, in *Pedagogy of the Oppressed* (1993), articulates both the ideas of praxis and conscientization in reflection and action for transformative change. Similarly, we believe that reflection bridges the gap between theory and practice by linking the two. The reflective process links practice and theory by requiring students and educators to value each other's work—that is, acknowledge the value of education in practice and valuing the expertise of practitioners in social work education (Mann, Byrnes, Power, Rich, & Winifreyda, 1999).

Anti-Colonialism, Anti-Racism, and Anti-Oppression

The critical ideas of anti-colonial, anti-racist, and anti-oppressive education also informed our stance as we developed and implemented the portfolio course. Our anti-colonial stance is influenced by scholars such as LaRocque's (2001) and Lawrence and Dua's (2005) work on decolonizing the academy. Other scholars argue that we must disrupt Eurocentric dominance in academia in order to make way for Aboriginal ways of knowing about and doing social work with First Nations families and communities (Baskin, 2008, 2009; Clarke, Pon, Benjamin, & Bailey, 2015; Dumbrill & Green, 2008; Hart, 2009; Sinclair, 2009). Disrupting the academic space of Eurocentric dominance allowed for the valuing of Aboriginal students' experiences as helpers and traditional teachers in their communities. This is crucial, since education was used as the pretext for removing Aboriginal children from their families and communities and placing them in residential schools. This forced removal ensured that they would not learn their language, culture, and traditional practices and teachings, and would instead be indoctrinated with Western/European knowledge and value systems (Absolon & Willett, 2005; Dumbrill & Green, 2008; Graveline, 1998; Sinclair, 2009). By embracing this stance, we contradict the conventional thinking that Eurocentric education is the only way of knowing.

Anti-racism is an action-oriented educational strategy that addresses issues of racism and the interlocking systems of social oppressions in society, through institutional and systemic change (Dei, 1996, 2008; Dei, James, Karumanchery, James-Wilson, & Zine, 2000). It is a proactive education strategy that calls for the creation of space for the lived experiences of subordinated groups to be incorporated into the education system. These ideas heavily influenced the creation of the portfolio course as a legitimate alternative to the traditional field practica, in order to address the needs of mature students.

Like anti-racism, anti-oppression looks at how power, privilege, and oppression are intersected in society and finds ways to challenge it. From this perspective, the portfolio course fits within our school's curriculum of anti-oppression, which requires students to interrogate structural and institutional barriers in their workplaces and everyday practice (Barnoff & Moffatt, 2007; Barnoff, 2011), address issues of power and dominant discourses (Fook, 2002; Foucault, 1997; Rossiter, 2005; Sinclair & Albert, 2008), and challenge intersecting privileges and oppression (Barnoff & Moffatt, 2007; Sakamoto & Pitner, 2005).

COURSE DESIGN AND IMPLEMENTATION: AN EXERCISE IN THINKING, REFLECTION, AND ACTION

Designing and implementing the self-reflexive portfolio course for both Aboriginal and non-Aboriginal students required different preparation, structure, processes, course content, and pedagogical approaches. Although all of our social work courses now contain some Aboriginal content, the portfolio course designed for Aboriginal students had a greater focus on First Nations issues and preparing for social work practice in First Nations communities.

In designing the course for Aboriginal students, one of the challenges was how to ensure that students were given the opportunity to meet the learning objectives of the field education course while also challenging the Eurocentric foundation of social work knowledge, values, and practice. To do this, the first author met with Aboriginal scholars, program coordinators, administrators, Elders, community members, and students. Together, they developed the course design, content, processes, and teaching approaches. The instructor gained valuable insights that were used to revise the course to meet the needs of Aboriginal students and fulfill the course objectives. The course was also delivered with the assistance of program administrators and Elders who were present in the classroom for the duration of the course. The process of collaboration allowed us to learn directly from the Aboriginal community, and to unlearn many of the Eurocentric practices and approaches that are often invisible in education. The knowledge gained was used to continuously modify the course in ways that speak to the lives and experiences of Aboriginal students. It also allowed us to question our own Eurocentric thinking and worldviews in order to improve our teaching practice.

Design/Structure

In designing the portfolio course, we took an anti-colonial, anti-racist, and anti-oppressive stance—a stance that values and respects diverse, mature students as self-directed learners, critical thinkers, and reflexive practitioners. Our stance also fits well with the theories of adult education, postmodern and critical thoughts on multiple "truths," different ways of knowing, and deconstruction (Fook, 2002; Leonard, 1994). This is particularly important in the portfolio course for Aboriginal students, as Eurocentric social work knowledge, values, and practice approaches have and continue to be implemented as *the* way of knowing, rather than one way of knowing. As critical pedagogues, we acknowledge that Western/European knowledge systems often appear as the "normal" and "natural" way of being and doing things (Yee & Dumbrill, 2003). The portfolio course is designed to disrupt and challenge this view by allowing students to meet the learning objectives of the field education credit in a different way—a way that values their experiences and honours their work and family responsibilities and commitments.

The portfolio course is offered to Aboriginal and non-Aboriginal undergraduate students in the third and fourth years of the program. To be eligible, students are required to have several years of paid, full-time employment in the human services sector and must reasonably expect to remain in full-time employment until the end of the course. This requirement for extensive work experience ensures that students are able to reflect upon past and current practice situations and work toward improving their practice in becoming reflective practitioners. Unlike the traditional field practica, which generally require students to be in a new field setting in the third and fourth years of the program, the portfolio course requires students to engage in reflective practice in their current place of employment. In the third year, this is typically 2 days per week for a total of 14 hours, and in the fourth year, 3 days per week, or 21 hours. In the portfolio course, students are expected to engage in critical thinking and reflection upon practice for similar durations. In addition, the course instructor meets with students individually at least once during the course and with students as a group at least four times over two semesters. Additional meetings may be required by instructor or student to address issues that arise in the field setting and the course.

The learning goals and objectives of the field education curricula form the central architecture for the portfolio course, including its content, expectations, and assessment methods. For third-year students, the broad learning goal is to develop micro-level intervention skills with individuals, families, and groups in various community contexts (SWP 36, 2011/2012). Six learning objectives frame the course and allow students to "gain a beginning understanding of the social work field through introduction to community agencies" (p. 1). Students learn to "develop practice skills, such as engagement, assessment, planning, implementation, termination and evaluation skills" (p. 1). Two core objectives are to "prepare a self-evaluating, knowledgeable and reflexive professional social work practitioner" who can "apply a critical understanding of existing social, economic and political forces and their implications for policy and practice ... [with] particular emphasis ... [on] issues of diversity, power, privilege, oppression, individualism, and transformative change" (p. 1). Similarly, course objectives are designed so that students can "gain a critical understanding of the practicum setting's response to manifestations of oppression from an anti-oppression framework and their implications for practice" and "apply critical self-reflexive knowledge about [their] social location and its implications for practice" (p. 1).

The fourth-year course is designed around four broad learning goals and six specific objectives. These goals and objectives frame the course and enable students to develop critical thinking, reflection, and evaluation skills for transformative change. The four goals are constructed to help students learn about the agency, social context, social work practices, and the self (SWP 51, 2010/2011, pp. 2–3). Through critical thinking and reflection in mandatory seminars, learning plan development, mid-term and final evaluations, and a reflective assignment, the portfolio course stimulates self-directed learning and narrows the classroom–practice divide, ultimately enhancing students' knowledge and skills in reflective practice.

Course Content

In the foundation of social work courses, students are introduced to an anti-oppression framework for practice. As we are preparing undergraduate students to work in a variety of complex community and organizational settings, portfolio course content must focus on micro-, mezzo-, and macro-levels of practice with individuals, families, groups, and communities. In third year, the focus is on micro-skills of engagement, assessment, planning, implementation, termination, and evaluation. In keeping with our theoretical underpinnings and pedagogy, students are exposed to content that addresses "issues of diversity, power, privilege, oppression, individualism, and transformative change" (SWP 36, 2011/2012, p. 1). Through individual and group discussions, reading materials, and assignments, students learn to interrogate, critically analyze, and deconstruct dominant discourses, and reflect upon organizational responses to social inequalities and various forms of oppression. Additionally, they learn to connect their own and others' experiences to broader social and political issues, and apply critical self-reflexive knowledge in practice.

The course content for Aboriginal students had a unique emphasis on cultural identity, the historical influences of colonialism, healing, spirituality, and decolonization. Course content critically examines the tenuous relationship between the Aboriginal community and the education system, beginning with Egerton Ryerson's role in the residential school system. Rather than the mainstream style of lecture and technology presentations, sharing circles and storytelling are often incorporated to encourage dialogue and acknowledge and value Aboriginal students' traditions and teachings. These formats also offer some relief from the intense reflective writing and documentary nature of the course. Through storytelling and dialogue we "encounter different points of view and differing ways of seeing and knowing, leading me to reflect on my own ways of seeing in light of the options and perspectives of others" (Ellsworth, 1997, p. 94). Dialogue also facilitates students' critical thinking and reflection and challenges the passive "banking" model of education (Freire, 2001). The assignments also provided a space for students to connect various ways of knowing and learning within "engaged pedagogy" (hooks, 1994, p. 15) and bridge the gap between professional knowledge and professional practice, or what happens in the classroom and the practice setting (Baines, 2006, 2011; Fook, 2002; Razack, 2002).

The content of the fourth-year course aims to prepare students for critical, anti-oppressive practice with individuals, families, groups, and communities. The focus is on the three levels of intervention: micro, mezzo, and macro. Through course content, class discussions, and assignments, we ensured that students made connections between course material and their experiences in the field. In keeping with our pedagogy and the objectives of the fourth-year curriculum, we also ensured that students learned to challenge large-scale structures and processes of oppression within and by societal institutions. Further, as noted in the Ryerson School of Social Work BSW Field Education Manual (2009/2010), we also ensured that they learned how to "implement strategies that influence the social, political and organizational contexts of social work practice [and] ... select, articulate and evaluate the social work practice theories and perspectives that inform their practice" (p. 2). Students were also expected to "demonstrate the use of research, policy, advocacy and mobilization in strategic and transformative change" (p. 2). By the end of the course, students were able to critically engage in reflection-in-action and reflection-on-action (Fejes, 2008; Schön, 1983, 1991). Throughout the course they continuously reflected upon their prior learning and their current practice—their everyday interaction with service users; their engagement with communities; analysis of power, privilege, and oppression; and the integration of new knowledge into future practice. As we engaged in this work with students, we simultaneously engaged in reflective practice or, as Mezirow (1991) points out, we both engaged in transformative learning.

IMPLICATIONS FOR SOCIAL WORK EDUCATION

The reflections and analyses on the portfolio course development and implementation in this chapter have a number of implications for social work education. In our experience, the portfolio course, within the context of social work field education, offers valuable insights into the benefits, challenges, and opportunities of using alternative teaching–learning approaches with diverse groups of students.

For social work students, portfolios reinforce skill development in reflection, critical thinking, and self-directed learning. As self-directed learners, students actively interrogate their own learning needs and work to change the way they think about practice and integrate new knowledge into practice. More importantly, the use of portfolio helps to promote depth of understanding in course content and practice situations, all of which facilitates the integration of professional knowledge and professional practice and bridges the classroom–practice divide. Portfolio also helps to shift the power imbalance in the instructor–student relationship by allowing mature students to be self-directed learners who actively engage in their own growth and development as professionals. In this course, the learners are the "experts" while instructors provide guidance and feedback that facilitate the learning process. Like Reeves and Reeves (1997), we see ourselves as "guides on the side" rather than "sages on the stage" (as cited in Rice-Green & Dumbrill, 2005, p. 172). Portfolio directly challenges the passive "banking" model of education (Freire, 2001) by encouraging students to actively participate in identifying their own learning needs, styles, and interests, which is a good fit with our anti-oppressive curriculum. Further, given the attention to critical self-reflection, power, privilege, and oppression that the portfolio course engenders (Barnoff & Moffatt, 2007; Sakamoto & Pitner, 2005), it fits well with our position as anti-racist, anti-oppressive, and anti-colonial pedagogues.

For the social work educator, the portfolio course is in line with our own anti-colonial, anti-racist, and anti-oppressive perspectives of education in terms of valuing students' voices in the teaching–learning process, sharing power in the classroom, supporting multiple ways of knowing and knowledge dissemination, and being comfortable with uncertainties. In this course, teaching and learning is a collective effort—a shared activity between students and instructors that promotes collective learning. This partnership fits well with our stance as educators, specifically for facilitating reflective practice in both students and instructors.

But the portfolio course, as social work education pedagogy, is not without its challenges. Over the past few years, we have observed that students experience a number of challenges, beginning with the idea of quality versus quantity. The sheer number of documents that students collect for their portfolio sometimes becomes the focus of the work, rather than the introspection and critical reflection needed to demonstrate and enhance knowledge and skill development. Some students also struggle to manage the self-directed, somewhat unstructured, and creative expectations of the portfolio course. Others struggle with the idea of writing about their accomplishments, strengths, weaknesses, and transformative moments. For these students, the portfolio presents an individualistic, competitive "showcasing" of their work, which conflicts with their values and perspectives. Finally, some students view the self-directed, learner-centred approach as faculty abdicating responsibility for the teaching–learning process. This is difficult for us because we want to promote the "learner as expert," but students expect the "teacher as expert" that is in keeping with the banking model of traditional education (Freire, 2001).

To conclude, the portfolio as an alternative pedagogical approach has many important implications for social work education. It challenges traditional field practica and offers instead an innovative approach that is creative, self-directed, and student-driven. Most of all, it offers opportunities for social work students to become self-directed, critical reflective practitioners who continuously think, reflect, and act upon course content and field practice to bridge the classroom–practice divide. We believe that the portfolio course is an appropriate response to the specific needs of mature students. Might portfolios be used in other courses, directed readings, or in preparation for research and thesis writing at the graduate level? We offer an urgent call for other educators to consider this alternative approach in their own curricula. While the portfolio course expands our understanding of an alternative pedagogical approach to meet part of the field education credit, we recommend that a formal evaluation of the course be undertaken to obtain students' experiences and perspectives in order to strengthen and improve it.

References

Abberley, P. (1987). The concept of oppression and the development of a social theory of disability. *Disability, Handicap & Society, 2*(1), 5–19.

Abele, F., Graham, K., Ker, A., Maioni, A., & Phillips, A. (1998). *Talking with Canadians: Citizen engagement and social union.* Ottawa, ON: Canadian Council on Social Development.

Abramovich, A. (2013). No fixed address: Young, queer, and restless. In S. Gaetz, B. O'Grady, K. Buccieri, J. Karabanow, & A. Marsolais (Eds.), *Youth homelessness in Canada: Implications for policy and practice* (pp. 387–404). Toronto, ON: Canadian Homelessness Research Network Press.

Absolon, K. (2009). Navigating the landscape of practice: Dbaagmowin of a helper. In R. Sinclair, M. A. Hart, & G. Bruyere (Eds.), *Wicihitowin: Aboriginal social work in Canada* (pp. 172–199). Halifax, NS: Fernwood Publishing.

Absolon, K., & Herbert, E. (1997). Community action as a practice of freedom: A First Nations perspective. In B. Wharf & M. Clague (Eds.), *Community organizing: Canadian experiences* (pp. 205–227). Toronto, ON: Oxford University Press.

Absolon, K., & Willett, C. (2005). Putting ourselves forward: Location in Aboriginal research. In L. Brown & S. Strega (Eds.), *Research as resistance* (pp. 97–126). Toronto, ON: Canadian Scholars' Press.

Adams, P., & Chandler, S. M. (2004). Responsive regulation in child welfare: Systemic challenges to mainstreaming the family group conference. *Journal of Sociology and Social Welfare, 31*(1), 93–116.

Adams, R. (2008). *Glass houses: Saving feminist anti-violence agencies from self-destruction.* Halifax, NS: Fernwood Publishing.

African Canadian Legal Clinic. (2012). *A report on the Canadian government's compliance with the international convention on the elimination of all forms of racial discrimination.* Toronto, ON: Author.

Afrikan Canadian Prisoner Advocacy Coalition. (2012). *Community communique: Potential human rights violations of Afrikan Canadian inmates in federal correctional institutions.* Retrieved from http://www.robertswright.ca/ACPACCommunique20120330.pdf.

Alafaro-LeFevre, R. (1995). *Critical thinking in nursing: A practical approach.* Toronto, ON: Saunders.

Alfred, T. (2009). Colonialism and state dependency. *Journal of Aboriginal Health, 5*(2), 42–60.

Alfred, T. (2011). Colonial stains on our existence. In M. J. Cannon & L. Sunseri (Eds.), *Racism, colonialism and Indigeneity in Canada* (pp. 3–11). Don Mills, ON: Oxford University Press.

Alfred, T., & Corntassel, J. (2005). Being Indigenous: Resurgences against contemporary colonialism. *Government and Oppression, 40*(4), 597–614.

Allan, B., & Smylie, J. (2015). *First Peoples, second class treatment: The role of racism in the health and well-being of Indigenous peoples in Canada.* Retrieved from http://www.wellesleyinstitute.com/wp-content/uploads/2015/02/Report-First-Peoples-Second-Class-Treatment-Feb-2015.pdf

Allen, M. (2014). *2012 police reported hate crime in Canada.* Retrieved from http://www. statcan.gc.ca/pub/85-002-x/2014001/article/14028-eng.pdf

Alvarez, A. R., & Moxley, D. P. (2004). The student portfolio in social work education. *Journal of Teaching in Social Work, 24*(1–2), 87–103.

American Psychiatric Association. (2013). *Diagnostic and statistical manual of mental disorders (DSM)* (5th ed.). Arlington, VA: Author.

Anastasiou, D., & Kauffman, J. (2013). The social model of disability: Dichotomy between impairment and disability. *Journal of Medicine and Philosophy, 38*, 441–459.

Armstrong, L. (2011). *An approach to engagement with youth in gangs: Participatory action projects.* (Unpublished master's thesis). Wilfrid Laurier University, Waterloo, ON.

Arnstein, S. (1969). A ladder of citizen participation. *Journal of the American Institute of Planners, 35,* 216–224.

Ashcroft, B. (2001). *Post-colonial transformation.* New York, NY: Routledge.

Ashcroft, B., Griffiths, G., & Tiffin, H. (Eds.). (1995). *The post-colonial studies reader: The key concepts.* New York, NY: Routledge.

Asselin, M. E. (2011). Using reflection strategies to link course knowledge to clinical practice: The RN-to-BSN student experience. *Journal of Nursing Education, 50*(3), 125–133.

Baikie, G. (2009). Indigenous-centred social work: Theorizing a social work way-of-being. In R. Sinclair, M. A. Hart, & G. Bruyere (Eds.), *Wicihitowin: Aboriginal social work in Canada* (pp. 42–61). Halifax, NS: Fernwood Publishing.

Bailey, M., Kandaswamy, P., & Richardson, M. U. (2006). Is gay marriage racist? In M. B. Sycamore (Ed.), *That's revolting: Queer strategies for resisting assimilation* (pp. 87–93). San Francisco, CA: Soft Skull Press.

Baines, D. (2004a). Seven kinds of work—only one paid: Raced, gendered and restructured work in social services. *Atlantis, 28*(2), 19–28.

Baines, D. (2004b). Pro-market, non-market: The dual nature of organizational change in social services delivery. *Critical Social Policy, 24*(1), 5–29.

Baines, D. (2006). "If you could change one thing": Social service workers and restructuring. *Australian Social Work, 59*(1), 20–34.

Baines, D. (2007). Anti-oppressive social work practice: Fighting for space, fighting for change. In D. Baines (Ed.), *Doing anti-oppressive practice: Building transformative, politicized social work* (pp. 13–42). Halifax, NS: Fernwood Publishing.

Baines, D. (Ed.). (2011). *Doing anti-oppressive practice: Social justice social work* (2nd ed.). Halifax, NS: Fernwood Publishing.

Baldwin, M. (2008). Promoting and managing innovation: Critical reflection, organizational learning and the development of innovative practice in a national children's voluntary organization. *Qualitative Social Work, 7*(3), 330–348.

Baluja, T., & Hammer, K. (2011, March 18). Mississauga high school bans gay-straight alliance. *The Globe and Mail.* Retrieved from http://www.theglobeandmail.com/news/toronto/ mississauga-high-school-bans-gay-straight-alliance/article573028/

Bansel, P., Davies, B., Gannon, S., & Linnell, S. (2008). Technologies of audit at work on the writing subject: A discursive analysis. *Studies in Higher Education, 33*(6), 673–683.

Barnartt, S. (2001). Using role theory to describe disability. In S. Barnartt & B. Altman (Eds.), *Exploring theories and expanding methodologies: Where we are and where we need to go* (pp. 53–75). Bingley, UK: Emerald Group Publishing.

Barnes, D. (2014). Causing disability, valuing disability. *Ethics, 125*(1), 88–113.

Barnes, M., Newman, J., Knops, A., & Sullivan, H. (2003). Constituting "the public" in public participation. *Public Administration, 81*(2), 379–399.

Barnoff, L. (2001). Moving beyond words: Integrating anti-oppression practice into feminist social services. *Canadian Social Work Review, 18*(1), 67–86.

Barnoff, L. (2002). *New directions for anti-oppression practice in feminist social service agencies*. (Unpublished doctoral dissertation). University of Toronto, Toronto, ON.

Barnoff, L. (2005). *Implementing anti-oppressive principles in everyday practice: Lessons from feminist social services*. (Unpublished report). Ryerson University, Toronto, ON.

Barnoff, L. (2011). Business as usual: Doing anti-oppressive organizational change. In D. Baines (Ed.), *Doing anti-oppressive practice: Social justice social work* (2nd ed., pp. 176–194). Halifax, NS: Fernwood Publishing.

Barnoff, L., & Coleman, B. (2007). Strategies for integrating anti-oppression principles: Perspectives from feminist agencies. In D. Baines (Ed.), *Doing anti-oppressive practice: Building transformative, politicized social work* (pp. 31–49). Halifax, NS: Fernwood Publishing.

Barnoff, L., George, P., & Coleman, B. (2006). Operating in "survival mode": Barriers to implementing anti-oppression practice within feminist social service agencies. *Canadian Social Work Review, 23*(1–2), 41–58.

Barnoff, L., & Moffatt, K. (2007). Contradictory tensions in anti-oppression practice within feminist social services. *Affilia, 22*(1), 56–70.

Baskin, C. (2003). Structural social work as seen from an Aboriginal perspective. In W. Shera (Ed.), *Emerging perspectives on anti-oppressive practice* (pp. 65–80). Toronto, ON: Canadian Scholars' Press.

Baskin, C. (2008). "I don't know what hurts more—to shut up or speak up": Aboriginal female learners in the academy. In A. Wagner, S. Acker, & K. Mayuzumi (Eds.), *Whose university is it, anyway? Power and privilege on gendered terrain* (pp. 27–43). Toronto, ON: Sumach Press.

Baskin, C. (2009). Evolution and revolution: Healing approaches with Aboriginal adults. In R. Sinclair, M. Hart, & G. Bruyere (Eds.), *Wichitowin: Aboriginal social work in Canada* (pp. 132–152). Halifax, NS: Fernwood Publishing.

Baskin, C. (2011). *Strong helpers' teachings: The value of Indigenous knowledges in the helping professions*. Toronto, ON: Canadian Scholars' Press.

Bauer G., & Scheim, A. (2015). *Transgender people in Ontario, Canada: Statistics to inform human rights policy*. Retrieved from Trans PULSE Project, http://transpulseproject.ca/research/statistics-from-trans-pulse-to-inform-human-rights-policy/

Baynton, D. (2013). Disability and the justification for inequality in American history. In L. J. Davis (Ed.), *The disability studies reader* (4th ed., pp. 17–33). New York, NY: Routledge.

Beck, E., & Pennell, J. (2013). Conferencing and restorative justice: The promise and challenge of restorative justice in the United States. In E. Zinsstag & I. Vanfraechem (Eds.), *Conferencing and restorative justice: International practices and perspectives* (pp. 137–151). Don Mills, ON: Oxford University Press.

Ben Moshe, L., Chapman, C., & Allison, C. (Eds). (2014). *Disability incarcerated: Imprisonment and disability in the United States and Canada*. New York, NY: Palgrave McMillan.

Benhabib, S. (1993). *From identity politics to social feminism: A plea for the nineties*. Retrieved from www.ed.uiuc.edu/EPS/PES-Yearbook/94_docs/BENHABIB.HTM

Benjamin, A. (2003). *The Black/Jamaican criminal: The making of ideology*. (Unpublished doctoral dissertation). University of Toronto, Toronto, Canada.

Benjamin, A. (2007). Doing anti-oppressive social work: The importance of resistance, history and strategy. In D. Baines (Ed.), *Doing anti-oppressive practice: Building transformative politicized social work* (pp. 196–204). Halifax, NS: Fernwood Publishing.

Benjamin, A. (2011). Doing anti-oppressive social work: The importance of resistance, history, and strategy. In D. Baines (Ed.), *Doing anti-oppressive practice: Social justice social work* (2nd ed., pp. 289–297). Halifax, NS: Fernwood Publishing.

Benner, P., Sutphen, M., Leonard, V., & Day, L. (2010). *Education nurses: A call for radical transformation*. San Francisco, CA: Jossey-Bass.

Berberoglu, B. (2011). The global capitalist crisis: Its origins, dynamics, and impact on the United States. *International Review of Modern Sociology, 37*(2), 159–184.

Beresford, P., & Croft, S. (1993). *Citizen involvement: A practical guide for change.* London, UK: Palgrave Macmillan.

Bernard, E. (2006). Organizing the organized. *Our Times Magazine, 25*(5), 18–19.

Bernard, W. T., & Hamilton-Hinch, B. (2006). Making diversity work: From awareness to institutional change. *Canadian Review of Social Policy, 56*, 131–139.

Bernhardt, A., Boushey, H., Bresser, L., & Tilly, C. (Eds.). (2008). *The gloves-off economy: Problems and possibilities at the bottom of America's labor market.* Champaign, IL: Labor and Employment Relations Association.

Bess, K. D., Prilleltensky, I., Perkins, D. D., & Collins, L. V. (2009). Participatory organizational change in community-based health and human services: From tokenism to political engagement. *American Journal of Community Psychology, 43*(1–2), 134–148.

Bessant, J. (2002). Risk and nostalgia: The problem of education and unemployment in Australia—A case study. *Journal of Education & Work, 15*(1), 31–51.

Bessant, J. (2003). Youth participation: A new mode of government. *Policy Studies, 24*(2–3), 87–100.

Bevan, D., & Thompson, N. (2003). The social basis of loss and grief. *Journal of Social Work, 3*(2), 179–194.

Bevan, R. (2011). *Changemaking: Tactics and resources for managing organizational change.* Seattle, WA: ChangeStart Press.

Bhabha, H. (1994). *The location of culture.* New York, NY: Routledge.

Bird, L. (2004). A queer diversity: Teaching difference as interrupting intersections. *Canadian Online Journal of Queer Studies in Education, 1*(1), 1–25.

Birnbaum, M. (1960). The right to treatment. *American Bar Association Journal, 46*, 499–504.

Blackstock, C. (2008, February). *The breath of life: When everything matters in child welfare.* Paper presented at the University of Victoria Aboriginal Child Welfare Research Symposium, Victoria, BC.

Blackstock, C. (2009). The occasional evil of angels: Learning from the experiences of Aboriginal peoples and social work. *First Peoples Child and Family Review, 4*(1), 28–37.

Blatt, B. (1974). *Christmas in purgatory.* Syracuse, NY: Human Policy Press.

Bourassa, C. (2009). *Reconceiving notions of Aboriginal identity. Aboriginal policy research series.* Ottawa, ON: Institute on Governance.

Boxall, H., Morgan, A., & Terer, K. (2012). *Evaluation of the FGC pilot program. AIC reports and public policy series 121.* Canberra, NSW: Australian Institute of Criminology.

Boyd, S. (2004). The perils of rights discourse: A response to Kitzinger and Wilkinson. *Analysis of Social Issues and Public Policy, 4*(1), 211–217.

Bracken, P., Thomas, P., Timimi, S., Asen, E., Behr, G., Beuster, C., ... & Yeomans, D. (2012). Psychiatry beyond the current paradigm. *The British Journal of Psychiatry, 201*(6), 430–434.

Brady, B. (2006). *Facilitating family decision making: A study of the family welfare conference services in the HSE western area.* Dublin, Ireland: Galway Child & Family Research and Policy Unit.

Breen, L., & O'Connor, M. (2007). The fundamental paradox in the grief literature: A critical reflection. *Omega, 55*(3), 199–218.

Brenner, N., Peck, J., & Theodore, N. (2010). Variegated neoliberalization: Geographies, modalities, pathways. *Global Networks, 10*(2), 182–222.

Brewer, P. (2003). The shifting foundations of public opinion about gay rights. *The Journal of Politics, 65*(4), 1208–1220.

Briskin, L. (2009). Cross-constituency organizing: A vehicle for union renewal. In J. Foley & P. Baker (Eds.), *Unions, equity, and the path to renewal* (pp. 137–156). Vancouver, BC: UBC Press.

Briskin, L., Genge, S., McPhail, M., & Pollack, M. (2013). *Making time for equality: Women as leaders in the Canadian labour movement.* Retrieved from http://womenunions.apps01. yorku.ca/wp-content/uploads/2012/10/OT1-pdf.pdf

Briskman, L., & Muetzelfeldt, M. (Eds.). (2003). *Moving beyond managerialism in human services.* Melbourne, VIC: InformIT.

Britzman, D. P. (2000). Teacher education in the confusion of our times. *Journal of Teacher Education, 51*(3), 200–205.

Brockett, R. G., & Hiemstra, R. (1991). *Self-direction in adult learning: Perspectives on theory, research, and practice.* New York, NY: Routledge.

Brockman, A. (2015, May 25). "Let kids be kids," say protesters against sex education curriculum. *Windsor Star.* Retrieved from http://blogs.windsorstar.com/news/let-kids-be-kids-protestors-rally-against-sex-education-curriculum

Broverman, A. (2009). ThisAbility #39: Gay and disabled in Canada? Back in the closet for you. *This Magazine.* Retrieved from http://this.org/blog/2009/11/03/gay-lesbian-disability/

Brown, C. (1994). Feminist postmodernism and the challenge of diversity. In A. Chambon & A. Irving (Eds.), *Essays on postmodernism and social work* (pp. 33–46). Toronto, ON: Canadian Scholars' Press.

Brown, C. G. (2012). Anti-oppression through a postmodern lens: Dismantling the Master's conceptual tools in discursive social work practice. *Critical Social Work, 13*(1), 34–65.

Brown, J., & Fraehlich, C. (2012). Assets for employment in Aboriginal community-based human services agencies. *Adult Education Quarterly, 62*(3), 287–303.

Brown, L. (2007). The adoption and implementation of a service innovation in a social work setting—a case study of FGC in the UK. *Social Policy and Society, 6*(3), 321–332.

Brown, L., & Strega, S. (Eds.). (2005). *Research as resistance.* Toronto, ON: Canadian Scholars' Press.

Brown, L., Callahan, M., Strega, S., Dominelli, L., & Walmsley, C. (2009). Manufacturing ghost fathers: The paradox of father presence and absence in child welfare. *Child and Family Social Work, 14*(1), 25–34.

Brown, W. (2002). Suffering the paradoxes of rights. In W. Brown & J. Halley (Eds.), *Left legalism/left critique* (pp. 420–434). Durham, NC: Duke University Press.

Bruyere, G. (2010). The decolonization wheel: An Aboriginal perspective on social work practice with Aboriginal peoples. In K. Brownlee, R. Neckoway, R. Delaney, & D. Durst (Eds.), *Social work and Aboriginal peoples: Perspectives from Canada's rural and provincial Norths* (pp. 1–11). Thunder Bay, ON: Lakehead University Centre for Northern Studies.

Buffett, P. (2013, July 27). The charitable-industrial complex. *The New York Times.* Retrieved from http://www.nytimes.com/2013/07/27/opinion/the-charitable-industrial-complex.html?smid=li-share&_r=1&

Burford, G., Connolly, M., Morris, K., & Pennell, J. (n.d.). *Introduction, principles, processes: Online annotated bibliography.* Retrieved from http://www.ucdenver.edu/academics/

colleges/medicalschool/departments/pediatrics/subs/can/FGDM/Research/Documents/Research%20Annotated%20Bibliography%202012%20Printable%20Version.pdf

Burford, G., & Hudson, J. (Eds.). (2000). *Family group conferencing: New directions in community-centered child and family practice*. New York, NY: Aldine de Gruyter.

Burke, B., & Harrison, P. (2002). Anti-oppressive practice. In R. Adams, L. Dominelli, & M. Payne (Eds.), *Social work: Themes, issues, and critical debates* (2nd ed., pp. 227–236). New York, NY: Palgrave MacMillan.

Burstow, B. (1992). *Radical feminist therapy: Working in the context of violence*. Thousand Oaks, CA: Sage.

Butler, J. (1993). *Bodies that matter: On the discursive limits of "sex."* New York, NY: Routledge.

Butler, J. (2004a). *Undoing gender*. New York, NY: Routledge.

Butler, J. (2004b). *Precarious life: The powers of mourning and violence*. New York, NY: Verso.

Butts, H. F. (1979). Frantz Fanon's contribution to psychiatry: The psychology of racism and colonialism. *Journal of the National Medical Association, 71*(10), 1015–1018.

Calhoun, C. (2000). *Feminism, the family, and the politics of the closet: Lesbian and gay displacement*. New York, NY: Oxford University Press.

Callahan, K. (2007). Citizen participation: Models and methods. *International Journal of Public Administration, 30*(11), 1179–1196.

Callister, L. C. (1993). The use of student journals in nursing education: Making meaning out of clinical experience. *Journal of Nursing Education, 32*(4), 185–186.

Cameron, G., & Vanderwoerd, J. (1997). *Protecting children and supporting families: Promising programs and organizational realities*. New York, NY: Aldine de Gruyter.

Camino, L., & Zeldin, S. (2002). From periphery to center: Pathways for youth civic engagement in the day-to-day life of communities. *Applied Developmental Science, 6*(4), 213–220.

Campbell, C., & Baikie, G. (2012). Beginning at the beginning: An exploration of critical social work. *Critical Social Work, 13*(1), 67–81.

Canadian Association for Social Work Education (CASWE). (2012). *Standards for accreditation*. Ottawa, ON: Author.

Canadian Centre for Accreditation. (2017). *About CCA*. Retrieved from https://www.canadiancentreforaccreditation.ca/about-cca/who-we-are

Canda, E. (1989). Religious content in social work education: A comparative approach. *Journal of Social Work Education, 25*(1), 36–45.

Cannon, M. J., & Sunseri, L. (2011). Glossary. In M. J. Cannon & L. Sunseri (Eds.), *Racism, colonialism, and Indigeneity in Canada* (pp. 275–279). Don Mills, ON: Oxford University Press.

Carbado, D. (2002). Straight out of the closet: Race, gender, and sexual orientation. In F. Valdes, J. McCristal Culp, & A. Harris (Eds.), *Crossroads, directions, and a new critical race theory* (pp. 221–242). Philadelphia, PA: Temple University Press.

Carniol, B. (2010). *Case critical: Social services and social justice in Canada* (6th ed.). Toronto, ON: Between the Lines Press.

Carniol, B., & Del Valle, V. (2010). "We have a voice": Helping immigrant women challenge abuse. In S. Hick, H. I. Peters, T. Corner, & T. London (Eds.), *Structural social work in action: Examples from practice*. Toronto, ON: Canadian Scholars' Press.

Carpenter-Aeby, T., & Aeby, V. (2009). Rewriting family stories during successful transition from an alternative school: One student's story of "violent female" to "phenomenal woman." *Journal of Human Behaviour in the Social Environment, 19*(3), 281–297.

Carpini, M. X. D., Cook, F. L., & Jacobs, L. (2004). Public deliberation, discursive participation and citizen engagement: A review of the empirical literature. *Annual Review of Political Science, 7*, 315–344.

Carlson, C. (2006). The Hampton experience as a new model for youth civic engagement. *Journal of Community Practice, 14*(1–2), 89–106.

Casey, C. (1995). *Work, self and society: After industrialism.* London, UK: Routledge.

Casey, C. (1999). "Come, join our family": Discipline and integration in corporate organizational culture. *Human Relations, 52*(2), 155–178.

CBC. (2010, October 29). *Bullying and sexual orientation by the numbers* (Editor's weblog comment). Retrieved from http://www.cbc.ca/news/canada/bullying-and-sexual-orientation-by-the-numbers-1.909444

Cesaire, A. (1972). *Discourse on colonialism.* New York, NY: Monthly Review Press.

Chamberlin, J. (1990). The ex-patients' movement: Where we've been and where we're going. *Journal of Mind and Behavior, 11*(3), 323–336.

Chambon, A. (1994). Postmodernity and social work discourse(s): Notes on the changing language of a profession. In A. Chambon & A. Irving (Eds.), *Essays on postmodernism and social work* (pp. 61–75). Toronto, ON: Canadian Scholars' Press.

Chambon, A. S. (1999). Foucault's approach: Making the familiar visible. In A. S. Chambon, A. Irving, & L. Epstein (Eds.), *Reading Foucault for social work* (pp. 51–81). New York, NY: Columbia University Press.

Chambon, A. (2012). Disciplinary borders and boundaries: Social work knowledge and its social reach, a historical perspective. *Social Work & Society, 10*(2), 1–12.

Chambon, A. (2013). Recognizing the other, understanding the other: A brief history of social work and otherness. *Nordic Social Work Research, 3*(2), 120–129.

Chandler, S. M., & Giovannucci, M. (2004). Family group conferences: Transforming traditional child welfare policy and practice. *Family Court Review, 42*(2), 216–231.

Chang, D. (2012). The neoliberal rise of East Asia and social movements of labour: Four moments and a challenge. *Interface: A Journal for and about Social Movements, 4*(2), 22–51.

Chappell, L. (2002). *Gendering government: Feminist engagement with the state in Australia and Canada.* Vancouver, BC: UBC Press.

Charlton, J. (1998). *Nothing about us without us.* Berkeley, CA: University of California Press.

Checkoway, B. N., & Gutiérrez, L. M. (2006). Youth participation and community change: An introduction. *Journal of Community Practice, 14*(1–2), 1–9.

Child and Family Services Statute Law Amendment Act. (2006). Retrieved from https://www.e-laws.gov.on.ca/html/source/statutes/english/2006/elaws_src_s06005_e.htm

Child Welfare Anti-Oppression Roundtable. (2009). *Anti-oppression in child welfare: Laying the foundation. A discussion paper.* Toronto, ON: Author.

Child Welfare Secretariat. (2005). *Child welfare transformation 2005: A strategic plan for a flexible, sustainable and outcome oriented service delivery model.* Toronto, ON: Ontario Ministry of Children and Youth Services.

Chrisjohn, J., & Young, S. (1997). *The circle game: Shadows and substance in the Indian residential school experience in Canada.* Penticton, BC: Theytus Books.

Ciszek, E. (2014). Cracks in the glass slipper: Does it really "get better" for LGBTQ youth, or is it just another Cinderella story? *Journal of Communication Inquiry, 38*(4), 325–340.

City of Toronto. (n.d.a). *Civic engagement.* Retrieved from http://www.toronto.ca/civic-engagement/index.htm

City of Toronto. (n.d.b). *Toronto youth cabinet.* Retrieved from http://www.thetyc.ca

Clark, A. (2008, January 24). Economic stimulus package gets bipartisan support. *The Guardian*. Retrieved from http://www.guardian.co.uk/world/2008/jan/24/usa.andrewclark/print

Clark, D. (2002). Neoliberalism and public service reform: Canada in comparative perspective. *Canadian Journal of Political Science, 35*(4), 771–793.

Clarke, J. (2012). Beyond child protection: Afro-Caribbean service users of child welfare. *Journal of Progressive Human Services, 23*(3), 223–257.

Clarke, J., & Newman, J. (1997). *The managerial state: Power, politics and ideology in the remaking of social welfare*. London: Sage.

Clarke, J., Pon, G., Benjamin, A., & Bailey, A. (2015). Ethnicity, race, oppression, and social work: The Canadian case. In J. Wright (Ed.), *International Encyclopedia of the Social & Behavioural Sciences* (2nd ed., Vol. 8, pp. 152–156). Waltham, MA: Elsevier.

Clarke, J., & Wan, E. (2011). Transforming settlement work: From a traditional to a critical anti-oppression approach with newcomer youth in secondary schools. *Critical Social Work, 12*(1), 14–26.

Clewett, N., Slowley, M., & Glover, J. (2010). *Making plans: Using family group conferencing to reduce the impact of caring on young careers*. Essex, UK: Barnardo's.

Coalition against Sanist Attitudes (CASA). (2011). Who coined sanism and what is sanism? Retrieved from http://www.freewebs.com/lindsaycasa/sanism.htm, link no longer active.

Coates, J. (2003). *Ecology and social work: Towards a new paradigm*. Halifax, NS: Fernwood Publishing.

Cocker, C., & Hafford-Letchfield, T. (2014). Introduction. In T. Hafford-Letchfield & C. Cocker (Eds.), *Rethinking anti-discriminatory and anti-oppressive theories for social work practice* (pp. 1–19). Hampshire, UK: Palgrave Macmillan.

Cohen, M. B., & Mullender, A. (1999). The personal in the political: Exploring the group work continuum from individual to social change goals. *Social Work with Groups, 22*(1), 13–31.

Coleman, H., Rogers, G., & King, J. (2002). Using portfolios to stimulate critical thinking in social work education. *Social Work Education, 21*(5), 583–595.

Connolly, M. (1994). An act of empowerment: The Children, Young Persons, and Their Families Act (1989). *British Journal of Social Work, 24*(1), 87–100.

Connolly, M. (2006). Up front and personal: Confronting dynamics in FGC. *Family Process, 45*(3), 345–357.

Conrad, P. (1992). Medicalization and social control. *Annual Review of Sociology, 18*, 209–232.

Contenta, S., Monsebraaten, L., & Rankin, J. (2014, December 11). Just 8% of Toronto kids are black. But 41% of kids in care are black. *Toronto Star*, pp. A1, A33.

Contenta, S., & Rankin, J. (2009, June 6). Suspended sentences: Forging a school-to-prison pipeline? *Toronto Star*. Retrieved from http://www.thestar.com/news/gta/2009/06/06/suspended_sentences_forging_a_schooltoprison_pipeline.html

Conway, S. (2007). The changing face of death: Implications for public health. *Critical Public Health, 17*(3), 195–202.

Corlett, J. (2000). The perceptions of nurse teachers, student nurses and preceptors of the theory–practice gap in nurse education. *Nursing Education Today, 20*, 499–505.

Corneau, S., & Stergiopoulos, V. (2012). More than being against it: Anti-racism and anti-oppression in mental health services. *Transcultural Psychiatry, 49*(2), 261–282.

Corntassel, J. (2008). Towards sustainable self-determination: Rethinking the contemporary Indigenous-rights discourse. *Alternatives, 33*, 105–132.

Corntassel, J. (2012). Re-envisioning resurgence: Indigenous pathways to decolonization and sustainable self-determination. *Decolonization Indigeneity, Education and Society, 1*(1), 86–101.

Coser, L. A. (1974). *Greedy institutions: Patterns of undivided commitment.* New York, NY: Free Press.

Cossman, B. (2002). Lesbians, gay men and the Canadian Charter of Rights and Freedoms. *Osgoode Hall Law Journal, 40*(3/4), 223–248.

Cossman, B., & Fudge, J. (2002). Privatization, law, and the challenge to feminism. In B. Cossman & J. Fudge (Eds.), *Privatization, law, and the challenge to feminism* (pp. 3–37). Toronto, ON: University of Toronto Press.

Couch, J., & Francis, S. (2006). Participation for all? Searching for marginalized voices: The case for including refugee young people. *Children, Youth and Environments, 16*(2), 272–290.

Coulthard, G. (2008). Beyond recognition: Indigenous self-determination as prefigurative practice. In L. Simpson (Ed.), *Lighting the eighth fire: The liberation, resurgence, and protection of Indigenous Nations* (pp. 187–204). Winnipeg, MB: Arbeiter Ring Press.

Crawford, C. (2013). *Disabling poverty and enabling citizenship: Understanding the poverty and exclusion of Canadians with disabilities.* Retrieved from http://www.ccdonline.ca/en/socialpolicy/poverty-citizenship/demographic-profile/understanding-poverty-exclusion

Crenshaw, K. (1994). Mapping the margins: Intersectionality, identity politics, and violence against women of color. In M. A. Fineman & R. Mykitiuk (Eds.), *The public nature of private violence* (pp. 93–118). New York, NY: Routledge.

Crenshaw, K. W. (2002). The first decade: Critical reflections, or "A foot in the closing door." In F. Valdes, J. McCristal Culp, & A. Harris (Eds.), *Crossroads, directions, and a new critical race theory* (pp. 9–31). Philadelphia, PA: Temple University Press.

Crow, L. (1996). Including all our lives: Renewing the social model of disability. In J. Morris (Ed.), *Encounters with strangers: Feminism and disability.* London: The Women's Press.

Cunning, S., & Bartlett, D. (2006). *Family group conferencing: Assessing the long-term effectiveness of an alternative approach in child protection. Final Report.* Toronto, ON: Centre for Excellence for Child Welfare, the George Hull Centre for Children and Families, Family Group Conferencing Project of Toronto.

Curry-Stevens, A. (2011). Persuasion: Infusing advocacy practice with insights from anti-oppression practice. *Journal of Social Work, 12*(4), 345–363.

Dalrymple, J., & Burke, B. (2006). *Anti-oppressive practice: Social care and the law* (2nd ed.). Maidenhead, UK: McGraw-Hill International.

Danso, R. (2009). Emancipating and empowering de-valued skilled immigrants: What hope does anti-oppressive social work practice offer? *British Journal of Social Work, 39*(1), 539–555.

Das Gupta, T. (2009). *Real nurses and others: Racism in nursing.* Halifax, NS: Fernwood Publishing.

Davies, B. (2000). *A body of writing 1990–1999.* Walnut Creek, CA: AltaMira Press.

Davies, B. (2005). The (im)possibility of intellectual work in neoliberal regimes. *Discourse: Studies in the Cultural Politics of Education, 26*(1), 1–14.

Davies, B., Browne, J., Gannon, S., Honan, E., & Somerville, M. (2005). Embodied women at work in neoliberal times and places. *Gender, Work and Organization, 12*(4), 343–362.

Davis, L. H. (1994). Relating work to adult higher education. *Journal of Continuing Higher Education, 42*(1), 17–22.

D' Cruz, H., Gillingham, P., & Mendez, S. (2007). Reflexivity, its meaning and relevance for social work: A critical review of the literature. *British Journal of Social Work, 37*, 73–90.

Deacon, L. (2000). Ethical issues in the assessment of the value base in social work students. *Journal of Practice Teaching in Health and Social Work, 3*(1), 55–61.

Dean, M. (1999). *Governmentality: Power and rule in modern society.* London: Sage.

Dean, M. (2014). Rethinking neoliberalism. *Journal of Sociology, 50*(2), 150–163.

Dei, G. S. (1996). *Anti-racism education: Theory and practice.* Halifax, NS: Fernwood Publishing.

Dei, G. S. (2000). Recasting anti-racism and the axis of difference: Beyond the question of theory. *Race, Gender & Class, 7*(2), 38–56.

Dei, G. S. (2008). *Racist beware: Uncovering racial politics in postmodern society.* Rotterdam, The Netherlands: Sense Publishers.

Dei, G. S., James, I. M., Karumanchery, L. L., James-Wilson, S., & Zine, J. (2000). *Removing the margins: The challenges and possibilities of inclusive schooling.* Toronto, ON: Canadian Scholars' Press.

DeMello, M. (1995). "Not just for bikers anymore": Popular representations of American tattooing. *Journal of Popular Culture, 29*(3), 37–52.

Department of Social Welfare. (1989). *Practice paper. Family decision making. Staff briefing paper.* Wellington, New Zealand: Author.

Desmeules, G. (2007). A sacred family circle: A family group conferencing model. In I. Brown, F. Chaze, D. Fuchs, J. Lafrance, S. McKay, & S. Thomas Prokop (Eds.), *Putting a human face on child welfare: Voices from the Prairies* (pp. 161–188). Retrieved from www.cecw-cepb.ca

Dewey, J. (1933). *How we think.* Boston, MA: D. C. Heath.

Dewey, J. (1938). *Experience and education.* New York, NY: Macmillan.

Dinshaw, D. M. (2010, March). *Immigrants and the Canadian mental health courts.* Retrieved from http://mentalhealthcourt.ca/pages/18/research.htm, link no longer active.

Dominelli, L. (1996). Deprofessionalizing social work: Anti-oppressive practice, competencies and postmodernism. *British Journal of Social Work, 26*, 153–175.

Dominelli, L. (1999). Neo-liberalism, social exclusion and welfare clients in a global economy. *International Journal of Social Welfare, 8*, 14–22.

Dominelli, L. (2004). *Social work: Theory and practice for a changing profession.* Cambridge: Polity Press.

Donaldson, L. P. (2005). Toward validating the therapeutic benefits of empowerment-oriented social action groups. *Social Work with Groups, 27*(2–3), 159–175.

Doolan, M. (2004). *The family group conference: A mainstream approach in child welfare decision-making.* Retrieved from https://pdfs.semanticscholar.org/d76a/bd23955b2cdc2f2a b83e058bd168ac2491ad.pdf

Dorf, M., & Tarrow, S. (2014). Strange bedfellows: How an anticipatory countermovement brought same-sex marriage into the public arena. *Law and Social Inquiry, 39*(2), 449–473.

Doss, E. (2002). Death, art and memory in the public sphere: The visual and material culture of grief in contemporary America. *Mortality, 7*(1), 63–82.

Doyle, R. (1990). Perspectives for purposive change. In R. Doyle & K. Rahi (Eds.), *Organization change toward multiculturalism* (pp. 26–36). Toronto, ON: Access Action Council.

Du Bois, W. E. B. (1903). *The souls of black folk.* Chicago, IL: A. C. McClurg & Company.

du Gay, P. (1996). Organizing identity: Entrepreneurial governance and public management. In S. Hall & P. du Gay (Eds.), *Questions of cultural identity* (pp. 151–169). London: Sage.

Dumbrill, G. (2006). Ontario's child welfare transformation: Another swing of the pendulum? *Canadian Social Work Review, 23*(1–2), 5–19.

Dumbrill, G., & Green, J. (2008). *Anti-oppressive social work: Theory and practice.* Basingstoke, UK: Palgrave Macmillan.

Dusenbury, P., Liner, B., & Vinson, E. (2000). *States, citizens and local performance management.* Retrieved from http://www.urban.org/sites/default/files/publication/62621/410068-States-Citizens-and-Local-Performance-Management.PDF

Edelman, M. (1988). *Constructing the political spectacle.* Chicago, IL: University of Chicago Press.

Elliott, N. (2003). Portfolio creation, action research and the learning environment: A study from probation. *Qualitative Social Work, 2*(3), 327–345.

Ellsworth, E. (1997). *Teaching positions: Difference, pedagogy and the power of address.* New York, NY: Teachers College Press.

Ellsworth, E. (2005). *Places of learning: Media, architecture, pedagogy.* New York, NY: RoutledgeFalmer.

Eng, D. (1997). Out here and over there: Queerness and diaspora in Asian American studies. *Social Text, 52/53*, 31–52.

Eskridge, W. (2000). Comparative law and the same-sex marriage debate: A step-by-step approach toward state recognition. *McGeorge Law Review, 1*(641), 1–19.

Espiritu, K. (2006). "Putting grief into boxes": Trauma and the crisis of democracy in Art Spiegelman's "In the shadow of no towers." *Review of Education, Pedagogy, and Cultural Studies, 28*, 179–201.

Evans, B., Richmond, T., & Shields, J. (2005). Structuring neoliberal governance: The nonprofit sector, emerging new modes of control and the marketisation of service delivery. *Policy and Society, 24*(1), 73–97.

Evans, S. (2004). *Forgotten crimes: The holocaust and people with disabilities.* Chicago, IL: Ivan R. Dee.

Fabricant, M. B., & Burghardt, S. (1992). *The welfare state in crisis and the transformation of social service work.* New York, NY: M. E. Sharpe.

Fabris, E. (2011). *Tranquil prisons: Chemical incarceration under community treatment orders.* Toronto, ON: University of Toronto Press.

Fairbrother, P. (2008). Social movement unionism or trade unions as social movements. *Employee Responsibilities and Rights Journal, 20*, 213–220.

Fairbrother, P., & Yates, C. (Eds.). (2003). *Trade unions in renewal: A comparative study.* London: Routledge.

Fanon, F. (1952/1991). *Black skin, white masks.* London: Pluto Press.

Fedosenko, K., & Leong, M. (2011, September 2). Sociology prof explores "post-gay" era. *Arts Wire.* Retrieved from http://students.arts.ubc.ca/sociology-prof-explores-post-gay-era/

Fejes, A. (2008). Governing nursing through reflection: A discourse analysis of reflective practices. *Journal of Advanced Nursing, 64*, 243–250.

Ferguson, S. A. (1996). Towards an anti-racist social service organization. *Journal of Multicultural Social Work, 4*(1), 35–48.

Fernando, S. (2012). Race and culture issues in mental health and some thoughts on ethnic identity. *Counselling Psychology Quarterly, 25*(2), 113–123.

Ferri, B., & Connor, D. (2014). Talking (and not talking) about race, social class, and dis/ability: Working margin to margin. *Race, Ethnicity, and Education, 17*(4), 471–493.

Filax, G., & Taylor, D. (Eds.). (2014). *Disabled mothers: Stories and scholarship by and about mothers with disabilities.* Bradford, ON: Demeter Press.

Fisher, J. (1980). *The response of social work to the depression.* Boston, MA: G. K. Hall.

Fisher, R., & Shragge, E. (2008). Challenging community organizing. *Journal of Community Practice, 8*(3), 1–9.

Fletcher, B., Jr., & Gapasin, F. (2008). *Solidarity divided: The crisis in organized labor and a new path toward social justice.* Berkeley, CA: University of California Press.

Foley, J. R., & Baker, P. (2009). *Unions, equity, and the path to renewal.* Vancouver, BC: UBC Press.

Fong, L. G. W., & Gibbs, J. T. (1995). Facilitating services to multicultural communities in a dominant culture setting: An organizational perspective. *Administration in Social Work, 19*(2), 1–24.

Fook, J. (2002). *Social Work: Critical Theory and Practice*. London: Sage.

Fook, J. (2003). Critical social work: The current issues. *Qualitative Social Work, 2*, 123–130.

Fook, J. (2012). S*ocial work: A critical approach to practice* (2nd ed.). Los Angeles, CA: Sage.

Fook, J., & Gardner, F. (2007). *Practising critical reflection: A handbook*. New York, NY: McGraw-Hill International.

Foote, C., & Frank, A. (1999). Foucault and therapy: The disciplining of grief. In A. Chambon, A. Irving, & L. Epstein (Eds.), *Reading Foucault for social work* (pp. 157–187). New York, NY: Columbia University Press.

Ford, T. (2004). Queering education from the ground up: Challenges and opportunities for educators. *Canadian Online Journal of Queer Studies in Education, 1*(1), 1–28.

Foucault, M. (1977). *Discipline and punish: The birth of the prison*. New York, NY: Vintage.

Foucault, M. (1991). Governmentality. In G. Burchell, C. Gordon, & P. Miller (Eds.), *The Foucault effect. Studies in governmentality. With two lectures by and an interview with Michel Foucault* (pp. 87–104). Chicago, IL: University of Chicago Press.

Foucault, M. (1994). Subjectivity and truth. In P. Rabinow (Ed.), *Michel Foucault. Ethics, subjectivity and truth. Essential works* (Vol. 1, pp. 87–92). New York, NY: New Press.

Foucault, M. (1997). The ethics of the concern for self as a practice of freedom. In P. Rabinow (Ed.), *Michel Foucault. Ethics: Subjectivity and truth* (pp. 281–302). London: Allen Lane.

Foucault, M. (2008). *The birth of biopolitics. Lectures at the College de France, 1978–1979.* (G. Burchell, Trans.; M. Senellart, Ed.). New York, NY: Palgrave Macmillan.

Fowler, K. (2008). "The wholeness of things": Infusing diversity and social justice into death education. *Omega, 57*(1), 53–91.

Frazee, C. (2014, March 30). A respectful postscript to Edward Fung's end-of-life letter. *Toronto Star*. Retrieved from http://www.thestar.com/opinion/commentary/2014/03/30/a_respectful_postscript_to_edward_hungs_endoflife_letter.html

Freeman, B. (2011). Indigenous pathways to anti-oppressive practice. In D. Baines (Ed.), *Doing anti-oppressive practice: Social justice social work* (2nd ed., pp. 116–131). Halifax, NS: Fernwood Publishing.

Freire, P. (1985). *The politics of education: Culture, power, and liberation*. South Hadley, MA: Bergin and Garvey Publishers.

Freire, P. (1993). *Pedagogy of the oppressed* (20th ed.). New York, NY: Continuum.

Freire, P. (2001). *Pedagogy of the oppressed* (M. B. Ramos, Trans., 30th ed.). New York, NY: Continuum.

Fung, A., & Wright, W. O. (2003). *Deepening democracy: Institutional innovations in empowered participatory governance*. New York, NY: Verso.

Galabuzi, G. E., & Block, S. (2011). *Canada's colour-coded labour market: The gap for racialized workers*. Toronto, ON: Wellesley Institute and Canadian Centre for Policy Alternatives.

Galambos, C., Dulmus, C. N., & Wodarski, J. S. (2005). Principles for organizational change in human service agencies. *Journal of Human Behaviour in the Social Environment, 11*(1), 63–78.

Gandhi, L. (1998). *Postcolonial theory: A critical introduction*. New York, NY: Columbia University Press.

Garavaglia, B. (2007). Avoiding the tendency to medicalize the grieving process: Reconciliation rather than resolution. *Social Work: The New Social Worker Online—Magazine for Social Work Students and Recent Graduates, 17*(4), 1–3.

Garrison, D. R. (1992). Critical thinking and self-directed learning in adult education: An analysis of responsibility and control issues. *Adult Education Quarterly, 2,* 136–148.

Gastil, J., & Levine, P. (2005) *The deliberative democracy handbook: Strategies for effective civic engagement in the twenty-first century.* San Francisco, CA: Jossey Bass.

Gavigan, S. (2006). Equal families, equal parents, equal spouses, equal marriage: The case of the missing patriarch. In S. McIntyre & S. Rogers (Eds.), *Diminishing returns: Inequality and the Canadian Charter of Rights and Freedoms* (pp. 291–316). Toronto, ON: LexisNexis Butterworths.

Gellatly, M. (2015). *Still working on the edge: Building decent jobs from the ground up.* Toronto: Workers Action Centre. Retrieved from http://www.workersactioncentre.org/press-room/policy-papers/

George, P., Coleman, B., & Barnoff, L. (2007). Beyond providing services: Voices of service users on structural social work practice in community-based social service agencies. *Canadian Social Work Review, 24*(1), 5–22.

George, P., & George, J. (2013). Interrogating the neoliberal governmentality of the Old Age Security Act: The case of sponsored immigrant seniors. *Canadian Social Work Review, 30*(1), 65–81.

Gilbert, K. (1996). "We've had the same loss, why don't we have the same grief?" Loss and differential grief in families. *Death Studies, 20*(2), 269–283.

Gilbert, S. (2015, June 12). After marriage equality, isn't gay kinda over? The waning of gay activism. *The Daily Xtra.* Retrieved from http://www.dailyxtra.com/world/news-and-ideas/opinion/marriage-equality-isn%E2%80%99t-gay-kinda-108932

Gilly, B. (2014). Joyous discipline: Native autonomy and culturally conservative two–spirit people. *American Indian Culture and Research Journal, 38*(2), 17–39.

Ginwright, S., & James, T. (2002). From assets to agents of change: Social justice, organizing, and youth development. *New Directions for Youth Development, 96,* 27–46.

Glisson, C. (2007). Assessing and changing organizational culture and climate for effective services. *Research on Social Work Practice, 17*(6), 736–747.

Goldberg, D. T. (1993). *Racist culture.* Cambridge, MA: Blackwell Press.

Goldstein, H. (1990). The knowledge base of social work practice: Theory, wisdom, analogue or art? *Families in Society: The Journal of Contemporary Human Services, 71,* 32–43.

Goldsworthy, K. (2005). Grief and loss theory in social work practice: All changes involve loss, just as all losses require change. *Australian Social Work, 58*(2), 167–178.

Golombek, S. B. (2006). Children as citizens. *Journal of Community Practice, 14*(1–2), 11–30.

Goodley, D. (2011). *Disability studies: An interdisciplinary introduction.* Los Angeles, CA: Sage.

Gorman, R. (2013). Mad nation? Thinking through race, class and mad identity politics. In B. LeFrancois, R. Menzies, & G. Reaume (Eds.), *Mad matters: A critical reader in Canadian Mad studies* (pp. 269–280). Toronto, ON: Canadian Scholars' Press.

Gould, N., & Harris, A. (1996). Student imagery in social work and teacher education: A comparative research approach. *British Journal of Social Work, 26,* 223–238.

Government of Ontario. (2006). *Child Family Services Act.* Retrieved from http://www.e-laws.gov.on.ca/html/statutes/english/elaws_statutes_90c11_e.htm

Government of Ontario. (2012). *Ontario's youth action plan.* Retrieved from http://www.children.gov.on.ca/htdocs/English/documents/youthandthelaw/youthactionplan/yap.pdf

Graham, G., & Megarry, B. (2005). The social care work portfolio: An aid to integrated learning and reflection in social care training. *The Board of Social Work Education, 24*(7), 769–780.

Grainger, R. (1998). Let death be death: Lessons from the Irish wake. *Mortality, 3*(21), 121–141.

Graveline, F. J. (1998). *Circleworks: Transforming Eurocentric consciousness.* Halifax, NS: Fernwood Publishing.

Gray, M. (2005). Dilemmas of international social work: Paradoxical processes in Indigenisation, universalism and imperialism. *International Journal of Social Welfare, 14*(3), 231–238.

Gray, M., & Coates, J. (2010). From "Indigenization" to cultural relevance. In M. Gray, J. Coates, & M. Yellow Bird (Eds.), *Indigenous social work around the world: Towards culturally relevant education and practice* (pp. 13–30). Surrey, UK: Ashgate.

Greenwood, M., & de Leeuw, S. (2007). Teachings from the land: Indigenous people, our health, our land, our children. *Canadian Journal of Native Education, 30*(1), 48–53.

Groce, N. (1985). *Everyone here spoke sign language.* Cambridge, MA: Harvard University Press.

Grue, L., & Laerum, K. (2002). "Doing motherhood": Some experiences of mothers with physical disabilities. *Disability & Society, 17*(6), 671–683.

Guilfoyle, M. (2005). From therapeutic power to resistance? Therapy and cultural hegemony. *Theory and Psychology, 15*(1), 101–124.

Gunderson, K. (2004). *Family group conferencing: Building partnerships with kin in Washington state.* American Humane Association FGDM in brief. Retrieved from http://www.ucdenver.edu/academics/colleges/medicalschool/departments/pediatrics/subs/can/FGDM/Documents/FGDM%20Web%20Pages/Resources/Issue%20Briefs/pc-fgdm-ib-washington-state.pdf

Gustafsson, C., & Fagerberg, I. (2004). Reflection, the way to professional development? *Journal of Clinical Nursing, 13*, 271–280.

Gutierrez, L., & Nagda, B. A. (1996). The multicultural imperative in human service organizations: Issues for the twenty-first century. In P. R. Raffoul & A. McNeece (Eds.), *Future issues for social work practice* (pp. 203–213). Boston, MA: Allyn and Bacon.

Habermas, J. (1996). Three normative models of democracy. In S. Benhabib (Ed.), *Democracy and difference: Contesting the boundaries of the political* (pp. 21–31). Princeton, NJ: Princeton University Press.

Hacking, I. (1999). *The social construction of what?* London: Harvard University Press.

Hacking, I. (2007). Kinds of people: Moving targets. *Proceedings of the British Academy, 151,* 285–318.

Hadad, M. (2008). *The ultimate challenge: Coping with death, dying and bereavement.* Toronto, ON: Nelson Education.

Haffner, B. (2001). Reflective practice. *West African Journal of Nursing, 12*, 42–48.

Halberstam, J. (2005). *In a queer time and place: Transgendered bodies, subcultural lives.* New York, NY: New York University Press.

Hall, S. (1996). When was "the post-colonial"? Thinking at the limit. In I. Chambers & L. Curti (Eds.), *The postcolonial question: Common skies, divided horizons* (pp. 242–260). London: Routledge.

Hall, S. (2005). New Labour's double-shuffle. *Review of Education, Pedagogy, and Cultural Studies, 27*(4), 319–335.

Halton, C., Murphy, M., & Dempsey, M. (2007). Reflective learning in social work education: Researching student experiences. *Reflective Practice, 8*(4), 511–523.

Halvorsen, K. E. (2003). Assessing the effects of public participation. *Public Administration Review, 63*(5), 535–543.

Hamer, H. P. (2011). *Inside the city walls: Mental health service users' journeys towards full citizenship.* (Unpublished doctoral dissertation). University of Auckland, New Zealand.

Hart, B., Sainsbury, P., & Short, S. (1998). Whose dying? A sociological critique of the "good death." *Mortality, 3*(1), 65–77.

Hart, M. A. (2002). *Seeking Mino-Pimatisiwin: An Aboriginal approach to helping.* Halifax, NS: Fernwood Publishing.

Hart, M. A. (2009). Anti-colonial Indigenous social work: Reflections on an Aboriginal approach. In R. Sinclair, M. A. Hart, & G. Bruyere (Eds.), *Wicihitowin: Aboriginal social work in Canada* (pp. 25–41). Halifax, NS: Fernwood Publishing.

Haudenosaunee Confederacy. (n.d.). *What is the Confederacy?* Retrieved from http://www. haudenosauneeconfederacy.com/whatisconfederacy.html

Haug, M. (2001). Combining service delivery and advocacy within humanitarian agencies: Experiences from the conflict in Sri Lanka. *International Working Paper 10.* Retrieved from www.lse.ac.uk/collections/CCS/pdf/iwp10.pdf

Head, B. W. (2011). Why not ask them? Mapping and promoting youth participation. *Children and Youth Services Review, 33*(4), 541–547.

Healy, K. (2005). *Social work theories in context: Creating frameworks for practice.* New York, NY: Palgrave Macmillan.

Hedtke, L. (2003). The origami of remembering. *International Journal of Narrative Therapy and Community Work, 4,* 57–62.

Helland, J. (2005). *FGC literature review.* Victoria, BC: International Institute for Child Rights and Development, University of Victoria.

Henry, F., & Tator, C. (2010). *The colour of democracy.* Toronto, ON: Nelson.

herising, F. (2005). Interrupting positions: Critical thresholds and queer pro/positions. In L. Brown & S. Strega (Eds.), *Research as resistance* (pp. 127–151). Toronto, ON: Canadian Scholars' Press.

Heron, B. (2005). Self-reflection in critical social work practice: Subjectivity and the possibilities of resistance. *Reflective Practice, 6*(3), 341–351.

Hick, S., & Pozzuto, R. (2005). Introduction: Towards "becoming" a critical social worker. In S. Hick, J. Fook, & R. Pozzuto (Eds.), *Social work: A critical turn* (pp. ix–xviii). Toronto, ON: Thompson Educational Publishing.

Hill Collins, P. (2000). It's all in the family: Intersections of gender, race and nation. In U. Narayan & S. Harding (Eds.), *Decentering the centre: Philosophy for a multicultural postcolonial, and feminist world* (pp. 156–176). Indianapolis, IN: Indiana University Press.

Hines, J. M. (2012). Using an anti-oppressive framework in social work practice with lesbians. *Journal of Gay and Lesbian Social Services, 24*(1), 23–39.

Hobson, B. (2003). Introduction. In B. Hobson (Ed.), *Recognition struggles and social movements* (pp. 1–17). Cambridge: Cambridge University Press.

Holley, L. C., Stromwall, L. K., & Bashor, K. H. (2012). Reconceptualizing stigma: Toward a critical anti-oppression paradigm. *Stigma Research and Action, 2*(2), 51–61.

Hollway, W., & Jefferson, T. (2000). *Doing qualitative research differently: Free association, narrative and the interview method.* London: Sage.

hooks, b. (1994). *Teaching to transgress: Education as the practice of freedom.* New York, NY: Routledge.

Houston, A. (2014, March 7). Opinion: What are we really talking about when we talk about "buck-naked men" at the Pride parade? *Toronto Life.* Retrieved from http://www.torontolife. com/informer/toronto-politics/2014/03/07/toronto-pride-sam-sotiropoulos-naked-men/, link no longer active.

Howarth, G. (2000). Dismantling the boundaries between life and death. *Mortality, 5*(2), 127–138.

Hoy, D. C. (2009). *The time of our lives: A critical history of temporality.* Cambridge, MA: MIT Press.

Hull, K. (2001). The political limit of the rights frame: The case of same-sex marriage in Hawaii. *Sociological Perspectives, 44*(2), 207–232.

Hull, K. (2003). The cultural power of law and the cultural enactment of legality: The case of same-sex marriage. *Law and Social Enquiry, 28*(3), 629–657.

Hunter, M. (2013). Race and the same-sex marriage divide. *Contexts, 12*(3), 74–76.

Huntsman, L. (2006). *Literature review: Family group conferencing in a child welfare context.* Centre for Parenting and Research, Funding & Business Analysis Division. NSW, UK.

Hutchinson, D. L. (2001). Identity crisis: Intersectionality, multidimensionality, and the development of an adequate theory of subordination. *Michigan Journal of Race and Law, 6,* 285–316.

Hyde, C. (2003). Multicultural organizational development in nonprofit human service agencies: Views from the field. *Journal of Community Practice, 11*(1), 39–59.

Hyde, C. (2004). Multicultural development in human services agencies: Challenges and solutions. *Social Work, 49*(1), 7–16.

Hyde, C. (2012). Organizational change rationales: Exploring reasons for multicultural development in human service agencies. *Administration in Social Work, 36*(1), 436–456.

Hyde, C., & Hopkins, K. (2004). Diversity climates in human service agencies: An exploratory assessment. *Journal of Ethnic and Cultural Diversity in Social Work, 13*(2), 25–43.

Ife, J. (2012). *Human rights and social work: Towards rights-based practice* (3rd ed.). New York, NY: Cambridge University Press.

Ignatieff, M. (2000). *The rights revolution.* Toronto, ON: House of Anansi Press.

Ingram, R. (2011). *Sanism in theory and practice.* Presentation for Second Annual Critical Inquiries Workshop, Vancouver, British Columbia.

Irving, A. (1994). From image to simulacra: The modern/postmodern divide and social work. In A. Chambon & A. Irving (Eds.), *Essays on postmodernism and social work* (pp. 19–32). Toronto, ON: Canadian Scholars' Press.

Irving, A., & Moffatt, K. (2002). Intoxicated midnights and carnival classrooms. *Radical Pedagogy, 4*(1), 1–14.

Jackson, B. W., & Holvino, E. (1988). *Multicultural organizational development.* (Unpublished paper). Ann Arbor, MI: Program on Conflict Management Alternatives.

James, C. E. (2005). Perspectives in multiculturalism in Canada: Opportunities, limitations and contradictions. In C. E. James (Ed.), *Possibilities and limitations: Multicultural policies and programs in Canada* (pp. 12–20). Winnipeg, MB: Fernwood Publishing.

James, C. E., Este, D., Bernard, W. T., Benjamin, A., Lloyd, B., & Turner, T. (2010). *Race and well-being: The lives, hopes, and activism of African Canadians.* Halifax, NS: Fernwood Publishing.

Jennings, L. B., Parra-Medina, D. M., Hilfinger-Messias, D. K., & McLoughlin, K. (2006). Toward a critical social theory of youth empowerment. *Journal of Community Practice, 14*(1–2), 31–55.

Jessop, B. (2003). From Thatcherism to new labour: Neo-liberalism, workfarism and labour-market regulation. In H. Overbeek (Ed.), *The political economy of European employment: European integration and the transnationalization of the (un)employment question* (pp. 137–153). London: Routledge.

Jindal, P. (2006). Sites of resistance or sites of racism. In M. Bernstein Sycamore (Ed.), *That's revolting: Queer strategies for resisting assimilation* (pp. 23–30). San Francisco, CA: Soft Skull Press.

Johns, C. (2007). *Becoming a reflective practitioner.* Malden, MA: Blackwell.

Johnson, A. (1996). Towards an equitable, efficient, and effective human service system. In C. E. James (Ed.), *Perspectives on racism and the human services sector: A case for change* (pp. 208–221). Toronto, ON: University of Toronto Press.

Johnston, B. (2004). Summative assessment of portfolios: An examination of different approaches to agreement over outcomes. *Studies in Higher Education, 29*(3), 395–412.

Johnston, D. M. (1986). The quest of the Six Nations Confederacy for self-determination. *University of Toronto Faculty Law Review, 44*(1), 1–32.

Johnston, P. (1983). *Aboriginal children and the child welfare system report.* Ottawa, ON: Department of Social Policy Development, Government of Canada.

Jones, E. (2010). Enhancing professionalism through a professional practice portfolio. *Reflective Practice, 11*(5), 593–605.

Jones, L., & Finnegan, D. (2003). Family unity meetings: Decision making and placement outcomes. *Journal of Family Social Work, 7*(4), 23–43.

Jones, P. (2009). Teaching for change in social work: A discipline-based argument for the use of transformative approaches to teaching and learning. *Journal of Transformative Education, 7*(1), 8–25.

Jordan, B. (2006). *Advanced feminist anti-racist anti-oppression organizational change and service delivery training curriculum.* Toronto, ON: Ontario Association of Interval and Transition Houses.

Kalinowski, C., & Risser, P. (2005). *Identifying and overcoming mentalism.* InforMed Health Publishing & Training. Retrieved from http://www.patrisser.com/Mentalism/Mentalism.pdf

Karabanow, J. (2004). Making organizations work: Exploring characteristics of anti-oppressive organizational structures in street youth shelters. *Journal of Social Work, 4*(1), 47–60.

Kear, M., & Bear, M. (2007). Using portfolio evaluation for program outcome assessment. *Journal of Nursing Education, 46*(3), 109–114.

Kellehear, A. (2007). The end of death in late modernity: An emerging public health challenge. *Critical Public Health, 17*(1), 71–79.

Kelly, C. (2010). Wrestling with group identity: Disability activism and direct funding. *Disability Studies Quarterly, 30*(3/4). Retrieved from http://dsq-sds.org/article/view/1279/1307

Kennedy, D. (2002). The critique of rights in critical legal studies. In W. Brown & J. Halley (Eds.), *Left legalism/left critique* (pp. 178–228). Durham, NC: Duke University Press.

Kennedy, B. (2010). Police knew of mental illness before fatal shooting, family says. *Toronto Star.* Retrieved from https://www.thestar.com/news/gta/2010/08/31/police_knew_of_mental_illness_before_fatal_shooting_family_says.html

Kerman, B., Freundlich, M., Lee, J. M., & Brenner, E. (2012). Learning while doing in the human services: Becoming a learning organization through organizational change. *Administration in Social Work, 36*(1), 234–257.

Khosla, P. (2014). *Working women, working poor.* Toronto: Women and Work Research Group and Toronto & York Region Labour Council.

Killian, M. L. (2010). The political is personal: Relationship recognition policies in the United States and their impact on services for LGBT people. *Journal of Gay and Lesbian Social Services, 22*, 9–21.

King, C. S., Feltey, K. M., & Susel, B. (1998). The question of participation: Toward authentic public participation in public administration. *Public Administration Review, 58*, 317–326.

King, T. (2003). *The truth about stories.* Toronto, ON: House of Anansi Press.

Kinney, E., & Merkel-Holguin, L. (2013). *Dads and paternal relatives: Using FGDM to refocus child welfare on the entire family constellation.* Retrieved from http://www.casaforchildren.org/site/c.mtJSJ7MPIsE/b.5547515/k.C805/Using_Family_Group_Decision_Making_to_Refocus_the_Child_Welfare_System_on_the_Entire_Family_Constellation.htm

Klarman, M. (2013). *From the closet to the altar: Courts, backlash, and the struggle for same sex marriage.* Don Mills, ON: Oxford University Press.

Knowles, M. (1975). *Self-directed learning: A guide for learners and teachers.* New York, NY: Cambridge Books.

Knowles, M. (1978). *The adult learner: A neglected species.* London: Gulf Publishing.

Knowles, M. (1980). *The modern practice of adult education: From pedagogy to andragogy.* New York, NY: Cambridge.

Kolb, D. A. (1984). *Experiential learning as the source of learning and development.* Englewood Cliffs, NJ: Prentice Hall.

Kolb, A. Y., & Kolb, D. A. (2005). Learning styles and learning spaces: Enhancing experiential learning in higher education. *Academy of Management Learning and Education, 4*(2), 193–212.

Kolb, A. Y., & Kolb, D. A. (2006). A review of multidisciplinary application of experiential learning theory in higher education. In R. Sims & S. Sims (Eds.), *Learning styles and learning: A key to meeting the accountability demands in education* (pp. 45–91). Hauppauge, NY: Nova Publishers.

Kumar, P., & Schenk, C. (Eds.). (2006). *Paths to union renewal: Canadian experiences.* Toronto, ON: University of Toronto Press.

Kundouqk [Thomas, J.] & Qwul'sih'yah'maht [Green, R.]. (2009). Children in the centre: Indigenous perspectives on anti-oppressive child welfare practice. In S. Strega & S. A. Esquao [J. Carriére] (Eds.), *Walking this path together: Antiracist and anti-oppressive child welfare practice* (pp. 29–44). Halifax, NS: Fernwood.

Laforest, R. (2004). Governance and the voluntary sector: Rethinking the contours of advocacy. *International Journal of Canadian Studies, 30,* 185–204.

Laforest, R., & Orsini, M. (2005). Evidence-based engagement in the voluntary sector: Lessons from Canada. *Social Policy & Administration, 39*(5), pp. 481–497.

Lahey, K. (1999). *Are we "persons" yet? Law and sexuality in Canada.* Toronto, ON: University of Toronto Press.

Lahey, K. (2010). Same-sex marriage, transnational activism, and international law: Strategic objectives beyond freedom to marry. *American Society of International Law Annual Proceedings, 104,* 380–383.

Langley, J. (2001). Developing anti-oppressive empowering social work practice with older lesbians and gay men. *British Journal of Social Work, 31*(6), 917–932.

Large, M., & Ryan, C. J. (2012). Sanism, stigma and the belief in dangerousness. *Australian New Zealand Journal of Psychiatry, 46*(11), 1099–1103.

Larner, W. (2000). Neo-liberalism: Policy, ideology, governmentality. *Studies in Political Economy, 63,* 5–25.

LaRocque, E. (2001). The colonization of a Native woman scholar. In C. Miller, P. Churchhryk, M. Smallface, M. B. Manyfingers, & B. Deering (Eds.), *Women of the First Nations: Power, wisdom, and strength* (pp. 11–18). Winnipeg, MB: University of Manitoba Press.

LaRocque, S. (2006). *Gay marriage: The story of a Canadian social revolution.* Toronto, ON: James Lorimer & Company.

La Rose, T. (2009). One small revolution: Unionization, community practice, and workload in child welfare. *Journal of Community Practice, 17*(1–2), 223–246.

Larson, G. (2008). Anti-oppressive practice in mental health. *Journal of Progressive Human Services, 19*(1), 39–54.

Latour, B. (2004). Why has critique run out of steam? From matters of fact to matters of concern. *Critical Inquiry, 30,* 225–248.

Lavallée, L. (2008). Balancing the Medicine Wheel through physical activity. *Journal of Aboriginal Health, 4*(1). Retrieved from hhttp://www.naho.ca/jah/english/jah04_01/09 MedicineWheel_64-71.pdf

Lavallée, L., & Poole, J. M. (2010). Beyond recovery: Colonization, health and healing for Indigenous people in Canada. *International Journal of Mental Health and Addiction, 8*(2), 271–281.

Lawrence, B., & Dua, E. (2005). Decolonizing antiracism. *Social Justice, 32*(4), 120–143.

Leckey, R. (2014). Must equal mean identical? Same-sex couples and marriage. *International Journal of Law in Context, 10*(1), 5–25.

LeFrancois, B. A. (2011). Supporting positive relationships in families where fathers suffer with mental distress. *Critical Social Work, 12*(1), 2–12.

LeFrancois, B. A. (2013). Queering child and adolescent mental health services: The subversion of heteronormativity in practice. *Children & Society, 27*(1), 1–12.

LeFrancois, B. A., Menzies, R., & Reaume, G. (Eds.). (2013). *Mad matters: A critical reader in Canadian Mad Studies.* Toronto, ON: Canadian Scholars' Press.

Lehr, V. (1999). *Queer family values: Debunking the myth of the nuclear family.* Philadelphia, PA: Temple University Press.

Lemay, R. (1999). *Roles, identities, and expectancies: Positive contributions to normalization and social role valorization.* Retrieved from http://socialrolevalorization.com/images/documents/Articles-resources/Lemay1999RolesExpectanciesAndSRV.pdf

Lemke, T. (2011). *Foucault, governmentality & critique.* London: Paradigm Publishers.

Leonard, P. (1994). Knowledge/power and postmodernism: Implications for the practice of a critical social work education. *Canadian Social Work Review, 11*(1), 11–26.

Liasidou, A. (2014). The cross-fertilization of critical race theory and disability studies; points of convergence/divergence and some education policy implications. *Disability & Society, 29*(5), 724–737.

Liddiard, K. (2014). The work of disabled identities in intimate relationships. *Disability & Society, 29*(1), 115–128.

Lindeman, E. (1980). Group work and democracy—A philosophical note. In A. Alissi (Ed.), *Perspectives on social group work practice* (pp. 77–82). New York, NY: The Free Press.

Linton, S. (2010). Reassigning meaning. In L. J. Davis (Ed.), *The disability studies reader* (3rd ed., pp. 223–236). New York, NY: Routledge.

Lockwood, S., Walker, C. A., & Tilley, D. S. (2009). Faculty perceptions of an accelerated baccalaureate nursing program. *Journal of Nursing Education, 48*(7), 406–410.

Longmore, P. K. (2003). Elizabeth Bouvia, assisted suicide and social prejudice. In *Why I burned my book and other essays on disability* (pp. 149–174). Philadelphia, PA: Temple University Press.

Lopes, T., & Thomas, B. (2006). *Dancing on live embers: Challenging racism in organizations.* Toronto, ON: Between the Lines Publishing.

Lorde, A. (1984). *Sister outsider: Essays and speeches.* Trumansburg, NY: Crossing Press.

Loughran, J. (2002). Effective reflective practice: In search of meaning in learning about teaching. *Journal of Teacher Education, 53*(1), 33–43.

Love, C. (2002). *Maori perspectives on collaboration and colonization in contemporary Aotearoa/New Zealand child and family welfare policies and practices.* Policy and Partnerships Conference, Wilfrid Laurier University, Waterloo, ON.

Lowndes, V., Pratchett, L., & Stoker, G. (2001). Trends in public participation: Part 2—citizens' perspectives. *Public Administration, 79*(2), 445–455.

Lucardie, R., & Sobsey, D. (2005). Portrayals of people with cerebral palsy in homicide news. *Developmental Disabilities Bulletin, 33*(1), 99–128.

Luchies, T. (2014). Anti-oppression as pedagogy; prefiguration as praxis. *Interface, 6*, 99–129.

Luluquisen, E. M., Trinidad, A. M. O., & Ghosh, D. (2006). Sariling Gawa youth council as a case study of youth leadership development in Hawai'i. *Journal of Community Practice*, *14*(1–2), 57–70.

Lundy, C. (2004). *Social work and social justice*. Toronto, ON: University of Toronto Press.

Lundy, C. (2011). *Social work, social justice and human rights: A structural approach to practice* (2nd ed.). Toronto, ON: University of Toronto Press.

Lupton, D. (1998). Going with the flow: Some central discourses in conceptualizing and articulating the embodiment of emotional states. In S. Nettleton & J. Watson (Eds.), *The body in everyday life* (pp. 82–100). London: Routledge.

Lyon, M., & Barbalet, J. (1994). Society's body: Emotion and the "somatization" of social theory. In T. Csordas (Ed.), *Embodiment and experience: The existential ground of culture and self* (pp. 48–68). Cambridge, MA: Cambridge University Press.

Maccormack, P. (2006). The great ephemeral tattooed skin. *Body & Society, 12*(2), 57–82.

MacKinnon, M., Pitre, S., & Watling, J. (2007). *Matching methods with policy purpose: Two case examples of public engagement*. Ottawa, ON: Canadian Policy Research Network.

Majury, D. (2002). The Charter, equality rights, and women: Equivocation and celebration. *Osgoode Hall Law Journal, 40*, 297–336.

Malacrida, C. (2009). Performing motherhood in a disablist world: Dilemmas of motherhood, femininity and disability. *International Journal of Qualitative Studies in Education, 22*(1), 99–117.

Malacrida, C. (2015). *A special hell: Institutional life in Alberta's eugenic years*. Toronto, ON: University of Toronto Press.

Malone, A. (2014). Ideal motherhood and surveillance: Young mothers with intellectual disabilities share their stories. In G. Filax & D. Taylor (Eds.), *Disabled mothers: Stories and scholarship by and about mothers with disabilities* (pp. 195–213). Bradford, ON: Demeter Press.

Mann, S., Byrnes, T., Power, C., Rich, M., & Winifreyda, A. (1999). Rhetoric to practice: The challenge of collaboration of academe and industry. *Journal of Nursing Education, 28*(1), 5–9.

Manuel, G., & Posluns, M. (1974). *The fourth world: An Indian reality*. New York, NY: Collier Macmillan Canada.

Marsh, P., & Crow, G. (2000). Conferencing in England and Wales. In G. Burford & J. Hudson (Eds.), *Family group conferencing: New directions in community-centered child and family practice* (pp. 206–217). New York, NY: Aldine De Gruyter.

Martinez, K. M., Green, C. E., & Sanudo, F. M. (2004). The CLAS challenge: Promoting culturally and linguistically appropriate services in health care. *International Journal of Public Administration, 27*(1–2), 39–61.

MASS LBP. (2008). *Profile*. Retrieved from http://www.masslbp.com/profile.php

Matsuda, M. (1995). Looking to the bottom: Critical legal studies and reparations. In K. Crenshaw, N. Gotanda, G. Peller, & T. Kendall (Eds.), *Critical race theory: The key writings that informed the movement* (pp. 63–79). New York, NY: The New Press.

Maurer, S. (2007). Thinking governmentality "from below": Social work and social movements as (collective) actors in movable/mobile orders. In M. A. Peters & T. A. C. Besley (Eds.), *Why Foucault: New directions in educational research* (pp. 125–137). New York, NY: Peter Lang.

May, K. (2014, August 27) Federal government on track to cut 35,000 public services jobs. *Ottawa Citizen*. Retrieved from http://ottawacitizen.com/news/national/federal-government-on-track-to-cut-35000-public-service-jobs

McBride-Johnson, H. (2003, February 16). Unspeakable conversations: Or how I spent one day as a token cripple at Princeton University. *New York Times Magazine*, 51–55, 74, 78–79.

McDonald, C. (2006). *Challenging social work: The institutional context of practice*. Basingstoke, UK: Palgrave Macmillan.

McIvor, S. D. (2004). Aboriginal women unmasked: Using equality litigation to advance women's rights. *Canadian Journal of Women and the Law, 16*, 106–136.

McKee, K. (2009). Post-Foucauldian governmentality: What does it offer critical social policy analysis? *Critical Social Policy, 29*(3), 465–486.

McLaughlin, K. (2005). From ridicule to institutionalization: Anti-oppression, the state and social work. *Critical Social Policy, 25*(3), 283–305.

McMullan, M., Endacott, R., Gray, M. A., Jasper, M., Miller, C. M., Scholes, J., & Webb, C. (2003). Portfolios and assessment of competence: A review of the literature. *Journal of advanced nursing, 41*(3), 283–294.

McRuer, R. (2003). As good as it gets: Queer theory and critical disability. *A Journal of Lesbian and Gay Studies, 9*, 79–105.

Mederos, F., & Woldeguiorguis, I. (2003). Beyond cultural competence: What child protection managers need to know and do. *Child Welfare, 82*(2), 125–142.

Memmi, A. (1991). *The colonizer and the colonized*. Boston, MA: Beacon Press.

Mercer, C., & Picard, S. (2011). Intellectual disability and homelessness. *Journal of Intellectual Disability Research, 55*(4), 441–449.

Merkel-Holguin, L. (2004). Sharing power with the people: FGC as a democratic experiment. *Journal of Sociology and Social Welfare, 31*(1), 155–173.

Merkel-Holguin, L., Nixon, P., & Burford, G. (2003). Learning with families: A synopsis of FGDM research and evaluation in child welfare. *Protecting Children, 18*(1–2), 2–11.

Meyer, M. (2008). Indigenous knowledge featured speakers. In M. P. Kumar (Ed.), *Seeing ourselves in the mirror: Giving life to learning. Executive summary and highlights* (pp. 30–33). University of Saskatchewan, Aboriginal Education Research Centre, Saskatoon, SK, and First Nations and Adult Higher Education Consortium, Calgary, AB. Retrieved from https://www.eboulearning.com/ccl/ablkc/AbLKCConf2008_Mar302009_SUMMARY_EN.pdf

Mezirow, J. (1991). *Transformative dimensions of adult learning*. San Francisco, CA: Jossey-Bass.

Mfoafo-M'Carthy, M. (2010). *Experience is the best teacher. Community treatment orders (CTOs) among ethno-racial minority communities in Toronto*. (Doctoral dissertation). Retrieved from University of Toronto. http://hdl.handle.net/1807/26490

Mfoafo-M'Carthy, M., & Williams, C.C. (2010). Coercion and community treatment orders (CTOs): One step forward, two steps back? *Canadian Journal of Community Mental Health, 29*(1), 69–80.

Midgley, J. (1999). Growth, redistribution, and welfare: Toward social investment. *Social Service Review, 73*(1), 3–21.

Midgley, J. (2014). *Social development: Theory & practice*. Los Angeles: Sage Publications.

Mifflin, M. (1997). *Bodies of subversion: A secret history of women and tattoo*. New York, NY: Juno.

Milkman, R. (2012). Immigrant workers, precarious work, and the US labour movement. In R. Munck, C. Schierup, & R. D. Wise (Eds.), *Migration, work and citizenship in the new global order* (pp. 113–124). New York, NY: Routledge.

Miller, P., & Rose, N. (2008). *Governing the present*. Cambridge, MA: Polity Press.

Mills, C. (2014). *Decolonizing global mental health: The psychiatrization of the majority world*. New York, NY: Routledge.

Minors, A. (1996). From uni-versity to poly-versity: Organizations in transition to anti-racism. In C. E. James (Ed.), *Perspectives on racism and the human services sector: A case for change* (pp. 196–208). Toronto, ON: University of Toronto Press.

Modesti, S. (2008). Home sweet home: Tattoo parlors as postmodern spaces of agency. *Western Journal of Communication, 72*(3), 197–212.

Moffatt, K. (1999). Surveillance and government of the welfare recipient. In A. Chambon, A. Irving, & L. Epstein (Eds.), *Reading Foucault for social work* (pp. 219–245). New York, NY: Columbia University Press.

Moffatt, K., Barnoff, L., George, P., & Coleman, B. (2009). Process as labour: Struggles for anti-oppressive/anti-racist change in a feminist organization. *Canadian Review of Social Policy, 62*(1), 34–54.

Monture-Angus, P. (1999). *Journeying forward: Dreaming First Nations independence.* Halifax, NS: Fernwood Publishing.

Morgaine, K., & Capous-Desyllas, M. (2015). *Anti-oppressive social work practice: Putting theory into action.* Los Angeles, CA: Sage.

Morley, C. (2008). Teaching critical practice: Resisting structural domination through critical reflection. *Social Work Education, 27*(4), 407–421.

Morris, J. (2001). Impairment and disability: Constructing an ethics of care that promotes human rights. *Hypatia, 16*(4), 1–16.

Mullaly, B. (2001). Confronting the politics of despair: Toward the reconstruction of progressive social work in a global economy and postmodern age. *Social Work Education, 20*(3), 303–319.

Mullaly, B. (2002). *Challenging oppression: A critical social work approach.* Don Mills, ON: Oxford University Press.

Mullaly, B. (2010). *Challenging oppression and confronting privilege* (2nd ed.). Don Mills, ON: Oxford University Press.

Murray, D. (2014). Real queer: "Authentic" LGBT refugee claimants and homonationalism in the Canadian refugee system. *Anthropologica, 56*(1), 21–32.

Murray, K., Low, J., & Waite, A. (2006). The voluntary sector and the realignment of government: A street-level study. *Canadian Public Administration, 49*(3), 375–393.

Murray, K. B. (2007). Governmentality and the shifting winds of policy studies. In M. Orsini & M. Smith (Eds.), *Critical policy studies* (pp. 161–184). Vancouver, BC: UBC Press.

Nairn, K., Sligo, J., & Freeman, C. (2006). Polarizing participation in local government: Which young people are included and excluded? *Children, Youth and Environments, 16*(2), 248–271.

Nangwaya, A. (2013). Fact sheet on police violence against the African community in Canada. *Toronto Media Co-op.* Retrieved from http://toronto.mediacoop.ca/blog/ajamu-nangwaya/18378

Nash, K. (2005). Human rights culture: Solidarity, diversity and the right to be different. *Citizenship Studies, 9*(4), 335–348.

Neimeyer, R. (2005/2006). Defining the new abnormal: Scientific and social construction of complicated grief. *Omega, 52*(1), 95–97.

Nettleton, S., & Watson, J. (1998). *The body in everyday life.* London: Routledge.

Ng, W. W. (2012) Pedagogy of solidarity: Educating for an interracial working class movement. *Journal of Workplace Learning, 24*(7/8), 528–537.

Nixon, P., Burford, G., Quinn, A., & Edelbaum, J. (2005). *A survey of international practices, policy and research on family group conferencing and related practices.* American Humane Association. Retrieved from http://www.americanhumane.org/assets/pdfs/children/fgdm/pc-fgdm-practices-survey.pdf, link no longer active.

Nybell, L. M., & Gray, S. S. (2004). Race, place, space: Meanings of cultural competence in three child welfare agencies. *Social Work, 49*(1), 17–26.

O'Donoghue, J. L., Kirshner, B., & McLaughlin, M. (2002). Introduction: Moving youth participation forward. *New Directions for Youth Development, 96,* 15–26.

O'Flynn, M. (2012). Capital accumulation and the historical decline of liberal individualism. *Critical Sociology, 39*(4), 493–509.

Office of the Auditor General of Ontario. (2006). *Reports on value for money (vfm) audits.* Retrieved from http://www.auditor.on.ca/en/content/annualreports/arreports/en06/302en06.pdf

Oliver, M. (1990). *The politics of disablement.* Basingstoke, UK: Macmillan.

Onishenko, D. (n.d.). *Equal rights discourse: A shifting terrain for sexual minority refugee claimants.* (Unpublished manuscript).

Onishenko, D., & Caragata, L. (2010). A theoretically critical gaze on the Canadian equal marriage debate: Breaking the binaries. *Journal of Gay and Lesbian Social Services, 21*(2/3), 91–111.

Ontario Association of Children's Aid Societies. (2008). *Child in care fact sheets.* Toronto, ON: Author.

Ontario Association of Social Workers. (2005a). *Role of social work in primary care—family health teams. Role statement.* Retrieved from http://www.oasw.org/membersite/pdfs/OASWPrimaryHealthCare-FHT-2005.pdf, link no longer active.

Ontario Association of Social Workers. (2005b). *Ontario Association of Social Workers (OASW) response to the review of the Child and Family Services Act.* Retrieved from http://www.oasw.org/en/membersite/pdfs/OASWResponseReviewC&FSAct-2005.pdf, link no longer active.

Ontario Ministry of Health and Long-Term Care. (2005, December 9). *McGuinty government announces creation of 31 new family health teams.* Retrieved from https://news.ontario.ca/archive/en/2005/12/09/McGuinty-Government-Announces-Creation-of-31-New-Family-Health-Teams.html

Ontario Ministry of Health and Long-Term Care. (2016). Family health teams. Retrieved from http://www.health.gov.on.ca/en/pro/programs/fht/

Osburn, J. (2006). An overview of social role valorization. *Social Role Valorization Journal, 1*(1), 4–13.

Osterman, P. L., Asselin, M. E., & Cullen, H. A. (2009). Returning for a baccalaureate: A descriptive exploratory study of nurses' perceptions. *Journal for Nurses in Professional Development, 25*(3), 109–117.

Palys, T. (2008). Purposive sampling. In L. Given (Ed.), *The Sage encyclopedia of qualitative research methods* (pp. 698–699). Thousand Oaks, CA: Sage.

Parada, H. (2004). Social work practices within the restructured child welfare system in Ontario: An institutional ethnography. *Canadian Social Work Review, 21*(1), 67–86.

Parks, C. (2010). A window illuminating the reservations of black men who have sex with men in fully embracing the institution of same-sex marriage. *Journal of Gay and Lesbian Social Services, 22,* 132–148.

Paterson, B. L., & Panessa, C. (2008). Engagement as an ethical imperative in harm reduction involving at-risk youth. *International Journal of Drug Policy, 19*(1), 24–32.

Patterson, C., Crooks, D., & Lunyk-Child, O. (2002). A new perspective on competencies for self-directed learning. *Journal of Nursing Education, 41*(1), 25–31.

Payne, M. (2005). *Modern social work theory* (2nd ed.). Chicago, IL: Lyceum.

Pearson, D. J., & Heywood, P. (2004). Portfolio use in general practice vocational training: A survey of GP registrars. *Medical Education, 38*(1), 87–95.

Peck, J. (2010). *Constructions of neoliberal reasoning.* Oxford: Oxford University Press.

Peck, J., & Tickell, A. (2002). Neoliberalizing space. *Antipode, 34*(3), 380–404.

Pender-Greene, M. (2007). Beyond diversity and multiculturalism: Towards the development of anti-racist institutions and leaders. *Journal for Nonprofit Management, 11*(1), 9–17.

Penna, S. (2004). Policy contexts of social work: "New" labour and the "new legal regime." *Social Work and Society, 1*(1), 1–19.

Pennell, J. (2005). Collaborative planning and ongoing training. In J. Pennell & G. Anderson (Eds.), *Widening the circle: The practice and evaluation of family group conferencing with children, youth, and their families* (pp. 73–87). Washington, DC: NASW Press.

Pennell, J. (2009). Widening the circle: Countering institutional racism in child welfare. In S. Strega & S. A. Esquao [J. Carriére] (Eds.), *Walking this path together: Antiracist and anti-oppressive child welfare practice* (pp. 78–92). Halifax, NS: Fernwood Publishing.

Perlin, M. L. (1992). On "sanism." *SMUL Review, 46,* 373–407.

Phillips, A. (2003). Recognition and the struggle for political voice. In B. Hobson (Ed.), *Recognition struggles and social movements: Contested identities* (pp. 263–273). Cambridge, MA: Cambridge University Press.

Phillips, C. B. (2009). Student portfolios and the hidden curriculum on gender: Mapping exclusion. *Medical Education, 43,* 847–853.

Phillips, S. D., & Orsini, M. (2002). *Mapping the links: Citizen involvement in the policy processes.* Retrieved from http://www.cprn.org/documents/11418_en.pdf

Pierson, M., & Kumari, S. (2000). Web-based student portfolios in a graduate instructional technology program. In D. Willis, J. Price, & J. Willis (Eds.), *Proceedings of Society for Information Technology & Teacher Education International Conference 2000* (pp. 1117–1121). Chesapeake, VA: Association for the Advancement of Computing in Education (AACE).

Ping, W. (2000). *Aching for beauty: Footbinding in China.* Minneapolis, MN: University of Minnesota Press.

Pink News. (2013, February). Organisation proposes replacing the "limiting" term LGBT with "more inclusive" GSD. Retrieved from http://www.pinknews.co.uk/2013/02/25/organisation-proposes-replacing-the-limiting-term-lgbt-with-more-inclusive-gsd/

Pollack, S. (2004). Anti-oppressive social work practice with women in prison: Discursive reconstructions and alternative practices. *British Journal of Social Work, 34*(1), 693–707.

Pon, G. (2009). Cultural competency as a new racism: Ontology for forgetting. *Journal of Progressive Human Services, 20*(1), 59–71.

Pon, G., Gosine, K., & Phillips, D. (2011). Immediate response: Addressing anti-Native and anti-Black racism in child welfare. *International Journal of Child, Youth and Family Studies, 3 & 4,* 385–409.

Poole, J. (2011). *Behind the rhetoric: Mental health recovery in Ontario.* Halifax, NS: Fernwood Publishing.

Poole, J. (2013). *On sanism.* Talk at the 2013 TEDxRyersonU event, November 25, 2013. Metro Toronto Reference Library, Toronto.

Poole, J. M., Jivraj, T., Arslanian, A., Bellows, K., Chiasson, S., Hakimy, H. & Reid, J. (2012). Sanism, "mental health," and social work/education: A review and call to action. *Intersectionalities: A Global Journal of Social Work Analysis, Research, Polity, and Practice, 1,* 20–36.

Poole, J., & Ward, J. (2013). Breaking open the bone: Storying, sanism and mad grief. In B. LeFrancois, R. Menzies, & G. Reaume (Eds.), *Mad matters: A critical reader in Canadian Mad studies* (pp. 94–104). Toronto, ON: Canadian Scholars' Press.

Porter, B. (2006). Expectations of equality. In S. McIntyre & S. Rogers (Eds.), *Diminishing returns: Inequality and the Canadian Charter of Rights and Freedoms* (pp. 23–44). Toronto, ON: LexisNexis Butterworths.

Pothier, D., & Devlin, R. (Eds.). (2006). *Critical disability theory: Essays in philosophy, politics, and law.* Vancouver, BC: UBC Press

Potter, C. C., & East, J. F. (2000). Developing reflective judgment through MSW education. *Journal of Teaching in Social Work, 20*(1–2), 217–237.

Potts, A. (2014, April 9). Bill to mandate gay-straight alliances in all schools fails in Alberta Canada. *GayStarNews.* Retrieved from http://www.gaystarnews.com/article/bill-mandate-gay-straight-alliances-all-schools-fails-alberta-canada090414

Powell, J. (2002). The changing conditions of social work research. *British Journal of Social Work, 32,* 17–33.

Prilleltensky, I. (2003). Understanding, resisting, and overcoming oppression: Toward psychopolitical validity. *American Journal of Community Psychology, 31*(1–2), 195–201.

Race, D. (1999). *Social role valorization and the English experience.* London: Whitehall & Birch.

Rankin, J., Rushowy, K., & Brown, L. (2013, March 22). Toronto school suspension rates highest for Black and Aboriginal students. *Toronto Star.* Retrieved from http://www.thestar.com/news/gta/2013/03/22/toronto_school_suspension_rates_highest_for_black_and_aboriginal_students.html

Rautkis, M. E., McCarthy, S., Krackhardt, D., & Cahalane, H. (2010). Innovation in child welfare: The adoption and implementation of family group decision making in Pennsylvania. *Children and Youth Services Review, 32*(5), 732–739.

Razack, N. (2000). North/South collaborations: Affecting transnational perspectives for social work. *Journal of Progressive Human Services, 11*(1), 71–91.

Razack, N. (2002). *Transforming the field: Critical antiracist and anti-oppressive perspectives for the human services practicum.* Halifax, NS: Fernwood Publishing.

Reaume, G. (2009). *Remembrance of patients past: Patient life in the Toronto Hospital for the Insane, 1870–1940.* Don Mills, ON: Oxford University Press.

Rehaag, S. (2008). Patrolling the borders of sexual orientation: Bisexual refugee claims in Canada. *McGill Law Journal, 53*(1), 59–102.

Reeves, T., & Reeves, P. (1997). Effective dimensions of interactive learning on the world wide web. In B. Khan (Ed.), *Web-based instruction* (pp. 59–66). Englewood Cliffs, NJ: Educational Technology Publications.

Reichert, E. (2011). *Social work and human rights: A foundation for policy and practice* (2nd ed.). New York, NY: Columbia University Press.

Reid, J., & Poole, J. (2013). Mad students in the social work classroom? Notes from the beginnings of an inquiry. *Journal of Progressive Human Services, 24*(3), 209–222.

Reid, M. (2009). Kaxlaya Gvila: Upholding traditional Heiltsuk laws, values and practices as Aboriginal people and allies. In R. Sinclair, M. A. Hart, & G. Bruyere (Eds.), *Wicihitowin: Aboriginal social work in Canada* (pp. 200–221). Halifax, NS: Fernwood Publishing.

Reimer, E. (2003). A reasonable grief: Discursive constructions of grief in a public conversation on raising the shipwrecked *M/S Estonia. Mortality, 8*(4), 325–341.

Rice-Green, J., & Dumbrill, G. C. (2005). A child welfare course for Aboriginal and non-Aboriginal students: Pedagogical and technical challenges. *Journal of Technology in Human Services, 23*(3/4), 167–181.

Robinson, B. A. (2004). *Same-sex marriage: Canadian public opinion polls 2003 to now.* Retrieved from http://www.religioustolerance.org/hom_maro.htm

Rogers, G., Finley, D. S., & Galloway, J. R. (2001). *Strategic planning in social services organizations: A practical guide*. Toronto, ON: Canadian Scholars' Press.

Roithmayr, D. (2001). Left over rights. *Cardozo Law Review, 22*, 1113–1134.

Rossiter, A. (2001). Innocence lost or suspicion found: Do we educate for or against social work? *Critical Social Work, 2*(1). Retrieved from http://www1.uwindsor.ca/criticalsocialwork/

Rossiter, A. (2005). Discourse analysis in critical social work: From apology to question. *Critical Social Work, 6*(1). Retrieved from http://www1.uwindsor.ca/criticalsocialwork/

Royal Commission on Aboriginal Peoples (RCAP). (1996). *Report of the Royal Commission on Aboriginal Peoples* (Vol. 1). Ottawa, ON: Supply and Services Canada.

Ruch, G. (2000). Self and social work: Towards an integrated model of learning. *Journal of Social Work Practice, 14*(2), 99–112.

Ruch, G. (2002). From triangle to spiral: Reflective practice in social work education, practice and research. *Social Work Education, 21*(2), 199–216.

Ruland, J. P., & Ahern, N. R. (2007). Transforming student perspectives through reflective writing. *Nursing Educator, 32*, 81–88.

Ruth-Sahd, L. (2003). Reflective practice: A critical analysis of data-based studies and implications for nursing education. *Journal of Nursing Education, 42*(11), 488–497.

Rutter, D., Manley, C., Weaver, T., Crawford, M. J., & Fulop, N. (2004). Patients or partners? Case studies of user involvement in the planning and delivery of adult mental health services in London. *Social Science & Medicine, 58*(10), 1973–1984.

Said, E. (1978). *Orientalism*. New York, NY: Pantheon.

Sakamoto, I. (2007). A critical examination of immigrant acculturation: Toward an anti-oppressive social work model with immigrant adults in a pluralistic society. *British Journal of Social Work, 37*(1), 515–535.

Sakamoto, I., & Pitner, R. O. (2005). Use of critical consciousness in anti-oppressive social work practice: Disentangling power dynamics at personal and structural levels. *British Journal of Social Work, 35*(4), 435–452.

Sandahl, C. (2003). Queering the crip or cripping the queer? Intersections of queer and crip identities. *GLQ: A Journal of Lesbian and Gay Studies, 9*(1–2), 25–56.

Sandau-Beckler, P., Salcido, R., Beckley, M.J., Mannes, M., & Beck, M. (2002). Infusing family-centered values into child protection practice. *Children and Youth Services Review, 24*, 719–741.

Sanders, D. (1994). Constructing lesbian and gay and lesbian rights. *Canadian Journal of Law and Society, 9*(2), 99–143.

Sanders, D. (1996). Getting gay and lesbian issues on the international agenda. *Human Rights Quarterly, 18*(1), 67–106.

San Martin, R. M., & Barnoff, L. (2004). Let them howl: The operations of imperial subjectivity and the politics of race in one feminist organization. *Atlantis: A Women's Studies Journal, 29*(1), 77–84.

Sayce, L. (1998). Stigma, discrimination and social exclusion: What's in a word? *Journal of Mental Health, 7*(4), 331–343.

Scanlon, E., & Harding, S. (2005). Social work and labor unions: Historical and contemporary alliances. *Journal of Community Practice, 13*(1), 9–30.

Schatz, M. C. S. (2004). Using portfolios: Integrating learning and promoting for social work students. *Advances in Social Work, 5*(1), 105–123.

Schmid, J., & Goranson, S. (2003). An evaluation of family group conferencing in Toronto. *Protecting Children, 15*(1–2), 110–112.

Schmid, J., & Pollack, S. (2004). Family group conferencing. A mechanism for empowerment. *Canadian Review of Social Policy, 54*, 128–134.

Schön, D. (1983). *The reflective practitioner: How professionals think in action.* New York, NY: Basic Books.

Schön, D. (1991). *The reflective turn: Case in and on educational practice.* New York, NY: Teachers College Press.

Schramm-Pate, S. L., & Lussier, R. (2003–2004). Teaching students how to think critically: The Confederate flag controversy in the high school social studies classroom. *High School Journal, 87*(2), 56–65.

Schwartz, D. (2012, May 30). "Gay-straight alliance" name forces debate in Ontario: Roman Catholic archbishop opposes requiring GSA name. *CBC News Canada.* Retrieved from http://www.cbc.ca/news/canada/gay-straight-alliance-name-forces-debate-in-ontario-1.1188147

Scourfield, P. (2007). Social care and the modern citizen: Client, consumer, service users, manager and entrepreneur. *British Journal of Social Work, 37,* 107–122.

Sennett, R. (1998). *The corrosion of character: The personal consequences of work in the new capitalism.* London: W. W. Norton.

Shaheen Shaikh, S. (2012). Antiracist feminist activism in women's social service organizations: A review of the literature. *Intersectionalities, 1*(1), 70–92.

Shakespeare, T. (2006). *Disability rights and wrongs.* New York, NY: Routledge.

Shakespeare, T. (2010). The social model of disability. In L. J. Davis (Ed.), *The disability studies reader* (3rd ed., pp. 266–273). New York, NY: Routledge.

Shavers, V. L., & Shavers, B, S. (2006). Racism and health inequity among Americans. *Journal of National Medical Association, 98*(3), 386–396.

Sheedy, A. (2008). *Handbook on citizen engagement: Beyond consultation.* Ottawa, ON: Canadian Policy Research Networks. Retrieved from http://www.cprn.org/documents/49583_EN.pdf

Sherrod, L. (2007). Civic engagement as an expression of positive youth development. In R. K. Silbereisen & R. M. Lerner (Eds.), *Approaches to positive youth development* (pp. 59–74). Thousand Oaks, CA: Sage.

Shildrick, M. (2012). Critical disability studies: Rethinking the conventions for the age of postmodernity. In N. Watson, A. Roulstone, & C. Thomas (Eds.), *Routledge handbook of disability studies* (pp. 30–41). New York, NY: Routledge.

Sidell, N. L. (2003). The course portfolio: A valuable teaching tool. *Journal of Teaching in Social Work, 23*(3–4), 91–106.

Simmons, M., & Dei, G. S. (2012). Reframing anti-colonial theory for the diasporic context. *Postcolonial Directions in Education, 1*(1), 67–99.

Simpson. L. (2014). Land as pedagogy: Nishnaabeg intelligence and rebellious transformation. *Decolonization Indigeneity, Education and Society, 3*(3), 1–25.

Sinclair, R. (2004). Aboriginal social work education in Canada: Decolonizing pedagogy for the seventh generation. *First Peoples Child and Family Review, 11,* 49–61.

Sinclair, R. (2007). Identity lost and found: Lessons from the Sixties Scoop. *First Peoples Child & Family Review, 3*(1), 65–82.

Sinclair, R. (2009). Identity or racism? Aboriginal transracial adoption. In R. Sinclair, M. A. Hart, & G. Bruyere (Eds.), *Wicihitowin: Aboriginal social work in Canada* (pp. 89–113). Halifax, NS: Fernwood Publishing.

Sinclair, R., & Albert, J. (2008). Social work and the anti-oppressive stance: Does the emperor really have new clothes? *Critical Social Work, 9*(1). Retrieved from http://www1.uwindsor.ca/criticalsocialwork/

Sinclair, R., Hart, M., & Bruyere, G. (Eds.). (2009). *Wicihitowin: Aboriginal social work in Canada.* Halifax, NS: Fernwood Publishing.

Singh, A. (2013). Transgender youth of color and resilience: Negotiating oppression and finding support. *Sex Roles, 68,* 690–702.

Skehill, C. (2007). Researching the history of social work: Exposition of a history of the present approach. *European Journal of Social Work, 10*(4), 449–463.

Smith, A. (2006). Heteropatriarchy and the three pillars of white supremacy. In INCITE! Women of Color Against Violence (Ed.), *Color of violence, the INCITE anthology* (pp. 66–73). Cambridge, MA: South End Press.

Smith, A. (2012). Indigeneity, settler colonialism, white supremacy. In D. Martinez-HoSang, O. LaBennett, & L. Pulido (Eds.), *Racial formation in the twenty first century* (pp. 66–90). Berkeley, CA: University of California Press.

Smith, L. T. (1999). *Decolonizing methodologies: Research and Indigenous peoples.* New York, NY: Zed Books.

Smith, M. (1999). *Lesbian and gay rights in Canada: Social movements and equality seeking* (pp. 1971–1995). Toronto, ON: University of Toronto Press.

Smith, M. (2005). Social movements and judicial empowerment: Courts, public policy, and lesbian and gay organizing in Canada. *Politics and Society, 33*(2), 327–353.

Smith, M. (2012). Split shifts and spinning solidarity: Library workers in the real world. *Our Times Magazine, 31*(3), 32–38.

Social Planning Council of Peel. (2007). *The Black community in Peel region: An exploratory study.* Mississauga, ON: Author.

Solleder, J. (2011, February 5). Are we entering a post-gay era? *Rage: Gay News and Entertainment.* Retrieved from http://www.ragemonthly.com/2011/02/05/are-we-entering-a-post-gay-era/

Spivak, G.C. (1988). Can the subaltern speak? In C. Nelson & L. Grossberg (Eds.), *Marxism and the interpretation of culture* (pp. 271–313). London: Macmillan.

St. Denis, V. (2011). Foreword. In M. J. Cannon & L. Sunseri (Eds.), *Racism, colonialism, and Indigeneity in Canada* (pp. vi–ix). Don Mills, ON: Oxford University Press.

Staller, K. M. (2010). Social problem construction and its impact on program and policy responses. In S. B. Kamerman, S. Phipps, & A. Ben-Arieh (Eds.), *From child welfare to child well-being: An international perspective on knowledge in service of policy making* (pp. 155–173). Dordrecht, The Netherlands: Springer Netherlands.

Stam, R. (1989). *Subversive pleasures: Bakhtin, cultural criticism, and film.* Baltimore, MD: Johns Hopkins University Press.

Stam, R., & Shohat, E. (2012). Whence and wither postcolonial theory? *New Literary History, 43,* 371–390.

Stanton, F., & Grant, J. (1999). Approaches to experiential learning, course delivery, and validation in medicine. A background document. *Medical Education, 33,* 515–520.

Starkman, M. (2013). The movement. In B. LeFrancois, R. Menzies, & G. Reaume (Eds.), *Mad matters: A critical reader in Canadian Mad Studies* (pp. 27–37). Toronto, ON: Canadian Scholars' Press.

Stienstra, D., & Wight-Felske, A. (Eds.). (2003). *Making equality: History of advocacy and persons with disabilities in Canada.* Concord, ON: Captus Press.

Stoker, G. (2006). *Why politics matters: Making democracy work.* Basingstoke, UK: Palgrave Macmillan.

Stoler, A.L. (2011). Colonial aphasia: Race and disabled histories in France. *Public Culture, 23*(1), 121–156.

Stoneman, D. (2002). The role of youth programming in the development of civic engagement. *Applied Developmental Science, 6*(4), 221–226.

Strega, S. (2005). The view from the poststructural margins. In L. Brown & S. Strega (Eds.), *Research as resistance* (pp. 199–235). Toronto, ON: Canadian Scholars' Press.

Strega, S. (2007). *Anti-oppressive practice in child welfare.* In D. Baines (Ed.), *Doing anti-oppressive practice* (pp. 67–82). Halifax, NS: Fernwood Publishing.

Strega, S., & Esquao, S. A. [Carrière, J.] (Eds.). (2009). *Walking this path together: Anti-racist and anti-oppressive child welfare practice.* Halifax, NS: Fernwood Publishing.

Strier, R., & Binyamin, S. (2010). Developing anti-oppressive services for the poor: Theoretical and organizational rationale. *British Journal of Social Work, 40*, 1908–1926.

Strier, R., & Binyamin, S. (2014). Introducing anti-oppressive social work practices in public services: Rhetoric to practice. *British Journal of Social Work, 44*(8), 2095–2112.

Stychin, C. (1995a). Novel concepts: A comment on *Egan and Nesbit v. The Queen. Constitutional Forum, 6*(4), 101–106.

Stychin, C. (1995b). Essential rights and contested identities: Sexual orientation and equality rights jurisprudence in Canada. *Canadian Journal of Law and Jurisprudence, III*(1), 49–66.

Subedi, B., & Daza, S. L. (2008). The possibilities of postcolonial praxis in education. *Race, Ethnicity and Education, 11*(1), 1–10.

Sullivan, N. (2003). *A critical introduction to queer theory.* New York, NY: New York University Press.

Sundell, K. (2000). Family group conferences in Sweden. In G. Burford & J. Hudson (Eds.), *Family group conferencing: New directions in community-centered child and family practice* (pp. 198–205). New York, NY: Aldine de Gruyter.

Sundell, K., & Vinnerljung, B. (2004). Outcomes of family group conferencing in Sweden. *Child Abuse & Neglect, 28*, 267–287.

Sundell, K., Vinnerljung, B., & Ryburn, M. (2001). Social workers' attitudes towards family group conferences in Sweden and the UK. *Child and Family Social Work, 6*, 327–336.

Swift, K. (1995). *Manufacturing "bad mothers."* Toronto, ON: University of Toronto Press.

Swift, K., & Callahan, M. (2009). At risk: Social justice in child welfare and other human services. Toronto, ON: University of Toronto Press.

Swigonski, M., Ward, K., Mama, R. S., Rodgers, J., & Belicose, R. (2006). An agenda for the future: Student portfolios in social work education. *Social Work in Education, 25*(8), 812–823.

Sycamore, M. B. (2006). Breaking glass. In M. B. Sycamore (Ed.), *That's revolting: Queer strategies for resisting assimilation* (pp. 1–11). San Francisco, CA: Soft Skull Press.

Sycamore, M. B. (2008). *That's revolting: Queer strategies for resisting assimilation* (2nd ed.). Berkeley, CA: Counterpoint Press.

Tam, L. (2013). Whither Indigenizing the Mad movement? In B. LeFrancois, R. Menzies, & G. Reaume (Eds.), *Mad matters: A critical reader in Canadian Mad Studies* (pp. 281–297). Toronto, ON: Canadian Scholars' Press.

Tamburro, A. (2010). *A framework and tool for assessing Indigenous content in Canadian social work curricula.* (Unpublished doctoral dissertation). Simon Fraser University, Surrey, BC.

Tang, K., & Peters, H. (2006). Internationalizing the struggle against neoliberal social policy: The experience of Canadian women. *International Social Work, 49*(5), 571–582.

Tatchel, P. (n.d.). Glad to be gay no more? The demise of gay identity is inevitable. *Human Rights, Democracy, Global Justice, LGBTI Freedom.* Retrieved from http://www.petertatchell.net/lgbt_rights/queer_theory/glad.htm

Tattersall, A. (2009). Using their sword of justice: The NSW Teachers 161 Federation and its campaign for public education between 2001 and 2004. In J. McBride & I. Greenwood (Eds.), *Community unionism: A comparative analysis of concepts and contexts* (pp. 161–186). Basingstoke, UK: Palgrave Macmillan.

Tauri, J. M. (1999). Family group conferencing: The myth of indigenous empowerment in New Zealand justice. *Justice as Healing, 4*(1), 1–6.

Taylor, C., & Peter, T., with McMinn, T. L., Schachter, K., Beldom, S., Ferry, A., Gross, Z., & Paquin, S. (2011). *Every class in every school: The first national climate survey on homophobia, biphobia, and transphobia in Canadian schools. Final report.* Toronto, ON: Egale Canada Human Rights Trust.

Taylor, I., Thomas, J., & Sage, H. (1999). Portfolios for learning and assessment: Laying the foundations for continuing professional development. *Social Work Education, 18*(2), 147–160.

Teitel, E. (2014a, March 15). The naked truth about Pride: In defence of public nudity. *Maclean's.* Retrieved from http://www.macleans.ca/society/the-naked-truth-about-pride/

Teitel, E. (2014b, June 30). LGBT baby boomers find themselves fighting homophobia again: The challenges facing aging gay, lesbian and trans seniors. *Maclean's.* Retrieved from http://www.macleans.ca/society/health/lgbt-baby-boomers-find-themselves-fighting-homophobia-again/

Tepper, M. (2000) Sexuality and disability: The missing discourse of pleasure. *Sexuality and Disability, 18*(4), 283–290.

Texas Department of Family and Protective Services. (2006). *Family group decision making: October 2006 final evaluation.* Austin, TX: Texas Department of Family and Protective Services.

Thobani, S. (2007). *Exalted subjects: Studies in the making of race and nation in Canada.* Toronto, ON: University of Toronto Press.

Thomas, B. (1987). *Multiculturalism at work: A guide to organizational change.* Toronto, ON: YMCA of Metropolitan Toronto.

Thompson, D. N., & Burns, H. K. (2008). Reflection: An essential element of evidence-based practice. *Journal of Emergency Nursing, 34,* 246–248.

Thornicroft, G. (2006). *Actions speak louder ... Tackling discrimination against people with mental illness.* London: Mental Health Foundation.

Timberlake, E. M., Farber, M. Z., & Sabatino, C. A. (2002). *The general method of social work practice* (4th ed.). Boston, MA: Allyn and Bacon.

Titchkosky, T. (2003). *Disability, self, and society.* Toronto, ON: University of Toronto Press.

Titchkosky, T. (2007). *Reading & writing disability differently: The textured life of embodiment.* Toronto, ON: University of Toronto Press.

Todd, S. (2005). Unfinished fictions: Becoming and unbecoming feminist community organizers. In S. Hick, J. Fook, & R. Pozzuto (Eds.), *Social work: A critical turn* (pp. 137–152). Toronto, ON: Thompson Educational Publishing.

Tolkien, J. R. R. (1954). *The lord of the rings: The fellowship of the ring.* Boston, MA: Houghton Mifflin.

Toronto Family Group Conferencing Project. (2006). *Family group conferencing manual.* Toronto, ON: George Hull Centre for Children and Families.

Toronto Star. (2012, August 19). Welcome probe into police shootings of the mentally ill. Retrieved from https://www.thestar.com/opinion/editorials/2012/08/19/welcome_probe_into_police_shootings_of_the_mentally_ill.html

Treasury Board of Canada Secretariat. (2007). *Cabinet directive on streamlining regulations.* Retrieved from http://www.tbs-sct.gc.ca/ri-qr/directive/directivetb-eng.asp

Trent, J. W. (1994). *Inventing the feeble mind.* Berkeley, CA: University of California Press.

Tritter, J. Q., & McCallum, A. (2006). The snakes and ladders of user involvement: Moving beyond Arnstein. *Health Policy, 76*(2), 156–168.

Trocmé, N., Knoke, D., & Blackstock, C. (2004). Pathways to the overrepresentation of Aboriginal children in Canada's child welfare system. *Social Service Review, 78*(4), 577–600.

Turner, T. (1994). Bodies and anti-bodies. In T. Csordas (Ed.), *Embodiment and experience: The existential ground of culture and self* (pp. 27–47). Cambridge, MA: Cambridge University Press.

Turpel-Lafond, M. E. (1997). Patriarchy and paternalism: The legacy of the Canadian state for First Nations women. In A. Caroline & S. Rogers (Ed.), *Women and the Canadian State* (pp. 174–192). Montreal, QC: McGill-Queen's University Press.

UN General Assembly. (2004). *Policies and programmes involving youth.* New York, NY: Author.

UNICEF. (2001). *The participation rights of adolescents: A strategic approach.* New York, NY: UNICEF Programme Division.

United Way of Greater Toronto. (1991). *Action, access, diversity! A guide to multicultural/anti-racist organizational change for social service agencies.* Toronto, ON: Author.

Valdes, F. (2003a). Teaching Asian Americans and the law: Insights and syllabi: Outsider jurisprudence, critical pedagogy and social justice activism: Marking the stirrings of critical legal education. *Asian Law Journal, 10*(65), 1–24.

Valdes, F. (2003b). Legal reform and social justice: An introduction to LatCrit theory, praxis and community. *The LatCrit Monograph Series,* 1–14.

Valentine, C. (2006). Academic constructions of bereavement. *Mortality, 11*(1), 57–78.

Vehmas, S., & Watson, N. (2014). Moral wrongs, disadvantages, and disability: A critique of critical disability studies. *Disability & Society, 29*(4), 638–650.

Velen, M., & Devine, L. (2005). Use of FGDM with children in care the longest: It's about time. *Protecting Children, 19*(4), 25–34.

Volkery, A. (2004). *Regulatory impact analysis in Canada.* Retrieved from: https://www.google.ca/url?sa=t&rct=j&q=&esrc=s&source=web&cd=1&cad=rja&uact=8&ved=0ahUKEwjGl-fUlKfUAhUq_IMKHay1B1kQFggoMAA&url=http%3A%2F%2Fwww.errada.gov.eg%2Fdownload.php%3Ffile_name%3Derrada_docs%2F2011-10%2Ff925e44c9bcb1c527b2880c1b1acbfe21317811091.pdf%26org_file_name%3DCanada%26type%3Dpdf&usg=AFQjCNF18LTI2_J9TbSYnWj-9nr1ykzexA&sig2=sJPR3pPSfOxurXbpnJ_x5Q

Wagner, A., & Yee, J. (2011). Anti-oppression in higher education. *Canadian Social Work Review, 28*(1), 89–105.

Waites, C., MacGowan, M. J., Pennell, J., Carlton-LaNey, I., & Weil, M. (2004). Increasing cultural responsiveness of family group conferencing. *Social Work, 49*(2), 291–300.

Wakefield, J. (2013). DSM-5: An overview of the change and controversies. *Clinical Journal of Social Work, 41*(2), 139–154.

Walcott, R. (2003). *Black like who? Writing Black Canada* (2nd ed.). Toronto, ON: Insomniac Press.

Walker, H. (1996). *Whanau (family) decision making: "Why do they not trust us?"* Paper presented at the Under Construction: Building a Better Future for Colorado's Children and Families Conference, Denver, CO.

Walker, R. (2004). "Queer"ing identity/ies: Agency and subversion in Canadian education. *Canadian Online Journal of Queer Studies in Education, 1*(1), 1–19.

Walkerdine, V. (2006). Workers in the new economy: Transforming as border crossing. *Ethos, 34*(1), 10–41.

Walkowitz, D.J. (1999). *Working with class: Social workers and the politics of middle class identity.* New York, NY: UNC Press.

Wall, C. (2009). Equity in unions: Political correctness or necessity for survival? In J. R. Foley & P. L. Barker (Eds.), *Unions, equity, and the path to renewal* (pp. 78–83). Vancouver, BC: UBC Press.

Walter, T. (1996). A new model of grief: Bereavement and biography. *Mortality, 1*(1), 7–25.

Walter, T. (2000). Grief narratives: The role of medicine in the policing of grief. *Anthropology & Medicine, 7*(1), 97–114.

Warner, M. (1999). *The trouble with normal: Sex, politics and the ethics of queer life.* New York, NY: Free Press.

Warner, R. (2006). *Theoretical framework for the racism, violence and health project: A working paper.* Retrieved from http://rvh.socialwork.dal.ca/resources.html, link no longer active.

Warner, T. (2002a). *Never going back: A history of queer activism in Canada.* Toronto, ON: University of Toronto Press.

Warner, T. (2002b). *Publics and counterpublics.* New York, NY: Zone Books.

Watson, J. (2005). Schizo-performativity? Neurosis and politics in Judith Butler and Felix Guattari. *Women: A Cultural Review, 16*(3), 305–320.

Watters, E. (2011). *Crazy like us: The globalization of the American psyche.* New York, NY: Simon and Schuster.

Weaver, S. (2007). Make it more welcome: Best-practice child welfare work with substance-using mothers—diminishing risks by promoting strengths. In S. Boyd & L. Marcellus (Eds.), *With child–substance use during pregnancy: A woman-centred approach* (pp. 76–90). Halifax, NS: Fernwood Publishing.

Wehbi, S. (2011a). Crossing boundaries: Foreign funding and disability rights activism in a context of war. *Disability and Society, 26*(5), 507–520.

Wehbi, S. (2011b). Anti-oppressive community organizing: Lessons from disability rights activism. In D. Baines (Ed.), *Doing anti-oppressive practice: social justice and social work* (2nd ed., pp. 133–145). Halifax, NS: Fernwood Publishing.

Wehbi, S., & Turcotte, P. (2007). Social work education: Neoliberalism's willing victim? *Critical Social Work, 8*(1). Retrieved from http://www1.uwindsor.ca/criticalsocialwork/

Weimer, M. (2002). *Learner-centered teaching: Five key changes to practice.* San Francisco, CA: Jossey-Bass.

Weisbrot, M. (2008, January 25). We're all Keynesians—again. *The Guardian.* Retrieved from http://www.guardian.co.uk/commentisfree/2008/jan/25/wereallkeynesiansagain/print

Wenzel, L. S., Briggs, K. L., & Puryear, B. L. (1998). Portfolio: Authentic assessment in the age of the curriculum revolution. *Journal of Nursing Education, 37*(5), 208–212.

Wharf Higgins, J. (1999). Citizenship and empowerment: A remedy for citizen participation in health reform. *Community Development Journal, 34*, 287–307.

Wheatley, T. (2013). *"And neither have I wings to fly": Labelled and locked up in Canada's oldest institution.* Toronto, ON: Inanna Publications & Education.

Whitaker, J. K. (2000). Foreword. In G. Burford & J. Hudson (Eds.), *Family group conferencing: New directions in community-centered child and family practice.* New York, NY: Aldine de Gruyter.

Wilding, P.M. (2008). Reflective practice: A learning tool for student nurse. *British Journal of Nursing, 17*, 720–724.

Williams, P. (1991). *The alchemy of race and rights.* Cambridge, MA: Harvard University Press.

Williams, P., & Nelson, C. (1995). *Kaswantha.* Paper No. 88a. Ottawa, ON: Royal Commission on Aboriginal Peoples.

Wilson, T. (2008). Reflecting on the contradictions: Governmentality in social work education and community practice. *Canadian Social Work Review, 25*(2), 187–202.

Wilson, T. E. (2011). Embodied liability: The usefulness of "at-risk youth." *Canadian Social Work Review, 28*(1), 49–68.

Winkel, H. (2001). A postmodern culture of grief? On individualization of mourning in Germany. *Mortality, 6*(1), 65–79.

Winter, R., & Maisch, M. (1996). *Professional competence and higher education: The ASSET Programme.* London: Falmer.

Withers, A. J. (2012). *Disability politics and theory.* Halifax, NS: Fernwood Publishing.

Wolfe, E. W., & Miller, T. R. (1997). Barriers to the implementation of portfolio assessment in secondary education. *Applied Measurement in Education, 10*(3), 235–251.

Wolfensberger, W. (1994). The growing threat to the lives of handicapped people in the context of modernistic values. *Disability & Society, 9*(3), 395–413.

Wolfensberger, W. (2000). A brief overview of social role valorization. *Mental Retardation, 38*(2), 105–123.

Wolfensberger, W. (2013). *Social role valorization: A high-order concept for addressing the plight of societally devalued people and for structuring human services* (4th ed.). Plantagenet, ON: Valor Press.

Wolfensberger, W., Thomas, S., & Caruso, G. (1996). Some of the universal "good things of life" which the implementation of social role valorization can be expected to make more accessible to devalued people. *SRV/VRS The International Social Role Valorization Journal, 2*(2), 12–14.

Wong, F., Wong, M., & Kan, E. (1997). An action research study into the development of nurses as reflective practitioners. *Journal of Nursing Education, 36*(10), 476–481.

Wong, R. Y. (2004). Knowing through discomfort: A mindfulness-based critical social work pedagogy. *Critical Social Work, 5*(1). Retrieved from http://www1.uwindsor.ca/criticalsocialwork/

Woodford, M. R. (2010). Successful community-government collaborative policymaking: A case study of a workgroup to improve income support services to victims of intimate violence. *Journal of Policy Practice, 9*, 96–113.

Woodford, M., Newman, P., Brotman, S., & Ryan, B. (2010). Northern enlightenment: Legal recognition of same-sex marriage in Canada strengthening social work's advocacy efforts. *Journal of Gay and Lesbian Social Services, 22*, 191–209.

Woodford, M., & Preston, S. (2011). Developing a strategy to meaningfully engage stakeholders in program/policy planning: A guide for human services managers and practitioners. *Journal of Community Practice, 19*(2), 159–174.

Woodford, M. R., & Preston, S. (2013). Strengthening citizen participation in public policy-making: A Canadian perspective. *Parliamentary Affairs, 66*(2), 345–363.

Xanthos, C. (2008). Racializing mental illness: Understanding African-Caribbean schizophrenia in the UK. *Critical Social Work, 9*(1). Retrieved from http://www1.uwindsor.ca/criticalsocialwork/

Yamamoto, E. (1997). Critical race praxis: Race theory and political lawyering practice in post-civil rights America. *Michigan Law Review, 95*, 821–900.

Yee, J. Y. (2015). Whiteness, white supremacy and social work. In J. D. Wright (Ed.), *International encyclopedia of the social and behavioral sciences* (2nd ed., Vol. 25). Oxford: Elsevier. doi:10.1016/B978-0-08-097086-8.28099-9

Yee, J. Y., & Dumbrill, G. C. (2003). Whiteout: Looking for race in Canadian social work practice. In A. Al-Krenawi & J. R. Graham (Eds.), *Multicultural social work in Canada— working with diverse ethno-racial communities* (pp. 98–121). Toronto, ON: Oxford University Press.

Yee, J. Y., Hackbusch, C., & Wong, H. (2015). An anti-oppression (AO) framework for child welfare in Ontario, Canada: Possibilities for systemic change. *British Journal of Social Work, 45*(2), 474–492.

Young, M. I. (1996). Communication and the other: Beyond deliberative democracy. In S. Benhabib (Ed.), *Democracy and difference: Contesting the boundaries of the political* (pp. 120–135). Princeton, NJ: Princeton University Press.

Young, R. J. C. (1990). *White mythologies: Writing history and the west*. London: Routledge.

Zeldin, S. (2004). Youth as agents of adult and community development: Mapping the processes and outcomes of youth engaged in organizational governance. *Applied Developmental Science, 8*(2), 75–90.

Zeldin, S., McDaniel, A. K., Topitzes, D., & Calvert, M. (2000). *A study on the impacts of youth on adults and organizations*. Madison, WI: University of Wisconsin.

Žižek, S. (2008, November 14). Use your illusions. *London Review of Books*. Retrieved from http://www.lrb.co.uk/2008/11/14/slavoj-zizek/use-your-illusions

Index